Complete

Daphne West

Revised by Marta Tomaszewski and
Michael Ransome

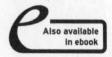

Contents

Acknowledgements

The author and publishers would like to thank Irina Vorobyova, Elena Selyanina, Tanya Shlyakhtenko-Deck, Frank Beardow, Tatyana Izmailova and Michael Ransome for their invaluable advice, criticism and suggestions. They would also like to thank VAAP for permission to reproduce material from: *Literaturnaia gazeta, Pravda, Zdorov'e, Sovetskii soyuz, Sputnik.*

About the authors

DAPHNE WEST

My passion for Russian began when it was offered at my school as an alternative to O-level Physics. At the University of Durham I gained a first-class honours degree in Russian with distinction in spoken Russian, and a PhD on the poet Mandelstam.

I have taught in schools and further education colleges; I was Head of Modern Languages at Sherborne School for Girls and Sevenoaks School, and Headmistress of the Maynard School in Exeter.

I have been Chief Examiner for GCSE and A-level Russian and my publications include three *Teach Yourself* titles, as well as A-level textbooks (*Poshli dal'she, Tranzit, Kompas*). In 1993 I was awarded the Pushkin Medal by the Pushkin Institute, Moscow, for contributions to the teaching of Russian. In the early 1990s I established an exchange which has flourished for nearly 20 years with School No. 7 in Perm (a city in the Urals closed to foreigners in Soviet times). Now I am a freelance teacher and writer; my former Russian students include teachers of Russian in schools and universities, as well those who have made their careers in Russia working for businesses and charitable organizations. In January 2010 I became the editor of *Rusistika*, the Russian journal of the Association of Language Learning.

DR MICHAEL RANSOME

Michael is Chief Examiner of Russian for the Edexcel examination board (A level and GCSE). He's the author of several school Russian courses (GCSE and GCE) and a teacher at Bristol Grammar School.

MARTA TOMASZEWSKI

Marta has taught Russian in schools for over ten years and is the co-author and co-editor of the leading GCSE Russian course used in schools – *Na Start, Vnimanie, Marsh!*

Introduction

A holiday, a business trip, an interest in world affairs or in the riches of Russian culture and history – there are many reasons for learning Russian, a language spoken by approximately 270 million people worldwide, of whom over 140 million live in the Russian Federation – a country which covers more than an tenth of the world's surface and has nine time zones.

The aim of this course is to equip the complete beginner with the skills needed to communicate in practical, everyday situations and to give some background information about Russia and the nature of Russian society. The units of the course are designed to teach specific uses of language. These are related to situations that visitors to Russia may encounter. For example, you will learn how to give and seek information about people and places, how to make requests, complaints, apologies, arrangements, how to express opinions and explain what has happened and what will happen. You will meet topics such as shopping, health, accommodation and entertainment, and learn how to cope with them in related settings – in a shop, with the doctor, in a hotel, at the theatre. A clear indication is given at the beginning of each unit of the language uses covered and of the setting of the dialogue which forms the basis of the unit.

Many dramatic changes have taken place in Russian society since the collapse of the Soviet Union in 1991, but the language you are learning through this course is very much the language used in Russia today.

How to use this course

First, work carefully through the sections on the Cyrillic alphabet and pronunciation before you attempt Unit 1. If you feel you need more practice in mastering the alphabet, there are lots of exercises which would help you in *Read and write Russian Script*. For more practice on specific grammatical points, you will find a lot of material in *Essential Russian Grammar*.

Each unit of *Complete Russian* follows the same pattern, starting with a culture point and Vocabulary builder, which contain key words and expressions necessary to understand the dialogue. Vocabulary lists throughout the units contain any extra words you will need. The main grammatical structures are explained and illustrated in the language discovery section.

Once you have grasped the meaning of the dialogue, read it through again until you are satisfied that it is clear. Then turn to the questions and test your understanding of the dialogue (you can check your answers in the Key to the exercises).

The Practice section will involve a range of activities: reading, asking, answering, looking (at pictures, maps, tables, forms) and writing. The answers to all the exercises can be found in the Key to the exercises.

The penultimate section is divided into three parts: Listen and understand, Reading and writing, and Speaking. The Listen and understand dialogues are based on the topic and language points of the unit's main dialogue, and they are accompanied by a set of questions. The texts in the Reading section give information about the geography, history, culture and society of Russia. You will meet new vocabulary here – you will not need to understand every word or every grammatical form in order to answer the questions, and the important vocabulary will be given for you before the text. Try to work out what you think the new words mean before you look at the vocabulary, and use the questions which follow the text to help you understand the passage more easily and concentrate on the main points. The Reading section is designed to improve your ability to understand written Russian, and the questions (and your answers) will always be in English. The Speaking sections give you a chance to put what you have learned into practice in realistic scenarios, and also provide useful revision of essential phrases in the unit.

In the course of each unit you will find Language tip boxes to help you understand and remember essential or tricky points, discovery questions to make you think and try to figure things out for yourself, and 'Your turn' (**Дава́йте**) boxes to try out new grammar points. The final part of each unit gives you an opportunity to test yourself on your overall understanding of the unit.

Using the course with the audio

All items with the sign 🎧 are on the audio. You will find it very helpful for your comprehension and pronunciation of Russian to listen to the audio as you work through the course. The more times you listen, the better. Try to concentrate on the pronunciation and intonation of the speakers. The dialogues can be used as listening comprehension exercises. Listen to the dialogue to get the general gist (do not worry about understanding every single word), look at the questions, then listen again before you try to answer them.

Learn to learn

The Discovery method

There are lots of approaches to language learning, some practical and some quite unconventional. Perhaps you know of a few, or even have some techniques of your own. In this book we have incorporated the Discovery method of learning, a sort of DIY approach to language learning. What this means is that you will be encouraged throughout the course to engage your mind and figure out the language for yourself, through identifying patterns, understanding grammar concepts, noticing words that are similar to English, and more. This method promotes language awareness, a critical skill in acquiring a new language. As a result of your own efforts, you will be able to retain more easily what you have learned, use it with confidence, and, even better, apply those same skills to continuing to learn the language (or, indeed, another one) on your own after you have finished this book.

Everyone can succeed in learning a language – the key is to know how to learn it. Learning is more than just reading or memorizing grammar and vocabulary. It is about being an active learner, learning in real contexts, and, most importantly, using what you have learned in different situations. Simply put, if you figure something out for yourself, you are more likely to understand it. And when you use what you have learned, you are more likely to remember it.

Since many of the essential but (let's admit it!) dull details, such as grammar rules, are taught through the Discovery method, you can have more fun while learning. Soon, the language will start to make sense and you will be relying on your own intuition to construct original sentences independently, not just listening and repeating.

Become a successful language learner

1 MAKE A HABIT OUT OF LEARNING

Study a little every day, between 20 and 30 minutes if possible, rather than two to three hours in one session. Give yourself short-term goals, e.g. work out how long you will spend on a particular unit and work within the time limit. This will help you to create a study habit, much in the same way you would a sport or music. You will need to concentrate, so try to create an environment suitable for learning which is calm and quiet and free from distractions. As you study, do not worry about your mistakes or the things you do not remember or understand. Languages settle differently in our brains, but gradually the language will become clearer as your brain starts to make new connections. Just give yourself enough time and you will succeed.

2 EXPAND YOUR LANGUAGE CONTACT

As part of your study habit, try to take other opportunities to expose yourself to the language. As well as using this book you could try listening to radio and television or reading articles and blogs. Remember that as well as listening to online radio live you can use catch-up services to listen more than once. Perhaps you could find information in Russian about a personal passion or hobby or even a news story that interests you. In time you will find that your vocabulary and language recognition deepen and you will become used to a range of writing and speaking styles.

3 VOCABULARY

▶ To organize your study of vocabulary, group new words under:
   a generic categories, e.g. food, furniture.
   b situations in which they occur, e.g. under *restaurant* you can write *waiter, table, menu, bill*.
   c functions, e.g. greetings, parting, thanks, apologizing.
   Say the words out loud as you read them.
▶ Write the words over and over again. Remember that if you want to keep lists on your smartphone or tablet you can usually switch the keyboard language to make sure you are able to type in Cyrillic.
▶ Listen to the audio several times.
▶ Cover up the English side of the vocabulary list and see if you remember the meaning of the word.
▶ Associate the words with similar-sounding words in English, e.g. **ресторáн** *restaurant*, **стул** *chair* and **нос** *nose*.
▶ Create flash cards, drawings and mind maps either on paper or using apps.
▶ Write words for objects around your house and stick them to objects.
▶ Pay attention to patterns in words, e.g. all nouns that end in **-а** in Russian are feminine; a **-л** on the end of a verb shows that it is in the past tense.

- Experiment with words. Use the words that you learn in new contexts and find out if they are correct. For example, when you learn that **ходи́ть** means *to walk/to go*, you will be able to see the same root (**ход**) in many other words, such as **вы́ход** *exit*, **вход** *entrance*, **перехо́д** *crossing* and **вездехо́д** *4x4 off-road vehicle*.
- Make the best of words you already know. When you start thinking about it you will realize that there are lots of Russian words and expressions which are taken from English: **футбо́л** *football*, **парк** *park*, **стадио́н** *stadium*, **би́знес** *business*, **о́фис** *office* and **марке́тинг** *marketing*.

4 GRAMMAR

- To organize the study of grammar, write your own grammar glossary and add new information and examples as you go along.
- Think about grammatical rules. Sit back and reflect on the rules you learn. See how they compare with your own language or other languages you may already speak. Try to find out some rules on your own and be ready to spot the exceptions. By doing this you will remember the rules better and get a feel for the language.
- Try to find examples of grammar in conversations or other articles.
- Keep a 'pattern bank' that organizes examples that can be listed under the structures you have learned.
- Use old vocabulary to practise new grammar structures.
- When you learn a new verb form, write the conjugation of several different verbs you know that follow the same form.

5 PRONUNCIATION

- When organizing the study of pronunciation keep a section of your notebook for pronunciation rules and practise those that trouble you.
- Repeat all of the conversations, line by line. Listen to yourself and try to mimic what you hear.
- Record yourself and compare yourself to a native speaker.
- Make a list of words that give you trouble and practise them.
- Study individual sounds, then full words.
- Do not forget that it is not just about pronouncing letters and words correctly, but using the right intonation. So, when practising words and sentences, mimic the rising and falling intonation of native speakers.

6 LISTENING AND READING

The conversations in this book include questions to help guide you in your understanding. But you can go further by following some of these tips.

▶ Imagine the situation. When listening to or reading the dialogues, try to imagine where the scene is taking place and who the main characters are. Let your experience of the world help you guess the meaning of the dialogue. For example, if a dialogue takes place in a snack bar you can predict the kind of vocabulary that is being used.

▶ Concentrate on the main part. When watching a foreign film you usually get the meaning of the whole story from a few individual shots. Understanding a foreign conversation or article is similar. Concentrate on the main parts to get the message and do not worry about individual words.

▶ Guess the key words; if you cannot, ask or look them up. When there are key words you do not understand, try to guess what they mean from the context. If you are listening to a Russian speaker and cannot get the gist of a whole passage because of one word or phrase, try to repeat that word with a questioning tone. The speaker will probably paraphrase it, giving you the chance to understand it. If, for example, you wanted to find out the meaning of the word **борщ** (a traditional Russian soup), you would ask **Что такóе 'борщ'?** *What is 'borshcht'?* or **'Борщ' – это какóй суп?** *'Borshcht' – what sort of soup is it?* This second example demonstrates how much you already know (*what sort of?* and *soup*) and this makes the guessing much easier.

7 SPEAKING

Rehearse in the foreign language. As all language teachers will assure you, the successful learners are those students who overcome their inhibitions and get into situations where they must speak, write and listen to the foreign language. Here are some useful tips to help you practise speaking Russian:

▶ Hold a conversation with yourself, using the conversations of the units as models and the structures you have learned previously.

▶ After you have conducted a transaction with a salesperson, clerk or waiter in your own language, pretend that you have to do it in Russian, e.g. buying groceries, ordering food, drinks and so on.

▶ Look at objects around you and try to name them in Russian.

▶ Look at people around you and try to describe them to a Russian.
▶ Try to answer all of the questions in the book out loud.
▶ Say the dialogues out loud then try to replace sentences with ones that are true for you.
▶ Try to role-play different situations in the book.

8 LEARN FROM YOUR ERRORS

Do not let errors interfere with getting your message across. Making errors is part of any normal learning process, but some people get so worried that they will not say anything unless they are sure it is correct. This leads to a vicious circle as the less they say, the less practice they get and the more mistakes they make.

Note the seriousness of errors. Many errors are not serious, as they do not affect the meaning. You will see that in Russian, many words change their endings depending on what they mean in the sentence, but a Russian will normally understand you even if you do not get the endings quite right. So concentrate on getting your message across and learn from your mistakes. The most important thing to remember though is BE BOLD! Getting it wrong at times is a huge part of your learning process and success.

9 LEARN TO COPE WITH UNCERTAINTY

▶ Do not over-use your dictionary. When reading a text in Russian, do not be tempted to look up every word you do not know. Underline the words you do not understand and read the passage several times, concentrating on trying to get the gist of the passage. If after the third time there are still words which prevent you from getting the general meaning of the passage, look them up in the dictionary.
▶ Do not panic if you do not understand. If at some point you feel you do not understand what you are told, do not panic or give up listening. Either try and guess what is being said and keep following the conversation or, if you cannot, isolate the expression or words you have not understood and have them explained to you. The speaker might paraphrase them and the conversation will carry on.
▶ Keep talking. The best way to improve your fluency in the foreign language is to talk every time you have the opportunity to do so. Keep the conversations flowing and do not worry about the mistakes. If you get stuck for a particular word, do not let the conversation stop. Paraphrase or replace the unknown word with one you do know, even if you have to simplify what you want to say.

The Cyrillic alphabet

Is Russian difficult? It is certainly very different from English – this is part of its fascination. An obvious difference is the Cyrillic alphabet – named after the ninth-century monk, St Cyril, its reputed author.

Using the Cyrillic alphabet to write Russian is actually a great deal easier than transliterating it – i.e. writing Russian in the English (Latin) alphabet – because two or more English letters are often needed to give a single letter in Russian. In the following example only two Russian letters are needed to provide the word meaning *cabbage soup*, while five are needed in English:

Cyrillic	**English transliteration**
щи	*shchi* (pronounced 'shchee')

Learning the alphabet is the first step to learning Russian.

Pronunciation

The alphabet can be divided into three different groups of letters:
- ▶ those which look and sound very much like English letters
- ▶ those which look like English letters but have different sounds
- ▶ those which neither look nor sound like English letters.

If you are familiar with Greek or Hebrew letters, you will recognize that some Russian letters have been developed from these sources.

00.01 Five letters fall into the first group (those which are equivalent to their English counterparts):

a	sounds slightly shorter than	*a*	in	*father*
к	sounds like	*k*	in	*kit*
м	sounds like	*m*	in	*motor*
о	sounds like	*aw/law*	in	*bore*
т	sounds like	*t*	in	*tired*

00.02 There are seven letters in the second group (those which look like English letters but which sound different):

в	sounds like	*v*	in	*visit*
е	sounds like	*ye*	in	*yet*
н	sounds like	*n*	in	*novel*
р	sounds like	*r*	in	*rat*
с	sounds like	*s*	in	*sip*
у	sounds like	*oo*	in	*shoot*
х	sounds like	*ch*	in	*loch* (Scots)

 00.03 The letters in the third group do not look like any English letters:

б	sounds like	*b*	in	*box*
г	sounds like	*g*	in	*goat*
д	sounds like	*d*	in	*daughter*
ё	sounds like	*yo*	in	*yonder*
ж	sounds like	*s*	in	*pleasure*
з	sounds like	*z*	in	*zoo*
и	sounds like	*ee*	in	*feet*
й	sounds like	*y*	in	*boy*
л	sounds like	*l*	in	*bottle*
п	sounds like	*p*	in	*peach*
ф	sounds like	*f*	in	*father*
ц	sounds like	*ts*	in	*quits*
ч	sounds like	*ch*	in	*chick*
ш	sounds like	*sh*	in	*shift*
щ	sounds like	*shch*	in	*posh china*

ъ hard sign – **твёрдый знак** – no separate sound, see below

ы	sounds like	*i*	in	*ill*

ь soft sign – **мягкий знак** – no separate sound, see below

э	sounds like	*e*	in	*let*
ю	sounds like	*yu*	in	*yule*
я	sounds like	*ya*	in	*yak*

The English equivalents given are only approximate and the best way to master Russian pronunciation is to listen to native speakers and try to imitate them – the audio will help you do this.

Ee Зз (handwritten)

00.04 Here is the alphabet in its proper order.

Аа Бб Вв Гг Дд Ее Ёё Жж Зз Ии Йй Кк Лл Мм Нн Оо Пп Рр Сс Тт Уу Фф Хх Цц Чч Шш Щщ ъ ы ь Ээ Юю Яя

HARD AND SOFT SOUNDS

00.05 Russian has ten letters denoting vowels and these fall into two groups:

Hard	а	э	ы	о	у
Soft	я	е	и	ё	ю

The soft sign (**ь**) usually softens the consonant that it follows. When the soft sign occurs between a consonant and a soft vowel it separates the two, so that they are pronounced separately: e.g. **семья** *family*.

The hard sign (**ъ**) is rarely used but also has a separating function. It keeps the consonant before it hard: e.g. **отъéзд** *departure*.

STRESS

00.06 Stress (indicated by an acute accent ´ over the vowel to be emphasized) is important. Every time you learn a new word, make sure you learn which syllable is stressed. In Russian the stressed vowel is 'given its full value' (it is pronounced quite distinctly) whereas the unstressed vowel is passed over quickly, almost 'thrown away'. This is heard most clearly with **o**. If an **o** comes immediately before the stressed syllable of the word, it is reduced to a sound rather like an **a**: e.g. **Москва́** *Moscow* looks as though it should be pronounced 'Moskva', but in fact a Russian would say it as 'Maskva', stressing the final letter. Note that the letter **ё** always carries the stress.

Note that stress marks are used here to help you as you learn; however, with a few rare exceptions, they are not used by Russians when writing. Stress marks should not be used when writing to Russians.

A final point about Russian pronunciation:

For all the challenge involved in learning a new alphabet, once you know it, Russian pronunciation is more reliable than English. Generally speaking, you say what you see – if there are four letters, there are four sounds. For example, **стол** *table* is pronounced 's-t-o-l'. This is unlike English, where the spelling can be very confusing, in words such as *drought* and *draught*; *I have read* and *I read after supper*; *I excuse you* and *What an excuse!*

Handwritten Russian

Although you will be dealing mostly with printed Russian, you need to also be aware that Russian handwriting, just like English, can look a little different from the printed page.

 Have a look at the following table and highlight any letters which look different in the handwritten form.

Printed capital	Handwritten capital	Printed small	Handwritten small
А	*А*	а	*а*
Б	*Б*	б	*б*
В	*В*	в	*в*
Г	*Г*	г	*г*
Д	*Д*	д	*д ∂*
Е	*Е*	е	*е*
Ё	*Ё*	ё	*ё*
Ж	*Ж*	ж	*ж*
З	*З*	з	*з*
И	*И*	и	*и*
Й	*Й*	й	*й*
К	*К*	к	*к*
Л	*Л*	л	*л*
М	*М*	м	*м*
Н	*Н*	н	*н*
О	*О*	о	*о*
П	*П*	п	*п*
Р	*Р*	р	*р*
С	*С*	с	*с*
Т	*Т*	т	*т, т*
У	*У*	у	*у*
Ф	*Ф*	ф	*ф*
Х	*Х*	х	*х*

Printed capital	Handwritten capital	Printed small	Handwritten small
Ц	*Ц*	ц	*ц*
Ч	*Ч*	ч	*ч*
Ш	*Ш*	ш	*ш*
Щ	*Щ*	щ	*щ*
Ъ		ъ	*ъ*
Ы		ы	*ы*
Ь		ь	*ь*
Э	*Э*	э	*э*
Ю	*Ю*	ю	*ю*
Я	*Я*	я	*я*

00.07 Here are some words given in both the printed and the handwritten form. Practise saying these words out loud and try copying them out. Pay special attention to the relative height of the letters:

	Printed	Handwritten	English
1	бага́ж	*багаж*	luggage
2	во́дка	*водка*	vodka
3	го́род	*город*	town
4	да	*да*	yes
5	друг	*друг*	friend
6	дя́дя	*дядя*	uncle
7	е́сли	*если*	if
8	лы́жи	*лыжи*	skis
9	мать	*мать*	mother
10	сад	*сад*	garden
11	тётя	*тётя*	aunt
12	футбо́л	*футбол*	football
13	хлеб	*хлеб*	bread
14	цирк	*цирк*	circus
15	ча́сто	*часто*	often

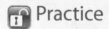 Practice

1 **Now that you have met the Cyrillic alphabet, try to work out these place names.**

   a Лондон
   b Вашингтон
   c Мадрид
   d Дублин
   e Амстердам

   f Абердин
   g Торонто
   h Бирмингем
   i Веллингтон
   j Мельбурн

2 **Here is the room allocation list for a group of tourists. Look at the second list in English and work out who is in which room.**

Дейвид Коган	201	Мигел Санчез	206
Шерул Кларк	202	Чад Харрисон	207
Мария Перез	203	Стеф Карлтон	208
Лили Макдоналд	204	Оливия Иохансен	209
Саймон Макензи	205	Ник Тэйлор	210

   a Steph Carlton
   b Cheryl Clark
   c Olivia Johanssen
   d Chad Harrison
   e Simon Mackenzie

   f Miguel Sanchez
   g David Cogan
   h Nick Taylor
   i Maria Perez
   j Lily McDonald

1 Ваш па́спорт, пожа́луйста!

Your passport, please!

In this unit you will learn how to:
▶ *respond to requests for personal information and identification.*
▶ *form simple sentences and questions.*
▶ *recognize which gender group a word belongs to.*
▶ *say I, you, he, she, it, we, you and they.*
▶ *say my and your.*

CEFR: (A1) *Can make an introduction and use basic greetings and leave-taking expressions; can introduce himself and others; can ask and answer questions about personal details.*

Russian names

As well as *surnames* (**фами́лия**) and *first names* (**и́мя**), Russians also have *patronymics* (**о́тчество**) – middle names derived from their father's first name and usually ending in **-овна** or **-евна** (for a woman) and **-ович** or **-евич** (for a man). Women's surnames usually end in **-а**.

First name	Surname	Father's name	Full name
Бори́с	Петро́в	Серге́й	Бори́с Серге́евич Петро́в
Ири́на	Его́рова	Никола́й	Ири́на Никола́евна Его́рова

Family members, close friends, children and young people address each other by the first name (or a diminutive version of it, e.g. the <u>diminutive</u> of **Светла́на** is **Све́та**). In more formal situations Russians use the first name and patronymic. So, **Гали́на Влади́мировна Петро́ва** would be known as **Гали́на** (or diminutive **Га́ля**) to her close friends and formally as **Гали́на Влади́мировна**.

Russians do not use equivalents of the English titles *Mr, Mrs, Ms* and *Miss*, although **господи́н** *Mr* (**госпожа́** (f.) *Mrs*) has come back into usage as an official way of addressing foreigners.

Cosmonaut Yuri Gagarin's full name was **Юрий Алексе́евич Гага́рин**. What was his father's first name?

Vocabulary builder

01.01 Look at the vocabulary and complete the missing English expressions. Then listen to the audio and repeat the Russian until you can say all the words with confidence.

НА́ДО ЗНАТЬ! *ESSENTIALS*

приве́т	*hi!* (inf.)
здра́вствуй	*hello* (inf.)
здра́вствуйте	*hello* (formal; pl.)
до свида́ния	*goodbye*
пожа́луйста	*please*
спаси́бо	*thank you*
да	*yes*
нет	*no*
я	*I*
ты	*you* (sing., inf.)
вы	*you* (sing., formal; pl.)
он	*he, it* (m.)
она́	*she, it* (f.)
мой/моя́	*my* (m./f.)
ваш/ва́ша	*your* (m./f.)

> **LANGUAGE TIP**
> **Здра́вствуйте** literally means *be healthy* and is used to greet a person/people you would call **вы**. The first **в** is not pronounced. To greet a person you usually call **ты**, say **Здра́вствуй!**

> **LANGUAGE TIP**
> Pronounce **до свида́ния** as though it were one word.

> **LANGUAGE TIP**
> **пожа́луйста** is also used to mean *don't mention it, you're welcome* when someone has said **спаси́бо** to you.

ВЫ - ТУРИ́СТ *TRAVEL ESSENTIALS*

па́спорт	_____
ви́за	_____
бага́ж	_____
биле́т	*ticket*
деклара́ция	*currency declaration*

НАЦИА́ЛЬНОСТИ И ЛЮ́ДИ *PEOPLE AND PLACES*

ру́сский/ру́сская	*Russian* (m./f.)
англича́нин/англича́нка	*English* (m./f.)
америка́нец/америка́нка	_____ (m./f.)
Москва́	*Moscow*
москви́ч/москви́чка	*Muscovite* (m./f.)
тури́ст/тури́стка	_____ (m./f.)

Dialogue

молодо́й челове́к	*young man*
как	*what?*
фами́лия	*surname*
хорошо́	*good, fine*
где	*where?*
вот	*here/there is/are*
де́вушка	*girl*

01.02 *Anna has just arrived at Sheremetyevo Airport in Moscow.*

1   What three questions does the young man ask Anna?

Молодо́й челове́к	Здра́вствуйте! Ваш па́спорт, пожа́луйста.
Áнна	Здра́вствуйте! Вот мой па́спорт.
Молодо́й челове́к	Вы тури́стка?
Áнна	Да, я тури́стка.
Молодо́й челове́к	Вы англича́нка, да?
Áнна	Да, я англича́нка.
Молодо́й челове́к	Как ва́ша фами́лия?
Áнна	Моя́ фами́лия – Принс.
Молодо́й челове́к	Хорошо́. Вот ваш па́спорт.
Áнна	Спаси́бо.
Молодо́й челове́к	Пожа́луйста.
Де́вушка	Где ваш бага́ж?
Áнна	Вот он.
Де́вушка	Пожа́луйста, где ва́ша деклара́ция?
Áнна	Вот она́.
Де́вушка	Хорошо́. Вот ва́ша деклара́ция.
Áнна	Спаси́бо.
Де́вушка	Пожа́луйста. До свида́ния.
Áнна	До свида́ния.

2   True or false?

a Anna is American.
b Her surname is Petrova.
c She is a tourist.

3 Answer the following questions.
   a Is Anna English?
   b What is her surname?

Language discovery

THE AND *A*

1 Find the expression in the dialogue that means *Are you a tourist?*
   What is the Russian word for *a/an***?**

There are no words in Russian for *the* (the definite article) or *a/an* (the indefinite article), so **турист** means *the tourist* or *a tourist* as well as just *tourist*.

I AM, YOU ARE …

2 In the same expression, which Russian word means *are***?**

I am, *you are* and so on (i.e. the verb *to be* in the present tense) are not used in Russian. So **Вы турист** (which means, literally, *you tourist*) is the way of saying *you are a tourist*. If both words separated by the 'missing' verb *to be* are nouns, a dash may be used: **Моя фамилия – Петрова**.

STATEMENTS AND QUESTIONS

3 Now look carefully at Anna's response to the question *Are you a tourist?* **How does the word order differ?**

The only difference between a statement and a question in written Russian is that a question ends with a question mark … and a statement does not! There is no change in word order.

Áнна туристка   *Anna is a tourist*

Áнна туристка?   *Is Anna a tourist?*

When asking questions, raise your voice on the part of the sentence that you are questioning. For example, in the sentence above, you want to know whether Anna is a <u>tourist,</u> so that is the word that should be stressed: **Áнна <u>туристка</u>?**

GROUPS OF NOUNS

 4 Look at the feminine versions of the words in the 'People and places' section in the Vocabulary builder. What do most of them have in common?

Nouns (words that name someone or something) are divided into different groups. In Russian there are three groups (also known as 'genders'): masculine, feminine and neuter (although there aren't many neuter nouns). The good news is that it is almost always possible to work out which group a Russian word belongs to by looking at its ending. The most common endings are:

Masculine words	end in	a consonant	**па́спорт**	*passport*
Feminine words	end in	**-а** or **-я**	**ви́за**	*visa*
			фами́лия	*surname*
Neuter words	end in	**-о**	**письмо́**	*letter*

Don't forget that sometimes a word has two forms to distinguish between males and females, e.g.

Бори́с – тури́ст	*Boris is a tourist*
А́нна – тури́стка	*Anna is a tourist*

HOW TO SAY *I, YOU, HE, SHE, IT, WE, YOU* AND *THEY*

The grammatical name for these words is the personal or subject pronoun.

 5 Complete the following with the Russian pronouns you have already met.

_____	*I*
ты	*you* (sing., informal)
_____	*he* (person), *it* (when referring to a masculine noun)
_____	*she* (person), *it* (when referring to a feminine noun)
мы	*we*
_____	*you* (sing., formal; pl.)
они́	*they*

ВЫ/ТЫ *YOU*

In Russian there are two ways of saying *you*. **Вы** is used for more than one person or for one person you don't know. Use **ты** if you are speaking to someone you know well.

You can switch from **вы** to **ты** when you get to know someone better, but it's usually best to wait for that person to invite you to do so (they'll probably say **давáй на ты** – *let's call each other* **ты**).

HOW TO SAY *MY* AND *YOUR*

6 **Find the expressions in the dialogue that mean** *Where is your luggage?* **and** *Where is your declaration?* **How do they differ?**

These words are known as 'possessive adjectives' because they are used for things you have. They change their endings to match what you have (masculine, feminine or neuter).

мой (for masculine words):	**мой пáспорт**	*my passport*
моя́ (for feminine words):	**моя́ декларáция**	*my declaration*
ваш (for masculine words):	**ваш багáж**	*your luggage* (i.e. belonging to **вы**)
вáша (for feminine words):	**вáша фами́лия**	*your surname*

Practice

1 **Look carefully at the form and then answer the questions that follow it.**

	№210
Национальность	*Русская*
Фамилия	*Воробьёва*
Имя, отчество	*Галина, Сергеевна*
Профессия	*консультант*

a What nationality is indicated on this form?
b What is the person's surname?
c What is her occupation?

журнали́ст	*journalist*
актёр/актри́са	*actor/actress*
инжене́р	*engineer*
студе́нт/студе́нтка	*student* (m./f.)
италья́нец/италья́нка	*Italian* (m./f.)
ирла́ндец/ирла́ндка	*Irish* (m./f.).

> **LANGUAGE TIP**
> The feminine forms of **журнали́ст** and **инжене́р** are derogatory in modern Russian usage.

2 **Make up sentences in Russian to describe the following people, giving their name, nationality and occupation.**

a Mark   American   journalist

<u>**Марк америка́нец. Он журнали́ст.**</u>

b Maria   English   student
c Maksim   Russian   engineer
d Zara   Irish   actress
e Silvio   Italian   student

3 **Which city features on the hotel emblem?**

ГОСТИНИЦА

> **LANGUAGE TIP**
> **гости́ница** means *hotel*.

САНКТ-ПЕТЕРБУРГ

4 Match each question with the correct answer.

a	Как ва́ша фами́лия?	**1**	Нет, она́ англича́нка.
b	Где ва́ша деклара́ция?	**2**	Да, мой.
c	Она́ ру́сская?	**3**	Вот она́.
d	Э́то ваш бага́ж?	**4**	Воробьёв.

LANGUAGE TIP
э́то means *it is/this is/these are.*

Listen and understand

ме́сто	*place, seat*
пять	*five*

01.03 *A Russian tourist has just boarded a plane at Sheremetyevo for a holiday in Yalta. He is talking to the flight attendant.*

1 What is the tourist's surname?

Стюарде́сса	Здра́вствуйте.
Тури́ст	Здра́вствуйте.
Стюарде́сса	Как ва́ша фами́лия?
Тури́ст	Цве́тов. Бори́с Влади́мирович Цве́тов.
Стюарде́сса	Где ваш биле́т?
Тури́ст	Вот он.
Стюарде́сса	Спаси́бо. Ва́ше ме́сто пять Б.
Тури́ст	Спаси́бо.
Стюарде́сса	Пожа́луйста.

2 What does the flight attendant ask him for?

3 Where does he sit?

Reading and writing

столи́ца	*capital*
Росси́и	*of Russia*
Кремль	*Kremlin*
там	*there*

Read the text, then answer the questions that follow.

Ви́ктор москви́ч.

Ви́ктор ру́сский. Он журнали́ст. Он москви́ч.

Москва́ – столи́ца Росси́и. Это центр поли́тики и культу́ры. Там Большо́й теа́тр, Моско́вский университе́т и Кремль.

1 True or false?

a Viktor is from Moscow.

b He is an engineer.

c Five famous places in Moscow are mentioned.

 2 Write answers to the following questions.

e.g. Где ваш па́спорт?   *Вот мой паспорт*

a Где ва́ша деклара́ция?

b Где ваш телефо́н?

c Где ва́ш бага́ж?

d Где ва́ш журна́л?

e Где ва́ша ви́за?

> **LANGUAGE TIP**
> журна́л means *magazine*; телефо́н means *telephone*. Remember that for *my* and *your* you need to use мой and ваш with masculine nouns, and моя́ and ва́ша with feminine nouns.

 ## Speaking

1 01.04 Play the part of the traveller in this conversation, then listen to the complete conversation on the audio.

Москвич	Как ва́ша фами́лия?
You	**a** *My surname is Prince.*
Москвич	Вы англича́нин/англича́нка?
You	**b** *Yes, I am English.*
Москвич	Вы студе́нт/студе́нтка?
You	**c** *Yes, I am a student.*

2 01.05 Can you remember how to say the following in Russian? Listen to the audio and practise saying each phrase.

a Your passport, please.

b What is your surname?

c Goodbye.

d Hello.

e Thank you.

Test yourself

1 How can you tell if a noun is feminine?

2 How do you say *the* in Russian?

3 What would you need to do to turn the following statement into a question? Виктор журналист.

4 Why would you say мой паспорт/ваш паспорт but моя виза/ваша виза?

5 What is a patronymic?

6 What should you say in reply if someone says Спасибо to you?

7 If you wanted to ask the question *where?*, would you use как? or где?

8 What is the Russian word for *goodbye*?

9 Can you give your nationality in Russian?

10 If you were being introduced to someone for the first time, would you call them вы or ты?

SELF CHECK

I CAN...
. . . respond to requests for personal information and identification.
. . . form simple sentences and questions.
. . . recognize which gender group a word belongs to.
. . . say *I, you, he, she, it, we, you* and *they*.
. . . say *my* and *your*.

2 Меня́ зову́т Йра

I'm called Ira

In this unit you will learn how to:

▶ *introduce yourself.*
▶ *say your name and ask someone else's name.*
▶ *say pleased to meet you.*
▶ *ask people where they live/work, and say where you live/work.*
▶ *say which languages you speak.*
▶ *form the present tense of verbs.*
▶ *recognize the nominative and prepositional cases.*

CEFR: (A1) *Can introduce himself and others, and can ask and answer questions about personal details such as where he lives and people he knows; can understand familiar names, words and very simple sentences.*

Major Russian cities

Moscow is, of course, the capital and most important city in Russia. St Petersburg was the capital of the Russian Empire before the revolution, and it remains a leading centre for culture and business. Both these leading cities are in north-western European Russia. Stretching as it does across nine time zones to the Far East, Russia has many other major cities. Vladivostok has, for a long time, been a regional centre and major port, giving access to China and Japan. In recent times, Ekaterinburg has become more important as a regional centre for the Urals, the mineral-rich mountain range dividing the continents of Europe and Asia.

Find these Russian cities on the map: **Арха́нгельск**, **Новосиби́рск**, **Владивосто́к**, **Омск**, **Екатеринбу́рг**, **Сама́ра**, **Москва́**, **Санкт-Петербу́рг**

Vocabulary builder

02.01 Complete the missing English expressions. Then listen to the audio and repeat the Russian until you can say all the words with confidence.

НА́ДО ЗНАТЬ! *ESSENTIALS*

дава́йте познако́мимся	*let's introduce ourselves*
меня́ зову́т	*I'm called (lit. they call me)*
о́чень прия́тно	*pleased to meet you*
как вас зову́т?	*what are you called? (lit. how do they call you?)*
вы уже́ хорошо́ говори́те по-ру́сски	*you already speak Russian well*
я изуча́ю	*I'm learning (I have been learning)*
ру́сский язы́к	*Russian (language)*
три го́да	*(for) three years*
я живу́	*I live*
в Москве́	*in Moscow*
где	*where*
вы живёте	*you _____*
в Ло́ндоне	*in _____*
вы рабо́таете	*you work*
я рабо́таю	*I work*
там	*there*

> **LANGUAGE TIP**
> **Дава́йте познако́мимся** literally means *let's get to know each other* and is used when you're introducing yourself (or a group of which you are a member).

в шко́ле	*in a/the _____*
я преподаю́	*I teach*
англи́йский язы́к	*English (language)*
здесь	*here*
в це́нтре	*in the _____*
в турагентстве	*in a/the tourist agency*
по-англи́йски	*(in) English*
по-испа́нски	*(in) Spanish*
по-неме́цки	*(in) German*
как	*how*
интере́сно	*_____*
знать	*to know*

Dialogue

02.02 *Anna meets her tour guide* (гид)*, Ira, for the first time in the hotel lobby.*

1 What does Ira tell Anna about herself? Give at least four details.

Йра	Дава́йте познако́мимся! Я – ваш гид. Меня́ зову́т Йра.
А́нна	О́чень прия́тно.
Йра	Как вас зову́т?
А́нна	Меня́ зову́т А́нна.
Йра	О́чень прия́тно, А́нна … Вы уже́ хорошо́ говори́те по-ру́сски!
А́нна	Спаси́бо. Я изуча́ю ру́сский язы́к уже́ три го́да. Йра, вы москви́чка?
Йра	Да, я живу́ в Москве́. Где вы живёте? В Ло́ндоне?
А́нна	Нет, я живу́ в Бри́столе. Я рабо́таю там в шко́ле, преподаю́ англи́йский язы́к. Где вы рабо́таете?
Йра	Здесь в це́нтре в турагентстве. Я хорошо́ говорю́ по-англи́йски, по-испа́нски и по-неме́цки.
А́нна	Как интере́сно!

2 True or false?

a Ira is a student.

b Anna speaks Spanish.

c Ira works in an office.

3 Answer the following questions.

   a How well does Anna speak Russian?

   b Where does Anna live?

   c What job does Anna do?

4 How do you say *in* a language **(e.g.** *in* Russian)**?**

5 When Ira introduces herself, saying Меня зовут Ира, one of the two words before her name literally means *me* **and one means** *they call***. Can you work out which is which and therefore give a direct translation of how Russians say** *my name is***?**

Language discovery

VERBS – FORMING THE PRESENT TENSE

The really good news is that Russian has only three main tenses of verbs: past, present and future. The past and the future are particularly easy, while the present tense has two main patterns with much in common between them.

1 Look at the dialogue. Can you spot five different verbs and give their English meaning? Some might appear in more than one form (e.g. the *I* **form and the** *you* **form).**

There are two main patterns (or conjugations) of verbs in Russian: (i) those whose infinitive (the *to do* part of the verb and how it will appear in a dictionary) ends in **-ать**, and (ii) those whose infinitive ends in **-ить**.

Verbs ending in -ать

Most verbs whose infinitive ends in **-ать** will work like the verb **рабóтать** *to work* in the present tense.

2 Look at the dialogue and find the Russian for *I work* **and** *you work* **to complete the verbs. (Hint: Look for я and вы with words that look similar to рабóтать.)**

я _____	*I work*	**мы рабóтаем**	*we work*
ты рабóтаешь	*you work*	**вы _____**	*you work*
он/онá/онó рабóтает	*he/she/it works*	**они́ рабóтают**	*they work*

Read and repeat out loud each part of the present tense for работать.

YOUR TURN (Давайте)

3 **Complete the rule for forming the present tense of most -ать verbs.**

Remove the **-ть** and add: **(я) -ю**; **(ты)** _____; **(он/она/оно)** _____; **(мы)** _____; **(вы) -ете**; **(они)** _____.

It really is worth taking some time to learn the present tense of **работать**, because then you will have a model to use for almost all verbs in Russian which end in **-ать**.

Verbs ending in -ить

Most verbs whose infinitive ends in **-ить** work like **говорить** _to speak_ in the present tense.

 4 **Using the -ать pattern, complete the missing letters to work out the endings for the -ить verb.**

я говорю	_I speak_	**мы говори**_____	_we speak_
ты говори_____	_you speak_	**вы говори**_____	_you speak_
он/она/оно говори_____	_he/she/it speaks_	**они говорят**	_they speak_

 Read and repeat out loud each part of the present tense for говорить.

You will notice that in **-ать** endings, the vowel **а** is always repeated, while in the **-ить** endings, the vowel **и** features only in four of the six endings.

 5 **What else do you notice when comparing the** _I_ **and** _they_ **endings for -ать and -ить verbs?**

YOUR TURN (Давайте)

6 **Complete the rule for forming the present tense of most -ить verbs.**

Remove the **-ить** and add: **я** _____; **ты** _____; **он/она/оно** _____; **мы** _____; **вы** _____; **они** _____.

Irregular verbs

Like other languages, Russian has some verbs which do not conform to the usual patterns (irregular verbs). However, even irregular Russian verbs have recognizable endings.

For example, **жить** *to live* has the following endings:

я живу́

ты живёшь

он́о живёт

мы живём

вы живёте

он́и живу́т

> **LANGUAGE TIP**
> Look carefully at the endings of this irregular verb to spot letters in the endings that are familiar from the **-ать** and the **-ить** patterns.

ENDINGS

One of the main differences between how English and Russian work is that, in English, word order is vital, but in Russian, it is the different endings that can be put on a word that matter. The different endings that can be put on Russian nouns, adjectives and pronouns are called cases. There are six cases in Russian, and we have already met one of them – the nominative case. This is the form always found in dictionaries and vocabularies.

The nominative case

This is used to talk about the person (or thing) doing an action (we call this the subject of the sentence).

YOUR TURN (Дава́йте)

7 Which word is the subject in each of the following sentences?
   a Я рабо́таю в о́фисе.
   b В Москве́ живёт И́ра.
   c А́нна говори́т по-ру́сски.

The prepositional case

8 Look at the dialogue again, and find the Russian for *I live in Moscow.* **Do you notice anything different about the word for** *Moscow* **here?**

Russians use the prepositions **в** to mean *in* and **на** to mean *on*. They then change the ending of the word that follows these prepositions to the prepositional case.

The prepositional is usually formed by adding the letter **e** to the end of a noun. However, if the noun ends in a vowel, remove this vowel first.

YOUR TURN

9 Use the examples given to help you complete the missing words

Nominative		Prepositional	
óфис	office	**в óфисе**	in the/an office
Лóндон	London	**в** _____	in London
Москва́	Moscow	**в Москве́**	in Moscow
ви́за	visa	**на** _____	on the/a visa
турага́нтсво	tour agency	**в турага́нтсве**	in the/a tour agency
письмо́	letter	**в** _____	in the/a letter

If you want to say *in* (a country), however, the prepositional ending is different if the country ends in **-ия**.

YOUR TURN

10 Complete the following.

Nominative		Prepositional	
Аме́рика	America	**в Аме́рике**	in America
Уэльс	Wales	**в** _____	in Wales
А́нглия	England	**в А́нглии**	in England
Росси́я	Russia	**в Росси́и**	in Russia
Испа́ния	Spain	**в** _____	in Spain
Шотла́ндия	Scotland	**в** _____	in Scotland
Ирландия	Ireland	**в** _____	in Ireland

> **LANGUAGE TIP**
> Very occasionally, the prepositional ending is irregular. The words you are most likely to come across where this happens are **в аэропорту́** and **в такси́**.

Practice

1 Which is the correct alternative?

a мы (рабо́таю/рабо́таем/рабо́тают)

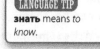

LANGUAGE TIP

знать means *to know.*

b она́ (изуча́ешь/изуча́ет/изуча́ют)

c вы (живу́/живёте/живёшь)

d они́ (зна́ете/зна́ю/зна́ют)

e я (говорю́/говори́те/говори́т)

2 Look at the café menu and answer the questions.

Кафе́ <<Класс>>

са́ндвич	100p
сала́т	150p
блины́	120p
шокола́дный торт	75p
лимона́д	35p
пепси	40p
минера́льная вода́	25p
ко́фе	45p
чай	15p
горя́чий шокола́д	30p
Телефо́н	292-00-50

a What is the name of the café?

b What costs 150 roubles?

c What can you have for dessert?

d What is the most expensive drink you can buy?

e What is the café's telephone number?

3 Who works where? Write sentences using the information given.

a Ви́ктор	рабо́тать	университе́т
b Са́ша	рабо́тать	Екатеринбу́рг
c Ты	рабо́тать	шко́ла
d Гали́на	рабо́тать	А́нглия
e Вы	рабо́тать	о́фис
f Я	рабо́тать	гости́ница
g Бори́с	рабо́тать	Москва́

Once you have checked your answers in the Key, practise saying each sentence out loud. If your ears, as well as your eyes, get used to the prepositional endings, it will be easier for you to remember them.

 4 Write some more sentences, using the information given.

a	Áнна	Брúстоль	по-англúйски
b	Я	Бúрмингем	по-англúйски
c	Никола	Парúж	по-францýзски
d	Мария и Рафал	Испáния	по-испáнски
e	Вы	Москвá	по-рýсски
f	Ты	Берлин	по-немецкй

Listen and understand

вот почемý	*that's why*
здесь	*here*
извинúте	*excuse me*
иногдá	*sometimes*
понятно	*I see* (lit. *it is understood*)
пять	*five*
тóже	*also*
тóлько	*only*

 02.03 *Michael Jones, a journalist, is met at St Petersburg airport by his guide.*

1 Why does Michael say that he needs to be able to speak Russian?

Гид	Извинúте, пожáлуйста, вы Майкл Джонс?
Майкл	Да, э́то я.
Гид	Здравствуйте! Я ваш гид. Меня зовýт Волóдя.
Майкл	Óчень приятно, Волóдя.
Гид	Вот наш автóбус, нóмер пять, Майкл.
Майкл	Спасúбо.
Гид	Скажúте, Майкл, вы англичáнин?
Майкл	Да, англичáнин.
Гид	Вы живёте в Лóндоне?
Майкл	Нет, нет, я живý в Óксфорде.
Гид	Как интересно. Вы рабóтаете в университéте?
Майкл	Нет, я журналúст.

Гид	Вы о́чень хорошо́ говори́те по-ру́сски.
Майкл	Спаси́бо. Я рабо́таю в О́ксфорде, но иногда́ в Росси́и то́же.
Гид	А, поня́тно … вот почему́ вы говори́те по-ру́сски.
Майкл	А где вы живёте, Воло́дя?
Гид	Я живу́ и рабо́таю здесь в Санкт-Петербу́рге.
Майкл	В це́нтре?
Гид	Да, да, в це́нтре … Ну, вот и ва́ша гости́ница.

2 True or false?

a Майкл Джонс живёт в Ло́ндоне.
b Майкл Джонс – журнали́ст.
c Майкл Джонс хорошо́ говори́т по-ру́сски.
d Майкл Джонс рабо́тает то́лько в О́ксфорде.
e Воло́дя живёт в Москве́.

Reading and writing

большо́й	*big*
Зи́мний дворе́ц	*Winter Palace*
кварти́ра	*flat*
коне́чно	*of course*
краси́вая архитекту́ра	*beautiful architecture*
наприме́р	*for example*
находи́ться	*to be situated*
пять миллио́нов	*5 million*
река́	*river*
ста́рый	*old*
та́кже	*also*
челове́к	*person*

Read the text and answer the questions that follow in English.

Еле́на Петро́вна Его́рова живёт в Санкт-Петербу́рге. Санкт-Петербу́рг о́чень большо́й го́род, культу́рный и администрати́вный центр. В Санкт-Петербу́рге живёт пять миллио́нов челове́к. Ле́на живёт в кварти́ре в це́нтре. Жить в це́нтре о́чень прия́тно! Там архитекту́ра о́чень краси́вая. Наприме́р, в це́нтре нахо́дятся Зи́мний дворе́ц и Эрмита́ж. И, коне́чно, в Санкт-Петербу́рге о́чень краси́вая река́ – Нева́.

В це́нтре та́кже нахо́дится о́чень большо́й, ста́рый университе́т, где Еле́на рабо́тает. Еле́на – профе́ссор.

- **a** What sort of city is St Petersburg?
- **b** What do we learn about the population?
- **c** Where exactly does Elena live?
- **d** What does she say about the architecture?
- **e** Where does she work?

 # Speaking

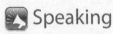 **02.04 Can you remember how to say the following in Russian? Listen to the audio and practise saying each phrase.**

- **a** What are you called?
- **b** I am called Anna.
- **c** Pleased to meet you.
- **d** I work in Moscow.
- **e** I live in London.

Test yourself

1 How do you say *I work, I speak, you work* and *you speak*?

2 How do you say *to live, I live* and *he lives*?

3 How would you reply if someone said the following to you: Как вас зову́т?

4 Can you remember how to say: *at the university, in the school, in the letter*?

5 How would you ask someone if they speak Russian?

6 There are some short words in this unit which come in very useful in all sorts of situations. Can you remember what the following mean: здесь, там, о́чень, да, нет?

7 When would you use the phrase о́чень прия́тно?

8 When would you use the phrase извини́те, пожа́луйста?

9 Explain in Russian where you live and work.

10 Can you remember how to say *my passport, my visa, your hotel*?

SELF CHECK

	I CAN...
⬤	. . . introduce myself.
⬤	. . . say my name and ask someone else's name.
⬤	. . . say *pleased to meet you*.
⬤	. . . ask people where they live/work, and say where I live/work.
⬤	. . . say which languages I speak.
⬤	. . . form the present tense of verbs.
⬤	. . . recognize the nominative and prepositional cases.

3 Где здесь гости́ница?

Where's the hotel?

In this unit you will learn how to:

▶ *ask* do you have …? *and answer* I have …
▶ *ask for and give simple directions.*
▶ *ask and say whether a place is far away or not.*
▶ *attract someone's attention.*
▶ *give and respond to thanks.*

CEFR: (A1) *Can recognize familiar words and basic phrases concerning concrete surroundings; can follow short, simple written directions.*

Russian addresses

Ле́нинский проспе́кт, дом 120, ко́рпус 3, кварти́ра 5

Russian addresses tend to look like this example, giving the number of the block of flats (**дом**), the individual building number (**ко́рпус**) – if the block of flats is made up of several sections – and finally the flat number itself (**кварти́ра**). Most Russians live on a street (**у́лица** – often abbreviated to **ул.**) or an avenue (**проспе́кт** – often abbreviated to **пр.**)

The blocks and wings, which all look very similar, are often built in large groups and will have their own shops, school, health centre and so on.

Whereas in the past it was typical to have a flat in town and a weekend cottage in the countryside – called a **да́ча** *dacha* – many wealthier Russians have now chosen to live permanently out of town. They often live in luxury out-of-town developments, which may also be gated communities, and commute into the city.

 You are given this address of a Russian colleague in Moscow: **ул. Бороди́нская, дом 145, ко́рпус 2, кварти́ра 67**. Which street would you look for, which block of flats, which individual building and, finally, which flat number?

24

Vocabulary builder

03.01 Complete the missing English expressions. Then listen to the audio and repeat the Russian until you can say all the words with confidence.

НАДО ЗНАТЬ! *ESSENTIALS*

извини́те	*excuse me*
вы не зна́ете …?	*you don't know …?*
гости́ница	*hotel*
я не зна́ю	_____
как пройти́ в?	*how do I/does one get to?*
куда́?	*where to?*
у вас есть?	*have you got?*
план	_____, *map*
у меня́ есть	_____
ну	*well …*
здесь	*here*
поня́тно	*understood*
ви́дите, ви́жу (ви́деть)	*you see, I see (_____)*
рестора́н	_____
вон там	*over there*
отту́да	*from there*
иди́те! (идти́)	*go! (to go on foot, to walk)*
напра́во	*on/to the right*
нале́во	*on/to _____*
пото́м	*then*
опя́ть	*again*
я понима́ю (понима́ть)	*I understand (_____)*
спаси́бо большо́е	*thank you very much*
её	*her*
а́дрес	_____
скажи́те	*tell me*
пря́мо	*straight on*
не́ за что	*don't mention it*

> **LANGUAGE TIP**
> Good ways of attracting someone's attention in Russian are to say **извини́те** (literally: *excuse*) or **скажи́те** (literally: *say/tell*). Add **пожа́луйста** to either of these if you want to be extra polite.

> **LANGUAGE TIP**
> Remember that **извини́те** can mean *sorry* as well as *excuse me*.

> **LANGUAGE TIP**
> To say *not*, put **не** in front of the word you want to make negative. This is often a verb: e.g. **я не понима́ю** (*I don't understand*). **Вы не зна́ете?** is a polite way of asking for information (roughly equivalent to *You don't know by any chance …?*).

Dialogue

прохо́жий	passer-by
Ле́нинский проспе́кт	Lenin Prospect (Avenue)
дом	house; block of flats
сто два́дцать	120
ко́рпус	block
три	three
кварти́ра	flat
пять	five
далеко́	a long way
о́чень	very
апте́ка	chemist's

03.02 *Ira, who lives near the hotel* Салю́т, *has invited Anna to her flat. Anna has some trouble in finding the flat and asks passers-by for help.*

1 What information does the first passer-by give Anna?

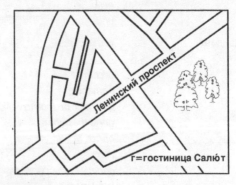

г = гостиница Салю́т

г = гости́ница Салю́т

. . . .

А́нна	Извини́те, пожа́луйста, вы не зна́ете, где гости́ница Салю́т?
Прохо́жий 1	Извини́те, не зна́ю.
А́нна	Извини́те, пожа́луйста, вы не зна́ете, как пройти́ в гости́ницу Салю́т?
Прохо́жий 2	Куда́?

Áнна	В гости́ницу Салю́т.
Прохо́жий 2	Зна́ю. У вас есть план?
Áнна	Да, у меня́ есть план. Вот он.
Прохо́жий 2	Ну, хорошо́. *(Points to map.)* Мы вот здесь. Поня́тно?
Áнна	Да, поня́тно.
Прохо́жий 2	Хорошо́. Вы ви́дите рестора́н вон там?
Áнна	Да, я ви́жу.
Прохо́жий 2	Хорошо́. Отту́да иди́те напра́во, пото́м нале́во, пото́м опя́ть нале́во.
Áнна	Хорошо́, я понима́ю: напра́во, нале́во, пото́м опя́ть нале́во. Спаси́бо большо́е.
Прохо́жий 2	Пожа́луйста.
Áнна	*(Follows instructions and arrives at* Салю́т.*)* Вот гости́ница Салю́т. А где живёт Йра? *(Looks in her bag for the address.)* Вот её а́дрес: Ле́нинский проспе́кт, дом 120, ко́рпус 3, кварти́ра 5. … Скажи́те, пожа́луйста, как пройти́ в дом 120? Это далеко́?
Прохо́жий 3	Нет, не о́чень. Ви́дите апте́ку, да? Отту́да иди́те пря́мо, пото́м нале́во.
Áнна	Спаси́бо большо́е.
Прохо́жий 3	Не́ за что.
Áнна	Ну, хорошо́, вот дом 120. А где ко́рпус 3? … Вот ко́рпус 1 … Вот корпус 2 … А вот ко́рпус 3!

LANGUAGE TIP

It might help you to remember which word means *on the left* and which *on the right* by remembering that **нале́во** (*on the left*) contains the letter *l* and **напра́во** (*on the right*) has an *r* in it.

2 True or false?

a Anna uses her phone to help her find the hotel.

b Anna goes right, then left, then right after finding the first landmark.

c It isn't far from the Hotel Salute to Ira's flat.

3 Answer the following questions.

a Which landmark does the second passer-by use for giving Anna directions?

b What is Ira's address?

c What directions does the third passer-by give Anna?

Language discovery

MORE ENDINGS

In the previous unit, you met the nominative case and the prepositional case.

 1 Can you remember what these cases are used for?

Now we meet the <u>accusative case</u>.

 2 Look at the dialogue again and find the Russian for *Do you see the restaurant?* **and** *Do you see the chemist's?* **What do you notice about the words for** *restaurant* **and** *chemist's* **here?**

The nominative is used for the person (or thing) doing an action; whereas the <u>object</u> of the action (e.g. *Do you see <u>the restaurant</u>?*) is in the accusative case.

YOUR TURN (Давáйте)

3 Which word is the object in each of the following sentences?

  a Вы вѝдите университéт?
  b Я знáю Москвý
  c Я вѝжу план

The good news is that for all neuter nouns and most masculine nouns, the accusative and the nominative are the same (see Unit 5 for more detail about the masculine nouns that do change).

All feminine nouns ending in **-a** or **-я** change their nominative endings to form the accusative:

	Remove	Add
Москвá	-a	-y
Он хорошó знáет Москвý	*He knows Moscow well*	
фамѝлия	-я	-ю
Он знáет её фамѝлию	*He knows her surname*	

(i.e. **-a → -y**; **-я → -ю**)

In Unit 2 we learned that **в** means *in* when followed by the prepositional case.

 4 Look back at the dialogue in this unit. How does the meaning of в change when it is followed by the accusative instead of the prepositional?

When you are describing motion towards, so that **в** means *to*, the accusative must be used.

Как пройти́ в гости́ницу?   *How do I get <u>to</u> the hotel?*

Russian has a special word for when you want to ask the question *where to?*: **куда́?** As a result, we need to remember the difference between this word and **где?** *where?*

> **LANGUAGE TIP**
>
> Note that there are also different words for *to there* (**туда́**) and *there* when it describes position (**там**).

▶ **Куда́** seeks information about a destination that you are going <u>to</u>: **Куда́ он идёт? – В теа́тр** *Where is he going? – To the theatre.*
▶ **Где?** seeks information about a place, a position: **Где вы живёте? – В Ло́ндоне** *Where do you live? – In London.*

VERBS

идти́ *to go on foot, to walk*

This is an irregular verb, though its endings follow a recognizable pattern.

YOUR TURN (Дава́йте)

5 Complete the verb forms for идти́ using what you learned in Unit 2.

я иду́ *I go (by foot)*; **ты идёшь** _____; **он/она́** _____ *he/she goes (by foot)*; **мы** _____ *we go (by foot)*; **вы** _____ *you go (by foot)*; **они́ иду́т** _____

в и́деть *to see*

YOUR TURN (Дава́йте)

6 Now complete the verb forms for в и́деть based on what you learned in Unit 2 and the я and вы forms given in the dialogue.

я _____ *I see*; ты ви́дишь *you see*; он/она́ _____ *he/she sees*; мы _____ *we see*; вы _____ *you see*; они́ ви́дят _____

7 Do you notice anything unusual about the spelling of one of these verb forms?

ИДИ́ТЕ! *GO!*

This is the command (or imperative) form of the verb. You have already met several of these (**здра́вствуйте**, **извини́те**, **скажи́те**). They are very straightforward to form: Take the **ты** form of the present tense and remove the last three letters – if you're left with a vowel, add **-йте** (if you're commanding **вы**; or just **-й** if you're commanding **ты**); and if you're left with a consonant, add **-ите** (or just **-и** if you're commanding **ты**).

рабóтаешь	→	рабóта-	→	+й/йте	→	рабóтай/ рабóтайте!
идёшь	→	ид-	→	+и/ите	→	иди́/иди́те!

Note that commands are usually followed by an exclamation mark in Russian.

У ВАС ЕСТЬ ... ? *DO YOU HAVE ... ?*

If you want to say *do you have?*, the phrase you use in Russian literally means *by you is there?* Take away the question mark and, of course, you get the statement *you have*.

Note that:

▶ This is not a verb; it is a phrase used instead of a verb.

▶ It is not essential to include the word **есть** (which means *there is/are*): **У меня́ план** and **У меня́ есть план** both mean *I have a plan*. **Есть** lends greater emphasis: i.e. *I do have a plan*.

 8 Complete the following with the correct English pronouns. Note the forms the pronouns take in this phrase.

ты	у тебя́	*you have*
он	у негó	_____ *has*
онá	у неё	_____ *has*
мы	у нас	_____ *have*
вы	у вас	_____ *have*
они́	у них	_____ *have*

 Practice

1 Choose the correct option in each sentence. Are you talking about *where you are* or *where you are going <u>to</u>*?

a (Кудá/Где) вы идёте?

b Онá живёт (в Омск/в Ómске).

c Мы рабóтаем (в университéт/в университéте).

d Сáша идёт (в аптéку/в аптéке).

e Волóдя рабóтает (в ресторáн/в ресторáне).

2 Choose the correct option. Do you need the nominative case or the accusative?

a Вы зна́ете (Москва́/Москву́)?

b (Ма́ша/Ма́шу) рабо́тает в рестора́не.

c Он ви́дит (О́льга/О́льгу).

3 Look at the following tweet, then answer the questions.

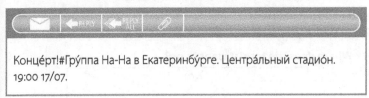

Конце́рт!#Гру́ппа На-На в Екатеринбу́рге. Центра́льный стадио́н. 19:00 17/07.

a What is the tweet about?

b Where and when should you go?

4 Who lives where? Look back at the Language discovery section in Unit 2 and write sentences using the information given, as in the example.

a О́льга/Самарка́нд →О́льга живёт в Самарка́нде

b Ви́ктор/Ки́ев

c Я/А́нглия

d Ты/Оде́сса

e Сла́ва и Ки́ра/Ита́лия

5 What question was asked for each of these answers?

a Меня́ зову́т А́нна.

b Я живу́ в А́нглии.

c Я рабо́таю в Бри́столе.

d Я иду́ в гости́ницу.

e Да, у меня́ есть план.

6 How would you say the following phrases in Russian?

a I have a passport.

b Do you have a passport?

c They have a visa.

d We have a visa.

Listen and understand

кинотеа́тр	*cinema*
туда́	*to there*
ничего́ (pronounced 'nichevo')	*never mind*
ста́нция метро́	*metro station*
музе́й космона́втики	*space museum*

 03.03 *A tourist stops a passer-by to ask for directions.*

1   Where does the tourist want to go?

проспект Мира

① станция метро
② гостинице
③ музей
④ кинотеатр

Тури́ст	Извини́те, пожа́луйста.
Прохо́жий	Да?
Тури́ст	Вы не зна́ете, где нахо́дится кинотеа́тр Ко́смос?
Прохо́жий	Кинотеа́тр Ко́смос? … ну, да … на проспе́кте Ми́ра.
Тури́ст	Спаси́бо. А как пройти́ туда́?
Прохо́жий	Вы зна́ете, где проспе́кт Ми́ра?
Тури́ст	Нет, не зна́ю. Я не о́чень хорошо́ зна́ю Москву́.
Прохо́жий	Ничего́. Кинотеа́тр Ко́смос не о́чень далеко́.
Тури́ст	Хорошо́!
Прохо́жий	Вы ви́дите ста́нцию метро́ вон там?
Тури́ст	Да, ви́жу.
Прохо́жий	Хорошо́. Отту́да иди́те напра́во. Это проспе́кт Ми́ра. Нале́во гости́ница Ко́смос.
Тури́ст	А кинотеа́тр то́же там?

Прохо́жий	Нет. Иди́те пря́мо. Напра́во нахо́дится музе́й космона́втики.
Тури́ст	Хорошо́, я понима́ю – гости́ница нале́во, музе́й напра́во.
Прохо́жий	Да. Иди́те пря́мо. Кинотеа́тр на углу́. Поня́тно?
Тури́ст	Да, спаси́бо большо́е.
Прохо́жий	Не́ за что.

> **LANGUAGE TIP**
>
> Because there is no word in Russian for *to be*, other verbs are sometimes used instead. When you are talking about where places are, you can use **находи́ться**, which really means *to find itself*.

2 Which three other places are mentioned in the directions given?

3 Choose the correct option to complete the sentences.

  a Кинотеа́тр Ко́смос нахо́дится
    1 в гости́нице Ко́смос
    2 в музе́е космона́втики
    3 на проспе́кте Ми́ра

  b Кинотеа́тр Ко́смос нахо́дится
    1 о́чень далеко́
    2 не о́чень далеко́
    3 в метро́

  c Вот ста́нция метро́. Отту́да
    1 тури́ст идёт напра́во
    2 тури́ст идёт нале́во
    3 тури́ст идёт в гости́ницу

  d Вот у́гол. Там нахо́дится
    1 кинотеа́тр
    2 гости́ница
    3 музе́й

Reading and writing

ва́нная	*bathroom*
в при́городе	*in the suburbs/on the outskirts*
гости́ная	*sitting room*

дочь (f.)	daughter
жена́	wife
зна́чит	that means, so
ита́к	and so
касси́рша	cashier
коне́чно	of course
ку́хня	kitchen
соба́ка	dog
спа́льня	bedroom
суперма́ркет	supermarket
типи́чная кварти́ра	typical flat
то есть	that is (i.e.)

 Read the text and answer the questions that follow in English.

Анато́лий Фёдорович Маша́тин – инжене́р. Он живёт в Москве́ не в це́нтре, а в при́городе . У него́ жена́, Валенти́на Никола́евна, дочь Мари́на и соба́ка Ша́рик. Валенти́на рабо́тает в апте́ке, а Мари́на уже́ три го́да рабо́тает в кинотеа́тре, она́ касси́рша. Ша́рик, коне́чно, не рабо́тает. Они́ живу́т в кварти́ре. Это типи́чная кварти́ра: ку́хня, ва́нная, спа́льня и гости́ная. Зна́чит, э́то не о́чень больша́я кварти́ра. В при́городе где они́ живу́т, нахо́дятся суперма́ркет, апте́ка, кинотеа́тр, шко́ла и ста́нция метро́. Валенти́на и Мари́на рабо́тают в при́городе, а Анато́лий рабо́тает в це́нтре, то есть о́чень далеко́.

> **LANGUAGE TIP**
> The Russian word **a** is sometimes translated into English as *and* and sometimes as *but*. Keep an eye out for **a** in this and other texts.

- **a** What is Anatoly's surname?
- **b** Where does his wife work?
- **c** How long has Marina worked at the cinema?
- **d** Where exactly do they live?
- **e** What is a typical urban Russian flat like?
- **f** What amenities are there in the area where Anatoly and his family live?

Speaking

03.04 You are asking a passer-by how to get to the chemist's. Play your part, then listen to the complete conversation on the audio.

Вы	**a** *Ask how to get to the chemist's.*
Прохо́жий	Иди́те пря́мо, пото́м нале́во.
Вы	**b** *Ask if it is far.*
Прохо́жий	Нет, не о́чень.
Вы	**c** *Say thank you very much.*
Прохо́жий	Не́ за что.

2 03.05 Can you remember how to say the following in Russian? Listen to the audio and practise saying each phrase.

a Thank you very much.
b Have you got a map?
c Tell me, please …
d How do I get to the theatre?
e Is it far?

⁇ Test yourself

1 How do you say *where to?* and *where?* in Russian?

2 Which three questions can you now ask that begin with the word как?

3 What do you do if you want to make a verb negative in Russian? (e.g. *I don't know*)

4 How do you say these useful everyday phrases: *excuse me, please; tell me, please* and *thank you very much*?

5 When seeking and giving information about where things are, how do you say *on the right, on the left, straight on* and *it is far*?

6 Can you remember the grammatical difference between the subject and the object of a verb?

7 Which case do you use for the object of a verb in Russian?

8 What changes would you make to the following nouns if they were in the accusative case: аптéка, ресторáн, метро?

9 Why is the word теáтр theatre spelled differently in the following phrases: Ивáн идёт в теáтр, Ивáн рабóтает в теáтре?

10 How do you ask *Do you have a dog?* and answer *Yes, I do have a dog?*

	SELF CHECK
	I CAN...
○	... ask *do you have ...?* and answer *I have ...*
○	... ask for and give simple directions.
○	... ask and say whether a place is far away or not.
○	... attract someone's attention.
○	... give and respond to thanks.

4 Здесь мо́жно фотографи́ровать?

Can you take photographs here?

In this unit you will learn how to:
▶ *ask/state whether something is permitted or not.*
▶ *ask/state whether something is possible, impossible or necessary.*
▶ *express regret.*

CEFR: (A1) *Can ask people for things; can make and respond to suggestions; can get simple information.*

 ## Музе́й *The museum*

Moscow and St Petersburg have many important museums, including world-class ones such as the Hermitage (**Эрмита́ж**) in St Petersburg and the Kremlin museums in Moscow. Some 'museums' cover whole geographical areas, such as **Коло́менское**, now a village but a former royal residence near Moscow. **Коло́менское** is called a **музе́й-запове́дник** – a museum and conservation area.

In each room of a Russian museum it is usual for an attendant to be on duty. This attendant is usually an expert on the museum's exhibits and also looks after the security of their room. Russian museums usually also have a group of highly-qualified and multi-lingual guides to help visitors see and appreciate the museum's highlights. In all but the smallest museums visitors are expected to leave their hats, coats and bags in the **гардеро́б** *cloakroom*, and there is no charge for this service. It is considered **некульту́рно** *uncivilized* to wear one's outdoor clothing in public places (e.g. theatres, restaurants). Very often, the floors of museum buildings are part of the exhibits and so visitors are required to put on disposable plastic overshoes (**та́почки**) so as not to cause damage as they walk around.

 What instruction are you being given in the following notice?
Не фотографи́ровать в музе́е зооло́гии!

Vocabulary builder

04.01 Complete the missing English expressions. Then listen to the audio and repeat the Russian until you can say all the words with confidence.

НА́ДО ЗНАТЬ В МУЗЕ́Е *MUSEUM ESSENTIALS*

здесь мо́жно фотографи́ровать	*here you can* _____
здесь мо́жно купи́ть биле́ты	*here you can buy tickets*
нельзя́ кури́ть	*no smoking*
в музе́е нельзя́ фотографи́ровать	_____
на́до идти́ в ка́ссу	*you need to go to the cash desk/ ticket office*
на́до купи́ть биле́ты	*you need to* _____
к сожале́нию …	*unfortunately …*

> **LANGUAGE TIP**
> Don't forget that all of these expressions can be turned into questions just by the addition of a question mark.

ВЫ – ТУРИ́СТ? НА́ДО ЗНАТЬ! *SIGHTSEEING ESSENTIALS*

како́е краси́вое ме́сто	*what a beautiful place*
зда́ния	*buildings*
це́рковь (f.)	*church*
я хочу́, ты хо́чешь (хоте́ть)	*I want,* _____ (_____)
посети́ть	*to visit*
я люблю́ (люби́ть)	*I like (_____)*
на́до	*it is necessary*
купи́ть	*to* _____
биле́ты	_____
в ка́ссе	*at the* _____
ла́дно	*OK*
мо́жно	*it is possible, one may*
откры́тки	*postcards*
вход	*entrance*
смотре́ть	*to look, watch*
ка́рта	*map*
действи́тельно	*really*
деревя́нный	*wooden*

> **LANGUAGE TIP**
> **Мо́жно** is a very useful word in Russian. It is usually followed by an infinitive, but if, for example, you wanted to ask if a seat on the bus/metro/tram or in a restaurant/theatre were free, just indicate it with your hand and say **Мо́жно?**

стул	*chair*
нельзя́	_____
ду́мать	*to think*
де́лать	*to do*

Dialogue

 04.02 *Ira has taken Anna to see a former royal estate on the banks of the Moskva river.*

1   What is the first question Anna asks Ira?

А́нна	Како́е краси́вое ме́сто!
И́ра	Да, здесь зда́ния о́чень краси́вые.
А́нна	А како́е э́то зда́ние, вон там, нале́во?
И́ра	Э́то о́чень ста́рая це́рковь. Краси́вая, да?
А́нна	Да, о́чень. Я хочу́ посети́ть музе́й. Мо́жно?
И́ра	Да, коне́чно.
А́нна	Хорошо́. Я о́чень люблю́ музе́и.
И́ра	Хорошо́ … На́до купи́ть биле́ты в ка́ссе.
А́нна	Ла́дно … Скажи́, И́ра, в ка́ссе мо́жно купи́ть откры́тки?
И́ра	Не зна́ю … *(Asks at ticket office.)* … Нет, нельзя́. Здесь мо́жно купи́ть то́лько биле́ты.
А́нна	Ничего́.
И́ра	Ну, вот вход в музе́й … Смотри́, А́нна, вон там напра́во, о́чень ста́рая ка́рта.
А́нна	Да, э́то действи́тельно интере́сная ка́рта. А э́то что?
И́ра	Э́то о́чень ста́рый деревя́нный стул.
А́нна	Скажи́, И́ра, здесь мо́жно фотографи́ровать?
И́ра	*(Asks the museum attendant.)* … Нет, А́нна, к сожале́нию в музе́е нельзя́ фотографи́ровать.
А́нна	*(Sighs.)* … Ну, ничего́ …

> **LANGUAGE TIP**
>
> Anna and Ira have clearly become friends and now address each other as **ты**; this can be seen because Anna uses **Скажи́**, rather than **Скажи́те**. Remember that **вы** is the polite form of address and on the whole it is better to use this unless a Russian invites you to change to **ты** (e.g. by saying **дава́й на ты**).

2 True or false?

   a Anna thinks that the church is beautiful.

   b You can't buy postcards at the ticket office.

   c You can take photographs in the museum.

3 Answer the following questions in Russian using the information in the dialogue.

   a Где надо купить билеты?

   b Что они видят в музее?

   c Что нельзя делать в музее?

Language discovery

PLURAL NOUNS

1 Looking back at the dialogue, what do you notice about the Russian words for *tickets* **and** *postcards***?**

The nominative plural of masculine or feminine nouns usually ends in **-ы** or **-и**.

You use **-ы** except for in the following two situations:

▶ you use **-и** if the noun is soft. This means that, in the nominative singular, the noun ends in **-ь**, **-й** or **-я**.

▶ you use **-и** if the letter before the ending is: **г**, **к**, **х**, **ж**, **ч**, **ш** or **щ**. This is an essential rule of spelling in Russian and applies whenever we need to use the letter **ы** (this also applies to **-ю** and **-я** – more on this later!)

2 Bearing these two situations in mind, complete the following.

Nom. sing.	Remove	Add	Nom. pl.	Meaning
университет	–	-ы	университеты	*universities*
газета	-а	_____	_____	*newspapers*
автомобиль	-ь	_____	автомобили	_____
дверь	_____	_____		*doors*
трамвай	-й	_____	_____	_____
станция	_____	_____	_____	_____
парк	–	-и	_____	_____
девушка	_____	_____		*girls*

> **LANGUAGE TIP**
> The spelling rule came about because it is quite difficult to pronounce the prohibited vowels (**ы**, **ю**, **я**) after **г**, **к**, **х**, **ж**, **ч**, **ш**, **щ** and easier to say the alternatives (**и**, **у**, **а**). Try repeating the sounds **г**, **к**, **х**, **ж**, **ч**, **ш**, **щ** out loud to memorize them.

The nominative plural of neuter nouns is **a** for hard nouns (i.e. those ending in **o**) and **я** for soft nouns (i.e. those ending in **e**).

Nom. sing.	Remove	Add	Nom. pl.	Meaning
письмó	-о	-а	пи́сьма	*letters*
зда́ние	-е	-я	зда́ния	*buildings*

Just as in English, there are some very irregular plurals. Here are some common ones (a fuller list is given in the Appendix).

Meaning	Singular	Plural
child	ребёнок	де́ти
person	челове́к	лю́ди
eye	глаз	глаза́
daughter	дочь	дочери
mother	мать	ма́тери
train	по́езд	поезда́
friend	друг	друзья́

The good news is that the accusative plural is exactly the same as the nominative plural for most nouns (see Unit 7 for more detail about the nouns that do change), e.g.:

Nom. pl.		Acc. pl.
Тури́сты	смо́трят	фи́льмы
The tourists	*are watching*	*films*

ADJECTIVES

Adjectives describe nouns. We have already met the following phrases that include adjectives:

интере́сный музе́й	*an interesting museum*
типи́чная кварти́ра	*a typical flat*
краси́вое ме́сто	*a beautiful place*

The famous **Большо́й теа́тр** includes an adjective – **большо́й** simply means *big*. In dictionaries and vocabularies adjectives are always given in the nominative masculine singular. The most important thing to remember about adjectives is that they must agree with the noun they describe in number (i.e. singular or plural), gender (masculine, feminine, neuter) and case (i.e. nominative, accusative, etc.). The most usual endings for adjectives in the nominative singular and plural are:

Masc. sing.	Fem. sing.	Neut. sing.	Pl.
-ый	-ая	-ое	-ые
типи́чный университе́т	типи́чная кварти́ра	типи́чное зда́ние	типи́чные тури́сты

Note that the plural ending is the same for masculine, feminine and neuter adjectives. Remember to be on the lookout for **г, к, х, ж, ч, ш, щ** as then the masculine singular ending will be **-ий** and the plural will be **-ие**:

ма́ленький университе́т   *a small university*

хоро́шие журна́лы   *good magazines*

You will notice that a very small number of adjectives have the masculine ending **-ой** (not **-ый**), e.g.:

большо́й дом   *a big house*

молодо́й актёр   *a young actor*

but don't worry – the remaining endings (feminine, neuter and plural) are all entirely regular.

КАКО́Й *WHICH?*

This adjective means either *which?/what sort of?* or *what a!*

YOUR TURN (Дава́йте)

3 How would you translate the following sentences?

**Како́й фильм ты хо́чешь   Кака́я краси́вая це́рковь!
смотре́ть?**

POSSIBILITY/IMPOSSIBILITY/NECESSITY

Мо́жно, нельзя́ and **на́до** are extremely common and very useful words. They are all used with an infinitive (such as *to smoke*).

**4 Look at the example, then work out what the other two
    sentences mean in English.**

В теа́тре нельзя́ кури́ть!   *No smoking in the theatre!*
В магази́не мо́жно купи́ть   _____
откры́тки
В Росси́и на́до посети́ть Кремль   _____
В Москве́!

SOME USEFUL IRREGULAR VERBS

Люби́ть *to like, love* is only irregular because it has an extra **л** in the **я** form.

YOUR TURN (Давайте)

5 Complete the rest of the forms for люби́ть.

я люблю́ *I like/love;* **ты лю́бишь** *you like/love;* **он/она́** _____ *he/she likes/loves;* **мы** _____ *we like/love;* **вы** _____ *you like/love;* **они́** _____ *they like/love*

The verb **гото́вить** *to prepare, cook* follows exactly the same pattern as **лю́бить**.

YOUR TURN (Давайте)

6 Complete the forms for гото́вить.

_____ *I prepare/cook;* _____ *you prepare/cook;* _____ *he/she prepares/cooks;* _____ *we prepare/cook;* _____ *you prepare/cook;* _____ *they prepare/cook*

Хоте́ть *to want* doesn't conform to the pattern of irregular verbs we have met so far. Because it is so irregular and because it is such a useful verb, it is worth learning it off by heart.

я хочу́	*I want*
ты хо́чешь	*you want*
он/она́ хо́чет	*he/she wants*
мы хоти́м	*we want*
вы хоти́те	*you want*
они́ хотя́т	*they want*

> **LANGUAGE TIP**
> Luckily, verb irregularities often sound so strange that they are easy to remember: **я хочу́** *I want* sounds rather like a sneeze, and the sound of **я люблю́** *I like/love* might remind you of the character in Andy Pandy – Looby Lou.

 Practice

1 Match the questions with the answers.

a Где мо́жно смотре́ть фи́льмы?   **1** в суперма́ркете

b Где мо́жно купи́ть вино́?   **2** в ка́ссе

c Где мо́жно смотре́ть бале́т?   **3** в кинотеа́тре

d Где мо́жно купи́ть биле́ты?   **4** в теа́тре

2 Look at the pictures and answer the questions.

These items are from a leaflet in a hotel room. What instructions are being given?

a В ли́фте нельзя́ кури́ть!   **b** В посте́ли не кури́ть!

c If **фа́брика** means *factory*, what sort of factory is being advertised?

Россия

шоколадная фабрика

СКАЗКИ ЛЕСА
КОНФЕТЫ

LANGUAGE TIP

Apart from helping you to learn the word **какой**, Exercise 3 is also designed to help you remember the different endings for masculine, feminine and neuter adjectives. If you were at all unsure about any of the endings, just check again with the Language discovery section.

3 Here are some answers. What were the questions? Complete the missing letters and words.

    a Какой э́то го́род?   Э́то большо́й го́род

    b Кака́я э́то _____?   Э́то ста́рая це́рковь

    c Как_____ э́то _____?   Э́то интере́сный музе́й

    d Как_____ э́то _____?   Э́то ма́ленькое зда́ние

    e _____?   Э́то но́вая кни́га

    f _____?   Э́то большо́й дом

4 Look at the map. Viktor is standing outside the school. Give the six instructions (indicated by the arrows) which will enable him to get to the **театр**.

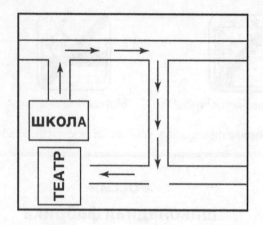

Идите _____, потом _____, потом _____, потом _____, потом _____, потом _____.

 5 Answer these questions about yourself.

a Как вас зовут?

b Где вы живёте?

c Где вы работаете?

d Вы живёте в доме или (or) в квартире?

e Какой у вас дом?/Какая у вас квартира?

Listen and understand

бесплатный	free
вечером	in the evening
дискотека	disco
завтракать	to eat breakfast
к сожалению	unfortunately
номер	hotel room
ночной клуб	night club
поп-музыка	pop music
чем помочь?	how can I help you?

04.03 *Julia has just arrived in St Petersburg for a holiday and is chatting to the receptionist (**администра́тор**).*

1 What is the first question Julia asks?

Ю́лия	Извини́те, пожа́луйста!
Администратор	Чем могу помо́чь?
Ю́лия	Интерне́т в но́мере - беспла́тный?
Администратор	Да, коне́чно. Вы хоти́те код?
Ю́лия	Мо́жно?
Администратор	Да, коне́чно. Код – Пи́тер 1.
Ю́лия	Спаси́бо. А что мо́жно де́лать ве́чером в гости́нице?
Администратор	У нас есть дискоте́ка.
Ю́лия	Да, интере́сно … но я не о́чень люблю́ поп-му́зыку.
Администратор	И, коне́чно, в гости́нице есть о́чень хоро́ший рестора́н.
Ю́лия	А ве́чером что мо́жно де́лать в го́роде?
Администратор	В городе? Ну, в го́роде есть, коне́чно, теа́тры, кинотеа́тры, рестора́ны, дискоте́ки и ночны́е клу́бы.
Ю́лия	Хорошо́. Скажи́те, пожа́луйста, мо́жно за́втракать в номере?
Администратор	Да, коне́чно мо́жно. Вот меню́.
Ю́лия	Хорошо́. Спаси́бо! Скажи́те, в ресторане мо́жно кури́ть?
Администратор	К сожа́лению, в рестора́не нельзя́ кури́ть!

2 True or false?
a Ю́лия рабо́тает в Санкт-Петербу́рге.
b В гости́нице интерне́т беспла́тный.
c Ю́лия лю́бит дискоте́ки.
d В го́роде нельзя́ смотре́ть фи́льмы.
e В гости́нице мо́жно за́втракать в номере.
f На́до кури́ть в рестора́не.

Reading and writing

ви́деть	*to see*
заво́д	*factory*
золото́й	*golden*

и … и	*both … and*
исто́рия	*history*
кольцо́	*ring*
красота́	*beauty*
ле́том	*in the summer*
огуре́ц	*cucumber*
огоро́д	*kitchen garden*
па́мятник	*monument*
пое́здка	*journey*
помидо́р	*tomato*
потому́ что	*because*
производи́ть	*to produce*
собо́р	*cathedral*
хотя́	*although*
хруста́ль (m.)	*crystal*

Read the text and answer the questions that follow in English.

МОСКВА – ВЛАДИМИР   ВЛАДИМИР – СУЗДАЛВ

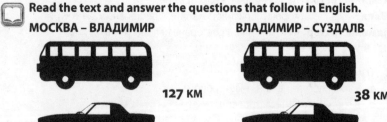

127 КМ   **38 КМ**

Пое́здка в Москву́, Влади́мир и Су́здаль? Кака́я хоро́шая иде́я! Почему́? Потому́ что Москва́– Влади́мир – Су́здаль – э́то «золото́е кольцо́» – зна́чит там и ру́сская исто́рия, и ру́сская культу́ра и ру́сская красота́. Мы уже́ зна́ем, что Москва́ – столи́ца Росси́и, но э́то та́кже, коне́чно, о́чень ста́рый ру́сский го́род. Влади́мир и Су́здаль то́же о́чень ста́рые ру́сские города́, краси́вые и истори́ческие. В Су́здале и Влади́мире есть краси́вые, ста́рые музе́и, це́ркви, собо́ры и па́мятники. Хотя́ Влади́мир о́чень ста́рый го́род, там та́кже нахо́дятся заво́ды, где произво́дят тра́кторы и компью́теры и де́лают краси́вый хруста́ль. Су́здаль – э́то музе́й-го́род – зна́чит там интере́сные музе́и, па́мятники, о́чень ста́рая, красивая архитекту́ра. В Су́здале есть краси́вые сады́ и огоро́ды, где летом можно видеть огурцы́ и помидо́ры.

- **a** What expression is used to describe the cities of Moscow, Vladimir and Suzdal?
- **b** What sort of cities are Vladimir and Suzdal?
- **c** What sort of buildings are to be found there?
- **d** What is produced in the factories in Vladimir?
- **e** Why is Suzdal called a 'museum town'?
- **f** What else is Suzdal famous for?

Speaking

1 04.04 You are trying to find your way round Kolomenskoye. Play your part, then listen to the complete conversation on the audio.

Вы	**a** *Say 'Excuse me, please'.*
Прохо́жий	Да?
Вы	**b** *Ask how to get to the church.*
Прохо́жий	Це́рковь вон там, нале́во.
Вы	**c** *Say 'Thank you' and ask where the museum is.*
Прохо́жий	Пря́мо, пото́м напра́во.
Вы	**d** *Ask where you can buy tickets.*
Прохо́жий	В ка́ссе, коне́чно.
Вы	**e** *Say 'Thank you' and 'Goodbye'.*
Прохо́жий	Пожа́луйста, до свида́ния.

2 04.05 Can you remember how to say the following in Russian? Listen to the audio and practise saying each phrase.

- **a** Where is it possible to buy postcards?
- **b** It is necessary to buy a ticket.
- **c** What sort of museum is it?
- **d** It's not possible (one may not) to smoke here.
- **e** OK.

? Test yourself

1 Which word would you use if you wanted to ask if something were possible?

2 What is the important thing to remember about the я form of the verb люби́ть?

3 What are the usual nominative plural endings for masculine and feminine nouns?

4 Adjectives must agree with the nouns they describe. So, if a noun is neuter, will the adjective describing it end in -ый, -ая or -ое?

5 If someone said Нельзя́! to you, what would you understand by this?

6 How would you say *which?* or *what sort of?* in Russian?

7 Челове́к is, of course, a very common word, but it has a very irregular plural. Can you remember what it is?

8 It is important to be able understand the question Вы хоти́те …? Can you remember what it means?

9 If you wanted to explain that you need to/must do something, would you use: мо́жно, на́до or нельзя́?

10 After which letters would you not use ы, ю or я?

SELF CHECK

I CAN…

- … ask/state whether something is permitted or not.
- … ask/state whether something is possible, impossible or necessary.
- … express regret.

Сколько стоит?

How much is it?

In this unit you will learn how to:

▶ *ask for and give simple information about cost and availability.*
▶ *ask for tickets to places and events.*
▶ *express location and distance from.*

CEFR: (A1) *Can handle numbers, quantities, cost and time.*

Покупки *Shopping*

In the former Soviet Union, shopping was often a difficult business, involving queuing, shortages and, at one stage, even rationing. Kiosks were a frequent feature on city streets, selling such things as flowers, postcards, maps and newspapers. Since the fall of the Soviet Union, shopping has changed radically for Russians. Shops have become far more attractive and shortages are definitely a thing of the past. Kiosks are still very much in business, but many have evolved into more permanent structures and sell a huge range of products. Most leading Western brands are on sale in Russia – both in the large department stores (**универма́ги**) and small, local stores. Markets remain a very good place to buy souvenirs and fresh produce, while supermarkets (**универса́мы** or **супермаркеты**), can be found on every street (though in city centres they tend to be smaller than in the West).

Match the following items to the shops in which you would buy them.

1 mp3 player   **a** Проду́кты

2 wine   **b** Фру́кты

3 designer clothes **c** Вино́

4 food   **d** Электро́ника

5 fresh fruit   **e** Мо́да

Vocabulary builder

оди́н	1	шесть	6	оди́ннадцать	11	шестна́дцать	16
два	2	семь	7	двена́дцать	12	семна́дцать	17
три	3	во́семь	8	трина́дцать	13	восемна́дцать	18
четы́ре	4	де́вять	9	четы́рнадцать	14	девятна́дцать	19
пять	5	де́сять	10	пятна́дцать	15	два́дцать	20

Complete the missing English expressions. Then listen to the audio and repeat the Russian until you can say all the words with confidence.

ВЫ – ТУРИ́СТ? TRAVEL ESSENTIALS

у вас есть биле́ты (в теа́тр/на о́перу)?	have you got any tickets for the _____/_____?
ско́лько сто́ит биле́т?	how much does a _____ cost?
с вас сто рубле́й	that costs 100 roubles
сле́ва от теа́тра	_____ of the theatre
недалеко́ от ста́нции метро́	_____ from the metro station
заказа́ть	to book, reserve
биле́ты на сего́дня на ве́чер	_____ for this evening
на како́й спекта́кль?	for which show?
на пье́су «Три сестры́»	for the play 'The Three Sisters'
два биле́та	two _____

НА́ДО ЗНАТЬ! ESSENTIALS

ещё	still
сего́дня (pronounced 'sivodnya')	today
за́втра	tomorrow
иногда́	sometimes
у́лица	street
шестьсо́т рубле́й	600 _____
да́йте	give (command form)
ты́сяча две́сти рубле́й	1,200 _____
у вас нет ме́лочи?	haven't you got any change?

> **LANGUAGE TIP**
> Note that **ме́лочь** (f.) is *small change* (in practice, lower denomination notes); the Russian word for money given to the buyer as change is **сда́ча**.

Dialogue

 05.02 *Anna is trying to get two tickets and tries first at the hotel service bureau* (**бюро́ обслу́живания**), *then at a kiosk.*

1 What does Anna plan to do this evening? Does she manage to do this?

А́нна	Скажи́те, пожа́луйста, здесь мо́жно заказа́ть биле́ты в теа́тр?
Де́вушка 1	Мо́жно.
А́нна	Хорошо́. У вас есть биле́ты на сего́дня на ве́чер?
Де́вушка 1	Нет. Но на сего́дня на ве́чер у нас ещё есть биле́ты в цирк. Хоти́те?
А́нна	Спаси́бо, нет, в цирк я не хочу́.
Де́вушка 1	У нас есть биле́ты в теа́тр, но то́лько на за́втра. Хоти́те?
А́нна	Спаси́бо, нет. Я хочу́ биле́ты на сего́дня на ве́чер.
Де́вушка 1	Зна́ете, иногда́ мо́жно купи́ть биле́ты в ка́ссе и́ли в кио́ске.
А́нна	В кио́ске?
Де́вушка 1	Да, кио́ск нахо́дится на у́лице, сле́ва от апте́ки, недалеко́ от ста́нции метро́.
А́нна	Спаси́бо. До свида́ния.
Де́вушка 1	Пожа́луйста.
А́нна	*(At the kiosk.)* Скажи́те, пожа́луйста, у вас есть биле́ты на сего́дня?
Де́вушка 2	На како́й спекта́кль?
А́нна	На бале́т «Жизе́ль».
Де́вушка 2	Нет. У нас оди́н биле́т на о́перу «Карме́н» и четы́ре биле́та на пье́су «Три сестры́» Че́хова.
А́нна	Ой, как хорошо́. Я Че́хова о́чень люблю́. Ско́лько сто́ит биле́т на пье́су?
Де́вушка 2	Шестьсо́т рубле́й.
А́нна	Да́йте, пожа́луйста, два биле́та на пье́су.
Де́вушка 2	Пожа́луйста … С вас ты́сяча две́сти рубле́й. *(Anna hands over two 1,000-rouble notes.)* У вас нет ме́лочи?
А́нна	Извини́те, нет. *(Receives change and tickets.)* Спаси́бо большо́е.
Де́вушка 2	Пожа́луйста.

2 True or false?

a Anna wants to buy tickets to the circus.

b You can't buy a ticket at the kiosk.

c Anna wants to buy two tickets.

3 Answer the following questions.

a Какие билеты мóжно купить в бюрó обслýживания на сегóдня на вéчер?

b Где нахóдится киóск?

c Скóлько стóит билéт на пьéсу?

Language discovery

НА + PREPOSITIONAL: *IN* OR *AT*

There is a group of words with which the preposition **в** is not used when expressing the position *in* or *at*. Unfortunately, we just have to learn these as exceptions. These words are mainly about events (e.g. a concert) or about places that are not just one enclosed space (e.g. railway station, south). With these words you must use **на** to mean *in* or *at*. Here are the most common (a fuller list is given in the Appendix):

вокзáл	на вокзáле	*at the (railway) station (terminus, main line)*
стáнция	на стáнции	*at the (bus/underground/small railway) station*
пóчта	на пóчте	*at the post office*
стадиóн	на стадиóне	*at the stadium*
плóщадь (f.)	на плóщади	*in/on the square*
ýлица	на ýлице	*in/on the street*
концéрт	на концéрте	*at the concert*
рабóта	на рабóте	*at work*
востóк	на востóке	*in the east*
зáпад	на зáпаде	*in the west*
сéвер	на сéвере	*in the north*
юг	на юге	*in the south*

> **LANGUAGE TIP**
>
> It is useful to know that **на** + accusative can mean *for the purpose of, intended for*. Did you notice how to say *a ticket for today* – **билéт на сегóдня**, and *a ticket for tomorrow* – **билéт на зáвтра**? The words for *today* and *tomorrow* are indeclinable (i.e. their endings never change).

THE GENITIVE CASE

Once you know this case, all sorts of possibilities are opened up! The principal meaning of this case is *of*. For example, if you want to say *A map of the town*, the way you do this is to put the word *town* into the genitive case.

> **LANGUAGE TIP**
>
> The genitive case in Russian is also used for the English apostrophe *s* (e.g. *Anna's ticket*) and *s* apostrophe (e.g. *tourists' tickets*) – because, of course, these could be reworded as *the ticket of Anna* and *the tickets of the tourists*.

Other main uses of the genitive case:

▶ after quantity words: e.g. **мно́го** *a lot (of)*; **ско́лько** *how many* and *how much (of)*; **буты́лка** *a bottle (of)*

▶ after several prepositions: **без** *without*; **от** *(away) from*; **для** *for*; **по́сле** *after*; **до** *until, before, as far as*; **с** *(down) from, since*; **из** *from (out of)*; **у** *by, near, at the house of*

▶ after numbers: after two, three and four the genitive singular is used; for numbers five and above, see later in this section, Unit 7 and Unit 20.

▶ in negative phrases: e.g. *I haven't got (any of)*

YOUR TURN (Дава́йте)

1 Complete the English meanings.

Use	Example	Meaning
of	**Это биле́т А́нны**	*This is Anna's* _____
quantity	**У вас мно́го багажа́!**	*You have* _____ *luggage!*
prepositions	**Недалеко́ от теа́тра**	*Not far from the* _____
numbers	**Два биле́та**	_____ *tickets*
negatives	**У меня́ нет биле́та**	*I haven't got a ticket*

The genitive singular of nouns is formed from the nominative in the following way.

2 Study the pattern and complete the following.

Nominative Masc.	Remove	Add	Genitive	Meaning
университе́т	–	-а	университе́та	*of (a/the) university*
автомоби́ль	-ь	-я	_____	*of (a/the) car*
трамва́й	-й	_____	трамва́я	*of (a/the) tram*
Fem.				
гости́ница	-а	-ы	гости́ницы	_____
неде́ля	-я	-и	_____	*of (a/the) week*

ста́нция	-я	-и	ста́нции	_____
дверь	_____	-и	две́ри	of (a/the) door
Neut.				
письмо́	-о	_____	пи́сьма́	of (a/the) letter
_____	-е	-я	мо́ря	of (a/the) sea
зда́ние	-е	-я	_____	of (a/the) building

Did you figure out the pattern? Each gender has hard and soft options (see Unit 4): the genitive singular forms of masculine and neuter nouns have the same endings (**а** or **я**); feminine nouns end in **ы** or **и**.

> **LANGUAGE TIP**
>
> Remember the spelling rule from Unit 4! When you remove the **-а** from the end of a feminine noun, if you are left with **г**, **к**, **х**, **ж**, **ч**, **ш**, or **щ**, you must add **-и**, not **-ы** (*three books* = **три кни́ги**).

The genitive case of personal pronouns is shown in the table:

Nom.	Gen.	Nom.	Gen.
я	меня́	оно́	**его́** (pronounced 'yevo')
ты	тебя́	мы	нас
он	**его́** (pronounced 'yevo')	вы	вас
она́	её	они́	их

Whenever **его́**, **её** or **их** is used after a preposition, then the letter **н** must be added: **у него́** *he has* – a phrase we met in Unit 3. If you want to say, for example, *Boris has a passport*, all you need to do is use **у** with the genitive of Boris: **У Бори́са есть па́спорт.**

ANIMATE ACCUSATIVE

We need to be careful with masculine animate nouns (i.e. people and animals) – they have their own special accusative ending. The good news is that this animate accusative ending is exactly the same as the genitive singular ending:

Subject (nom.)	Verb	Object (acc.)	Meaning
Вы	зна́ете	Бори́са?	*Do you know Boris?*
Я	зна́ю	Ви́ктора	*I know Viktor*
Я	люблю́	тигр	*I like the tiger*

Similarly, the genitive form of the personal pronouns is also their accusative form:

Оля зна́ет тебя́   *Olya knows you*

NUMBERS

You have now met the numbers 1–20. However, you will probably need larger numbers when shopping:

30 **три́дцать**	80 **восемьдесят**	400 **четыреста**	900 **девятьсо́т**
40 **со́рок**	90 **девяносто**	500 **пятьсо́т**	1,000 **ты́сяча**
50 **пятьдесят**	100 **сто**	600 **шестьсо́т**	2,000 **две ты́сячи**
60 **шестьдесят**	200 **двести**	700 **семьсо́т**	5,000 **пять ты́сяч**
70 **семьдесят**	300 **три́ста**	800 **восемьсо́т**	10,000 **де́сять ты́сяч**

Оди́н has masculine, feminine and neuter forms and agrees with the word it describes:

оди́н биле́т	**одна́ неде́ля**	**одно́ письмо́**
one ticket	*one week*	*one letter*

Два has two forms – **два** is used with masculine and neuter nouns, but it changes to **две** before feminine nouns:

два биле́та	**две неде́ли**	**два письма́**
two tickets	*two weeks*	*two letters*

Apart from **три** and **де́сять** (linked to the English word *decimal*), Russian numbers do not bear much resemblance to their English counterparts. With the teens of numbers, it might help you to think, for example, that the idea behind **трина́дцать** *13* is 'three on ten'.

One of the most frequent uses of numbers is when you're dealing with money, so it's important to know how to use the word *rouble*, Russia's main unit of currency:

оди́н рубль	*one rouble*
два (три, четыре) рубля́	*two (three, four) roubles*

Numbers above four are followed by the genitive plural (see Unit 7), but as the genitive plural form of *rouble* is so frequently used, it is worth noting it now:

шестьсо́т рубле́й	*600 roubles*

> **LANGUAGE TIP**
> In theory, there are 100 *kopeks* to the *rouble*, but, in practice, these are never used in modern-day Russia.

СКÓЛЬКО СТÓИТ? *HOW MUCH DOES IT COST?*

The verb *to cost, to be worth* – **стóить** – is a regular second conjugation verb, like **говори́ть**; remember to use the 3rd person plural (*they*) form of the verb if you're asking the price of more than one item:

Скóлько стóит билéт? *How much is a ticket?*

Скóлько стóят билéты? *How much are the tickets?*

WORD ORDER

Note how flexible word order is in Russian – it's quite acceptable to vary the position of, for example, subjects and objects in a sentence:

Я óчень люблю́ Чéхова
Я Чéхова óчень люблю́ } *I really like Chekhov*

У вас нет мéлочи?
Мéлочи у вас нет? } *Haven't you got any change?*

Practice

1 How many times is the genitive singular used in this sentence?

У Áнны два билéта на пьéсу Чéхова «Три сестры́».

2 What Russian question was asked for each of these answers?

  a У меня́ нет пáспорта.
  b Киóск нахóдится недалекó от стáнции метрó.
  c План гóрода стóит дéсять рублéй.
  d Он рабóтает на завóде.
  e Да, я óчень люблю́ Чéхова.

05.03 Check your answers by listening to the audio.

3 Look at the kiosk signs and decide which one you would be most likely to visit if you like listening to music.

  a | ТАБАК |

  b | КОМПАКТ-ДИСКИ |

  c | ЛОТО |

4 Look at the list, then write sentences explaining what each person has or hasn't got. The first one has been done for you.

Кто?	Соба́ка	Автомоби́ль	Телефо́н
a Óльга	✓	✗	✓
b Вади́м	✗	✓	✓
c Ни́на	✓	✓	✗
d Алексе́й	✗	✓	✓

a **У Óльги есть соба́ка и телефо́н, но у неё нет автомоби́ля.**

5 Which of the two alternatives in each of these sentences is correct and why?

a Вы ви́дите (Ви́ктор/Ви́ктора)?

b Это (пье́са/пье́су) Че́хова.

c Она́ о́чень лю́бит (о́пера/о́перу).

d Я хочу́ купи́ть биле́т на (пье́са/пье́су).

e Вот (Влади́мир/Влади́мира).

Listen and understand

минера́льная вода́	*mineral water*
буты́лка	*bottle*
сто	*a hundred*
что ещё?	*anything else?*
бу́лочка	*roll*
по́рция	*portion*
мину́точку	*just a moment*
пиро́жное	*cake, bun*

05.04 *Hungry and thirsty after a day's sightseeing, Igor visits a* **кафе́**.

1 What does Igor buy at the café counter, and how much does it cost in total?

И́горь	Скажи́те, пожа́луйста, у вас есть минера́льная вода́?
Де́вушка	Есть.
И́горь	Ско́лько сто́ит одна́ буты́лка?
Де́вушка	Сто рубле́й.
И́горь	Да́йте, пожа́луйста, две буты́лки.
Де́вушка	Пожа́луйста. А что ещё?

Игорь	Дáйте, пожáлуйста, три бýлочки .
Дéвушка	Суп хотúте?
Игорь	Да, дáйте, пожáлуйста, три пóрции сýпа.
Дéвушка	Пожáлуйста. Это всё?
Игорь	Гм … минýточку … У вас есть шоколáд?
Дéвушка	Нет, у нас сегóдня нет шоколáда.
Игорь	Гм … Дáйте, пожáлуйста, однó пирóжное.
Дéвушка	Пожáлуйста. Это всё?
Игорь	Да, спасúбо, это всё. Скóлько с меня?
Дéвушка	С вас семьсóт рублéй.
Игорь	Вот … тысяча.
Дéвушка	Мéлочи у вас нет?
Игорь	Минýточку … да … есть. *(Gives her 700 exactly.)*
Дéвушка	Спасúбо большóе.
Игорь	Пожáлуйста.

2 Choose the correct option to complete the sentences.

a Игорь хóчет купúть
   1 винó
   2 вóдку
   3 вóду

b Однá бутылка стóит
   1 10 рублéй
   2 100 рублéй
   3 1,000 рублéй

c В кафе сегóдня нет
   1 сýпа
   2 шоколáда
   3 воды

d У Игоря
   1 есть мéлочь
   2 нет мéлочи
   3 тóлько сто рублéй

LANGUAGE TIP

Did you notice the phrase **две бутылки** in the conversation? **Бутылка** is a feminine noun, so remember that we need to use the feminine form **две**, not **два** (which is only to be used with masculine and neuter nouns).

Reading and writing

Днепр	*Dniepr (river)*
ке́мпинг	*campsite*
«мать ру́сских городо́в»	*'The mother of Russian cities'*
мотоци́кл	*motorbike*
находи́ться	*to be situated*
но и	*but also*
одна́ко	*however*
отдыха́ть	*to rest, have a holiday*
оте́ль	*luxury hotel*
па́мятник	*monument*
приме́рно	*approximately*
самолёт	*aeroplane*
Украи́на	*Ukraine*

Read the text, then answer the questions that follow in English.

Ки́ев – столи́ца Украи́ны. Это о́чень ста́рый го́род, «мать ру́сских городо́в». В Ки́еве живёт, приме́рно три миллио́на челове́к. Ки́ев о́чень краси́вый го́род. Он нахо́дится на берегу́ Днепра́. Тури́сты о́чень лю́бят отды́хать в Ки́еве. Здесь есть па́рки, леса́ и сады́, ке́мпинги, гости́ницы, оте́ли, истори́ческие и архитекту́рные па́мятники. Одна́ко, Ки́ев – не то́лько туристи́ческий центр, но та́кже администрати́вный, экономи́ческий и культу́рный центр Украи́ны. В Ки́еве нахо́дятся больши́е заво́ды, где де́лают самолёты, телеви́зоры, мотоци́клы.

a Of which country is Kiev the capital?

b What is Kiev known as?

c How many people live there?

d Why do tourists like it?

e What do Kiev's factories produce?

Speaking

05.05 Can you remember how to say the following in Russian? Listen to the audio and practise saying each phrase.

a Have you got any tickets?

b How much does a ticket cost?

c How much do I owe you?

d Not far from the theatre.

e To the left of the school.

Test yourself

1 When out shopping, how would you say: *How much does it cost?* and *How much do I owe you?*

2 What is a *rouble* and a *kopek?*

3 Why does the number *one* have alternative forms in Russian?

4 What happens in terms of case to nouns that follow the numbers *two, three* and *four?*

5 What is the main use of the genitive case?

6 Can you remember the eight prepositions that need to be followed by the genitive case?

7 Why do we use the genitive case in the following phrases? мно́го багажа́, полкило́ са́хара, буты́лка вина́, нет молока́

8 How would you say *far from/not far from?*

9 What do we need to remember about animate masculine nouns?

10 How do you say that you want to buy an opera ticket for tomorrow?

6

Я предпочитáю плáвать

I prefer to swim

In this unit you will learn how to:
▶ *talk about likes and dislikes.*
▶ *ask people about their preferences.*

CEFR: (A2) *Can explain what he likes or dislikes.*

 ## Sport and fitness in Russia

Russians play much the same range of sports as in Western Europe, though, of course, much is dependent on the weather. Football and other games played on grass are only really practical in summer in Russia, but the climate there does favour winter sports and the playing of ice hockey in particular. When Russians refer to hockey, it is usually this form of the game they have in mind. Russians also continue to love figure skating and skiing, especially cross-country. In recent years, tennis has become more popular, with several female Russian tennis players regularly featuring in the world's top ten. In the Soviet Union sport was effectively used as a Cold War weapon against the West, with Soviet athletes routinely topping the Olympic medal tables. Nowadays in Russia fewer resources are devoted to sport, but privately run fitness centres and indoor sports facilities are becoming ever more popular.

Can you match the English and Russian words for the following sports?

1 бадминтóн	**2** баскетбóл	**3** волейбóл	**4** лы́жный спорт
5 тéннис	**6** фигу́рное катáние	**7** футбóл	**8** хоккéй

a volleyball	**b** football	**c** skiing	**d** tennis
e basketball	**f** hockey	**g** badminton	**h** figure skating

Vocabulary builder

06.01 Complete the missing English expressions. Then listen to the audio and repeat the Russian until you can say all the words with confidence.

НАДО ЗНАТЬ! *ESSENTIALS*

предпочитáть	*to prefer*
бóльше всегó (pronounced 'fsyevó')	*most of all*
мне (óчень) нрáвится	*I (really) like*
скýчно	*boring*
ну, …	*well, …*
всё	*everything*
прóсто	*simple*
игрáть в хоккéй	*to play* _____
ужé	*already*
три часá	*for* _____ *hours*
мне хóчется	*I would like to …*
пить (irregular: пью, пьёшь … пьют)	*to drink*
дýмать	*to think*
спасúбо большóе за	*thank you* _____ *for*
ýтро	*morning*
фрукто́вый сок	_____ *juice*
что тебé?	*what would* _____ *like?*
	(lit. what for _____ *?)*

ВЫ – ТУРИ́СТ? *TRAVEL ESSENTIALS*

пейзáж	*landscape*
портрéт	_____
замечáтельная (замечáтельный)	*splendid*
картúна	*picture*
показáть	*to show*
пойдём	*let's go*
что ты!	*what next!*
такúе интерéсные	*so* _____
худóжник	*artist*
нам порá идтú	*it's time for us to go*
пойдёмте	*let's go*
номерóк	*tag, metal disc*

> **LANGUAGE TIP**
> Literally meaning *that you*, **Что ты!** is a useful way of expressing surprise, indignation or objection in response to what someone has said. **Что вы!** would, of course, be required if addressing more than one person or using the polite form.

Dialogue

 06.02 *Anna has spent the morning at the museum with Ira and Ira's friend, Volodya.*

1   What do Ira, Anna and Volodya each think of their morning out?

И́ра	Что ты предпочита́ешь, А́нна, пейза́жи и́ли портре́ты?
А́нна	Бо́льше всего́ я люблю́ пейза́жи, но мне о́чень нра́вится э́тот портре́т, вон там.
И́ра	Ах, да, портре́т Ре́пина, замеча́тельная карти́на … Я о́чень хочу́ показа́ть её Воло́де, а где он?
Воло́дя	*(Sitting in the corner, yawning.)* Ой, как ску́чно!
И́ра	Ну, что ты, Воло́дя! Здесь всё так интере́сно! И карти́ны таки́е интере́сные! Я тебя́ не понима́ю!
Воло́дя	Ну, И́ра, всё о́чень про́сто. Ты худо́жник – зна́чит в свобо́дное вре́мя ты лю́бишь смотре́ть карти́ны. А я предпочита́ю игра́ть в хокке́й … А ты, А́нна, лю́бишь хокке́й?
А́нна	*(Embarrassed.)* Нет, не о́чень … Я предпочита́ю пла́вать … И́ра, здесь о́чень интере́сно и карти́ны о́чень краси́вые. Но мы здесь уже́ три часа́ …
Воло́дя	Пра́вда! Мы уже́ три часа́ смо́трим карти́ны. Тепе́рь мне хо́чется пить … Я ду́маю, что нам пора́ идти́, И́ра.
И́ра	Но я хочу́ показа́ть А́нне ещё … *(Volodya groans.)* … Ну ла́дно, пойдёмте в гардеро́б … А́нна, да́й мне твой номеро́к, пожа́луйста.
А́нна	Вот он, И́ра … и спаси́бо большо́е за о́чень интере́сное у́тро.
И́ра	Зна́чит, тебе́ нра́вится э́тот музе́й?
А́нна	Да, о́чень.
Воло́дя	А сейча́с пойдём в буфе́т! Мне фрукто́вый сок. А тебе́ что, А́нна?
А́нна	Мне чай, пожа́луйста.
Воло́дя	А тебе́, И́ра?
И́ра	Мне то́же чай, пожа́луйста.

2 True or false?

a Anna prefers landscapes to portraits.

b Ira doesn't understand why Volodya is bored.

c Anna and Volodya both like hockey.

d They have been in the museum for four hours.

e Ira thinks that it is time for them to go.

3 Answer the following questions.

a Воло́дя лю́бит музе́й?

b Что есть в музе́е?

c Почему́ И́ра лю́бит карти́ны?

d Что А́нна хо́чет пить?

Language discovery

В + ACCUSATIVE *TO PLAY (AT)*

A further use of **в** + accusative is found in the construction **игра́ть в** *to play (at)*. Note that this is used for games and sports.

YOUR TURN (Дава́йте)

1 Complete the second expression.

игра́ть в ша́хматы   *to play chess*

игра́ть в футбо́л   _____

If you want to talk about a musical instrument, **в** + accusative is not used; **на** + prepositional is required.

YOUR TURN (Дава́йте)

2 Complete the second expression.

игра́ть на фле́йте   *to play the flute*

игра́ть на гита́ре   _____

HAS/HAVE BEEN …

In order to say that you have been doing an action for a certain period of time (i.e. an action which is still going on at the moment of speaking), Russian simply uses the present tense and no word for *for*.

YOUR TURN (Дава́йте)

3 Bearing this in mind, how would you translate the following phrase?

Мы уже́ два часа́ игра́ем

СПАСИ́БО ЗА … *THANK YOU FOR …*

The way that Russians say *thank you for (something)* is:

Спаси́бо за журна́л	*Thank you for the magazine*
Спаси́бо за кни́гу	*Thank you for the book*
Спаси́бо за письмо́	*Thank you for the letter*

 4 Which case do you think you need to use after за when using спаси́бо за in this way?

DATIVE CASE

The principal meaning of the dative case is *to* or *for*. For example, if you want to say *Olya gives the tickets <u>to Viktor</u>*, then the way to do this is to put Viktor into the dative case:

Subject (nom.)	Verb	Object (acc.)	Indirect object (dat.)
Olya	*gives*	*the tickets*	*to Viktor*
О́ля	**даёт**	**биле́ты**	**Ви́ктору**

> **LANGUAGE TIP**
>
> In English the indirect object is not always obvious, because we do not always include the word *to*: *Olya gives Viktor the tickets*.

 5 Study the pattern and complete the table of dative singular forms.

Nominative	Remove	Add	Dative	Meaning
Masc.				
брат	–	-у	**бра́ту**	*to/for (a/the) brother*
учи́тель	-ь	-ю	_____	*to/for (a/the) teacher*
Алексе́й	-й	_____	**Алексе́ю**	*to/for Alexei*
Fem.				
соба́ка	-а	-е	**соба́ке**	_____
О́ля	-я	-е	_____	*to/for Olya*
Мари́я	-я	-и	**Мари́и**	_____
дверь	_____	-и	**две́ри**	*to/for (a/the) door*
Neut.				
окно́	-о	_____	**окно́**	*to/for (a/the) window*
_____	-е	-ю	**мо́рю**	*to/for (a/the) sea*
зда́ние	-е	-ю	_____	*to/for (a/the) building*

Did you figure out the pattern for forming dative singular forms? The dative singular forms of masculine and neuter nouns have the same endings (either **-у** or **–ю**); feminine nouns end in **-е** or **-и**.

The dative case of personal pronouns is shown in the following table:

Nom.	Dat.	Nom.	Dat.
я	мне	онó	емý
ты	тебé	мы	нам
он	емý	вы	вам
онá	ей	они́	им

The dative case is also used:

▶ with the prepositions **к** and **по** in the following ways:

к нам	*towards us/to our house*
к И́ре	*to Ira's (to Ira's house)*
по у́лице	*along/down/up the street*
по гóроду	*around/throughout the town*
по телеви́зору	*on the television*

▶ with **мóжно** *it is possible, one may*; **нельзя́** *it is impossible, one may not*; **нáдо** *it is necessary* and **порá** *it is time to*:

Dative of person	(e.g.) порá	infinitive
Волóде	порá	идти́

It's time for Volodya to go

И́ре	мóжно	купи́ть биле́т

Ira can buy a ticket

Нам	нельзя́	кури́ть в музе́е

We are not allowed to smoke in the museum

▶ idiomatically in phrases with **нрá вится** (*to express liking*). **Я люблю́** and **мне нрá вится** both express liking, but **я люблю́** is more intense (*I love*) and tends to apply in general (e.g. **Я люблю́ мý зыку** *I love/like music*), whereas **мне нрá вится** is less intense (*I like*) and tends to apply to a particular occasion or instance

(**Мне нра́вится э́тот портре́т** *I like this portrait*). The verb **хо́чется** can be used in a similar way, to express *wanting, feeling like* in a less intense way than *I like*, etc. (e.g. **Мне хо́чется пить** *I feel like a drink / I feel thirsty*).

YOUR TURN (Давайте)

6 Complete the English meanings.

Use	Example	Meaning
to	Оля даёт биле́ты Ви́ктору	*Olya gives the _____ to Viktor*
for	Мне ко́фе, пожа́луйста	*Coffee for _____, please*
к	Я иду́ к Ви́ктору	*I'm going _____*
по	Она́ говори́т по телефо́ну	*She's talking on the _____*
на́до	Мне на́до рабо́тать	*I've got to _____*
нельзя́	Тебе́ нельзя́ кури́ть	*You mustn't _____*
нра́вится	Мне о́чень нра́вится э́та пье́са	*_____ really like this play*
хо́чется	Воло́де хо́чется отдыха́ть	*Volodya wants _____*

Э́ТОТ *THIS*

Э́тот means *this* and it must agree with the word it describes (a list of case endings of **э́тот** is given in the Appendix):

э́тот университе́т	*this university*
э́та гости́ница	*this hotel*
э́то зда́ние	*this building*
э́ти теа́тры	*these theatres*

> **LANGUAGE TIP**
> Note that the neuter form **э́то** is identical to the word for *it is/this is/ these are.*

Practice

1 Choose a word/words from the box to complete each sentence or to answer the question.

>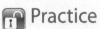
> багажа́   Да, вот он   Да, мо́жно
> зна́ете   рабо́таете   Бори́су
> Да, вот она́   рабо́тает

a Извини́те, пожа́луйста, вы не _____, где метро́?

b У вас есть па́спорт? _____

c У меня́ в но́мере телефо́н не _____

d Здесь мо́жно фотографи́ровать? _____

e У вас мно́го _____ ?

f _____ нельзя́ кури́ть.

2 Put the words in brackets in the correct form.

a Я предпочита́ю ко́фе без _____ (молоко́).

b Сего́дня ве́чером мы идём к _____ (Бори́с).

c Зна́ете, Ве́ра, _____ (мы) уже́ пора́ идти́.

d Нет, музе́й не о́чень далеко́ от _____ (гости́ница).

e (Я) _____ о́чень хо́чется отдыха́ть.

> **LANGUAGE TIP**
>
> It is helpful to think grammatically in order to work out what the sentence will mean when you complete it, and therefore what case the bracketed word requires. We have recently met the genitive and dative cases – can you remember their main uses?

3 Look at the pictures and write a sentence about the preferences of each person. The first one has been done for you.

a <u>Бори́с предпочита́ет игра́ть в те́ннис.</u>

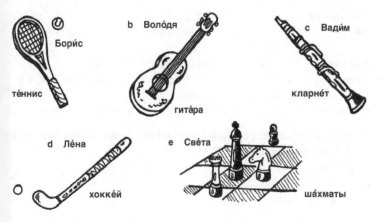

b **Воло́дя**

c **Вади́м**

Бори́с

те́ннис

гита́ра

кларне́т

d **Ле́на**

e **Све́та**

хокке́й

ша́хматы

Listen and understand

 матема́тика   *mathematics*

бассе́йн   *swimming pool*

спортза́л   *sports hall*

 06.03 *A journalist from the newspaper «Спорт» is visiting a university and he interviews a student there.*

1 **What do you think the journalist will write about Lena? Note at least five points.**

Журнали́ст	Здра́вствуйте, Ле́на. Меня́ зову́т Ви́ктор. Я журналист газе́ты «Спорт».
Ле́на	Здра́вствуйте.
Журнали́ст	Скажи́те мне, Ле́на, вы изуча́ете матема́тику, да?
Ле́на	Да, матема́тику.
Журнали́ст	Вам нра́вится курс?
Ле́на	Да, курс о́чень интере́сный.
Журнали́ст	А что вы де́лаете в свобо́дное вре́мя?
Ле́на	Ну, я смотрю́ телеви́зор, чита́ю мно́го, и о́чень люблю́ пла́вать.
Журнали́ст	Вы ча́сто пла́ваете?
Ле́на	Нет, не ча́сто, потому́ что бассе́йн нахо́дится далеко́ от до́ма.
Журнали́ст	А здесь, в университе́те, есть спортза́л?
Ле́на	Да, есть. Э́то небольшо́й спортза́л, где мо́жно игра́ть в волейбо́л и баскетбо́л.

2 **Choose the correct options based on the conversation between the journalist and Lena.**

a Ле́на изуча́ет

1 ру́сский язы́к

2 матема́тику

3 му́зыку

4 англи́йский язы́к

b Она́ ду́мает, что

1 курс о́чень ску́чный

2 курс не о́чень интере́сный

   3 курс не о́чень хоро́ший

   4 курс о́чень интере́сный

c Ле́на пла́вает не о́чень ча́сто потому́, что

   1 у неё мно́го рабо́ты

   2 ей не о́чень нра́вится пла́вать

   3 она́ предпочита́ет игра́ть в волейбо́л

   4 бассе́йн далеко́ от её до́ма

Reading and writing

изве́стный	*famous*
Третьяко́вская галере́я	*Tretyakov Gallery*
основа́тель (m.)	*founder*
век	*century*
бога́тый	*rich*
купе́ц	*merchant*
уника́льный	*unique*
колле́кция	*collection*
жи́вопись (f.)	*painting*
изобража́ть	*to depict*
жизнь (f.)	*life*
пробле́ма	*problem*

Read the text, then answer the questions that follow in English.

В Москве́ нахо́дится изве́стная Третьяко́вская галере́я. Э́то о́чень краси́вое и типи́чно ру́сское зда́ние. Оно́ нахо́дится в це́нтре го́рода, недалеко́ от ста́нции метро́ «Третьяко́вская». Основа́тель галере́и – Серге́й Миха́йлович Третьяко́в (XIX ве́ка) – бога́тый моско́вский купе́ц. В галере́е уника́льная колле́кция ру́сской жи́вописи. Там, наприме́р, мо́жно ви́деть изве́стные карти́ны Ре́пина, Су́рикова и Ива́нова (Ре́пин, Су́риков, Ива́нов – худо́жники XIX ве́ка). Там есть портре́ты и пейза́жи, о́чень изве́стные и популя́рные, потому́ что они́ изобража́ют жизнь и пробле́мы Росси́и XIX ве́ка.

  a How is the Tretyakov Art Gallery building described?

  b Where exactly is it situated?

  c Who was the founder of the gallery?

  d Why are Repin, Surikov and Ivanov popular?

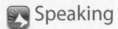 Speaking

 1 **06.04 You are asking about museums in the city at Reception in your hotel. Play your part, then listen to the complete conversation on the audio.**

Вы	**a** *Ask if there are any museums in the city.*
Дéвушка	Конéчно! У нас мнóго.
Вы	**b** *Ask if these museums are near the hotel.*
Дéвушка	Да, недалекó отсю́да (from here) есть большóй музéй.
Вы	**c** *Ask what there is in the museum.*
Дéвушка	В музéе красúвые картúны и стáрая мéбель (furniture).
Вы	**d** *Ask how much a ticket to the museum costs.*
Дéвушка	Двéсти пятьдесят рублéй.
Вы	**e** *Say 'thank you very much. Goodbye'.*
Дéвушка	Нé за что. До свидáния.

 2 **06.05 Can you remember how to say the following in Russian? Listen to the audio and practise saying each phrase.**

   a What do you prefer?
   b Most of all, I like footballl.
   c I prefer to play the guitar.
   d Do you like this picture?
   e Do you like sport?

Test yourself

We have now covered the nominative, accusative, genitive, dative and prepositional endings for singular nouns, so it's time to review their uses. Look at the following ten questions and check that you understand the answers.

1 If you want to ask whether Boris preferred opera or ballet, which case ending will you use for opera and ballet?

2 If you want to tell someone you work in an office, which case ending will you use for office?

3 If you want to say that your house is a long way from the railway station, which case ending will you need for railway station?

4 If you want to explain that the book belongs to Olga, which case will you need for Olga?

5 If you want to ask whether someone is going to the hotel, which case ending will you need for hotel?

6 If you want to explain that it is necessary for Vladimir to work today, which case ending would you need for Vladimir?

7 These prepositions have something in common – the case with which they must be used. Can you remember which case it is for без *without*; для *for*; у *by, near*?

8 If you want to say thank you for something, which case will follow Спасибо за?

9 If you want to explain that you like playing tennis, which case ending will you need after играть в?

10 If you want to ask someone if they're going to Anna's this evening, which case ending will you need for Anna?

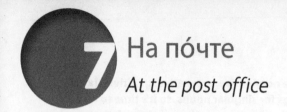

7 На по́чте

At the post office

In this unit you will learn how to:

▶ *request information about cost, availability and necessity.*
▶ *give information about cost, availability and necessity.*
▶ *give instructions.*

CEFR: (A1) *Can handle numbers, quantities and cost. Can ask people for things and give people things.*

На по́чте *At the post office*

Post offices in Russia have longer opening hours than those in the West and are often open in the evenings and on Sundays. It is possible to buy traditional items such as stamps, postcards and pre-paid envelopes, but in the post-Soviet period, Russian post offices have in fact become much more like convenience stores, selling a wide range of everyday staple goods at reasonable prices. With such a wide range of goods and services on offer, it is, of course, a very good idea that you choose the right counter for the service you require.

Postboxes in Russia are blue and sometimes have more than one slot, so look out for the slot with **междунаро́дные** *international* above it. Russian envelopes normally have a space for the sender's address in the top left-hand corner. It is a good idea to send postcards in an envelope to ensure delivery, especially as most postcards do not have a space for the destination address. It is always worth paying the small extra amount to send post by air rather than surface mail.

 Here are possible stamp prices for postcards, letters or parcels to various destinations. What information do you think is given in the brackets?

Австра́лия: 1,400 р (авиа.)   Великобрита́ния: 120 р (авиа.)

Кана́да: 100 р (наземн.)   Ирла́ндия: 25 р (авиа.)

Vocabulary builder

07.01 Complete the missing English expressions. Then listen to the audio and repeat the Russian until you can say all the words with confidence.

НА́ДО ЗНАТЬ НА ПО́ЧТЕ *POST OFFICE ESSENTIALS*

что тебе́ / вам ну́жно?	*what do you need?*
конве́рт	*envelope*
по два́дцать пять рублей	*at _____ roubles each*
око́шко	*counter, position (in a post office or bank)*
прода́жа	*sale*
иди́(те) скажи́(те) де́вушке	*go and say to the girl (go and tell the girl)*
кро́ме	*apart from*
всегда́	*always*
посла́ть име́йл	*to send an _____*
домо́й	*home (lit. to home, homewards)*
тебе́/вам что́-нибудь ну́жно?	*do you _____ anything?*
для моего́ сосе́да	*for my neighbour*

LANGUAGE TIP

Note that the word **де́вушка** *girl* is a very useful one. Here it is being used to denote the post office employee; as there are no Russian equivalents for *Miss, Madam*, etc. it is also the way of attracting the attention of a shop assistant, waitress or any female (between the ages of about 15 and 50!) who you don't know. **Молодо́й челове́к** *young man* is the masculine equivalent.

LANGUAGE TIP

The word **дом** *house, home* is unusual in that it has forms not found in other words when it means *home*, namely: **до́ма** *at home*; **домо́й** *to home*. Note that **в до́ме** means *in the house* and **в дом** means *into the house*.

Dialogue

 07.02 *Anna has asked Ira to go with her to the post office to help her buy stamps, envelopes and postcards..*

1 What does Anna need to buy?

Йра	Скажи, Анна, что тебе нужно?
Анна	Я хочу купить конверты, марки и открытки.
Йра	Сколько открыток хочешь?
Анна	Шесть красивых открыток и шесть марок.
Йра	Куда ты хочешь послать эти открытки? В Англию?
Анна	Да, в Англию.
Йра	Значит, шесть открыток и шесть марок по двадцать пять рублей. Сколько конвертов хочешь?
Анна	Пять. А где можно купить всё это?
Йра	Вон там … видишь окошко? … «Продажа марок, конвертов, открыток». Иди скажи девушке: Дайте, пожалуйста, шесть марок в Англию, шесть открыток и пять конвертов.
Анна	Понятно.
Йра	А ещё что тебе нужно, кроме открыток, марок и конвертов?
Анна	Ничего, потому что можно всегда послать имейл домой, если я хочу. А тебе что-нибудь нужно?
Йра	Да, марки для моего соседа.

 2 Did you notice the word кроме in the dialogue and how it changes the words that follow it? Can you work out what it means from the context?

> **LANGUAGE TIP**
>
> **Кроме** is another preposition which must be followed by the genitive case. In the Appendix you will find a useful list of prepositions and the cases which must follow them.

3 True or false?

a Anna wants to buy only stamps.

b Anna wants to send postcards to England.

c Ira wants to buy envelopes.

4 Answer the following questions.

a Какие открытки Анна хочет купить?

b Сколько конвертов она хочет?

c Куда Анна хочет послать имейл?

Language discovery

NOUNS – GENITIVE PLURAL

In the dialogue, and previously in Unit 5, we met several examples of the genitive plural (e.g. **шесть красивых открыток, сколько конвёртов**).

1 Complete the following table, which shows how to form the genitive plural from the nominative.

Nom. sing. Masc.	Nom. pl.	Remove	Add	Gen. pl.	Meaning
билет	билеты	-ы	-ов	билетов	of tickets
автомобиль	автомобили	-и	-ей	_____	of cars
музей	музеи	-и	-ев	музеев	of _____
Fem.					
гостиница	гостиницы	-ы	–	гостиниц	of hotels
неделя	_____	-и	-ь	недель	of weeks
станция	станции	-и	-ий	станций	of _____
дверь	двери		-ей	дверей	of doors
Neut.					
место	места	-а	–	мест	of places
море	моря		-ей	морей	of seas
здание	здания	-ия	-ий	_____	of buildings

Feminine nouns ending in **a** and neuter nouns ending in **o** simply lose the last letter of the nominative; when the result is a cluster of consonants at the end of the word this sometimes leads to the insertion of an **o**, **ё** or an **e**. Here are some common examples:

марка	**шесть марок**	*six stamps*
окно	**шесть окон**	*six windows*
девушка	**шесть девушек**	*six girls* (i.e. **e** after **ш**)
деньги	**много денег**	*a lot of money* (i.e. **e** replaces soft sign)
сестра	**пять сестёр**	*five sisters*

Some nouns which have an irregular nominative plural also have an irregular genitive plural. Here are the most common (a full list of irregulars is given in the Appendix):

Meaning	Nom. sing.	Nom. pl.	Gen. pl.
child	ребёнок	дети	детей
friend	друг	друзья	друзей
person	человек	люди	людей

ADJECTIVES – GENITIVE SINGULAR AND PLURAL

We have seen that adjectives must agree with the nouns they describe in number (singular or plural) and gender (masculine, feminine or neuter) – they must also agree with the noun they describe in case (nominative, accusative, genitive, etc.)

Adjectives – genitive singular

In the dialogue we saw the phrase **для моего соседа** *for my neighbour*. The preposition **для** must be followed by the genitive case, so both the noun (**сосед**) and the adjective (**мой**) have been put into the genitive singular. Learning the genitive singular adjective endings is not too complicated.

 2 Complete the table for forming genitive singular adjectives.

	Nom. sing.	Remove	Add	Gen. sing.	Pronounced
Masc.	ста́рый	_____	-ого	ста́рого	'starovo'
Fem.	ста́рая	_____	-ой	ста́рой	'staroy'
Neut.	ста́рое	_____	-ого	ста́рого	'starovo'

A common exception to the general genitive singular pattern is the adjective **хоро́ший**, which is affected by a second spelling rule: when you are dealing with adjectives whose stem (i.e. what's left when you've removed the last two letters) ends in: **ж, ч, ц, ш, щ**, these letters can never be followed by an unstressed **о**. So, the adjective **хоро́ший** has the following endings:

	Nom. sing.	Remove	Add	Gen. sing.
Masc.	хороший	-ий	-его	хорошей
Fem.	хорошая	-ая	-ей	хорошей
Neut.	хорошее	-ее	-его	хорошего

The letters involved in this new spelling rule are not the same as for the first rule (see Unit 4). In summary: it is fine to have a stressed **о** after **ж, ц, ч, ш** and **щ** (e.g. **большо́й**), but never try to put an unstressed **о** after these letters. Very occasionally you may see an unstressed **o** after these letters in words of foreign origin e.g. **шоссе́** *highway*; **Шотла́ндия**.

The possessive adjectives **мой**, **твой**, **наш**, **ваш** also all take this second kind of ending:

Это пода́рок для моего́ бра́та   *This is a present for my brother*

Adjectives – genitive plural

The genitive plural of adjectives is rather more straightforward – here, whatever the gender of the noun you are describing, there are only two possible endings: **-ых** and **-их**. Always use the first (**-ых**) unless you are dealing with an adjective whose stem ends in one of the letters which may never be followed by **-ы** (**г, к, х, ж, ч, ш, щ**):

Nom. pl.	Remove	Add	Gen. pl.
ста́рые	-ые	-ых	ста́рых
ма́ленькие	-ие	-их	ма́леньких

ACCUSATIVE PLURAL

Now that you have met the genitive plural, you will be able to deal with all nouns and adjectives in the accusative plural as well.

All inanimate (i.e. not alive) nouns and their adjectives in the plural look exactly the same as they do in the nominative:

Я о́чень люблю́ чита́ть   *I really like reading Russian*
ру́сские газе́ты   *newspapers*

All animate plural nouns and their adjectives look exactly the same as they do in the genitive:

Я о́чень люблю смотре́ть   *I really like watching Russian*
ру́сских балери́н   *ballerinas*

So, although the genitive plural of nouns is a bit complicated, at least there is more than one use for the endings. Notice in particular that in the plural you need to use the animate accusative for all animate objects (i.e. not just for masculine, as in the singular).

NUMBERS

In Unit 5 we met all the numbers up to 10,000. Compounds of numbers are formed simply by putting one number after another, but without any hyphens or the word *and*.

два́дцать три	23
сто де́сять	110
три ты́сячи пятьсо́т три	3,503

In Unit 5 we saw how numbers are used with the word **рубль** (Russia's main unit of currency). To recap, when you are dealing with the number one or compounds of one, the noun that follows stays in the nominative singular – i.e. it agrees with one:

три́дцать оди́н рубль	*31 tickets*
два́дцать одна́ кни́га	*21 books*

The numbers two, three and four and their compounds are always followed by the genitive singular of nouns:

три́дцать два рубля́	*32 roubles*
два́дцать три кни́ги	*23 books*

All other numbers are followed by the genitive plural of nouns.

YOUR TURN (Дава́йте)

3 Translate the numbers.

пятьсо́т рублей	_____ *roubles*
оди́ннадцать маро́к	_____ *stamps*
сто тури́стов	_____ *tourists*

See the Appendix for more information about numbers.

ПО ПЯТЬСО́Т РУБЛЕ́Й *500 ROUBLES EACH*

The preposition **по**, followed by a number, is used to express price per item, e.g.:

Э́ти кни́ги по 500 рубле́й	*These books are 500 roubles each*

🔓 Practice

1 How would you say that you have the following? The first one is done for you.

   a ма́ленькие конве́рты – 10
   b театра́льные биле́ты – 5
   c килогра́мм помидо́ров – 1
   d ру́сские сувени́ры - 20

e буты́лка во́дки – 3

f краси́вые ма́рки – 26

a **У меня́ де́сять ма́леньких конве́ртов**

2 The following people want to buy stamps. How many stamps do they need to buy and at what price? Look at the example, then write similar sentences for the others.

Кто	Куда́?	Ско́лько ма́рок?	Каки́е ма́рки?
a Джейк	А́нглия	5	50р
b Па́трик	Аме́рика	6	75р
c Ты	И́ндия	3	20р
d Мы	Испа́ния	7	35р
e Са́ша	Петербу́рг	2	20р
f Я	Кана́да	10	100р

a **Джейк хо́чет купи́ть пять ма́рок в А́нглию. Зна́чит ему́ на́до купи́ть пять ма́рок по пятьдеся́т рубле́й.**

3 Who likes doing what? Match the following information and statements.

a Ли́дия о́чень лю́бит кни́ги.

b Бори́с о́чень лю́бит мо́ре.

c Ле́на не лю́бит рабо́тать.

d Вади́м о́чень лю́бит фи́льмы.

e А́лла о́чень лю́бит спорт.

1 Зна́чит, он лю́бит пла́вать.

2 Зна́чит, она́ лю́бит отдыха́ть.

3 Зна́чит, она́ лю́бит чита́ть.

4 Зна́чит, она́ лю́бит игра́ть в те́ннис.

5 Зна́чит, он лю́бит смотре́ть телеви́зор.

4 Use appropriate question words to complete the questions.

a _____ вас зову́т?

b _____ биле́тов вы хоти́те?

c _____ вы идёте?

d Вы не зна́ете, _____ метро́?

e _____ ва́ша фами́лия?

f _____ фи́льмы ты лю́бишь смотре́ть?

Listen and understand

приве́т	*hello* (inf.)
непло́хо	*not bad*
пода́рок	*present, gift*
день (m.) **рожде́ния**	*birthday*
по по́чте	*by post*

посы́лка	*parcel*
свитер	*sweater*
сестра́	*sister*

 07.03 *In town one day Natasha meets her friend Olya.*

1 Where are Natasha and Olya going and why?

Óля	Ната́ша, приве́т! Как дела́?
Ната́ша	Неплóхо. А ты куда́ идёшь, Óля?
Óля	Я иду́ на пóчту.
Ната́ша	И я тóже! Что тебе́ там ну́жно?
Óля	Мне? Тóлько конве́рты. А тебе́ что ну́жно?
Ната́ша	Мне на́до посла́ть э́тот пода́рок бра́ту на его день рожде́ния.
Óля	А где живёт твой брат?
Ната́ша	В Ку́рске. Зна́чит, мне на́до посла́ть ему́ пода́рок по пóчте.
Óля	Поня́тно. Но кака́я больша́я посы́лка!
Ната́ша	Да, пра́вда, больша́я.
Óля	Интере́сно, какóй э́то пода́рок?
Ната́ша	Свитер.
Óля	Кака́я ты хорóшая сестра́, Ната́ша!
Ната́ша	(*Laughs.*) Да, пра́вда, хорóшая!

2 Based on Olya and Natasha's conversation, choose the correct option for each statement.

a Óля идёт
  1 на вокза́л
  2 в шкóлу
  3 на пóчту
  4 на стадиóн

b Óля хóчет купи́ть
  1 конве́рты и ма́рки
  2 тóлько откры́тки
  3 тóлько конве́рты
  4 откры́тки и ма́рки

c Ната́ша хóчет посла́ть
  1 имéйл домóй
  2 пода́рок бра́ту
  3 откры́тку сестре́
  4 письмó бра́ту

Reading and writing

автомагистра́ль (f.)	*motorway*
кру́пный	*major, large*
оте́ц	*father*
посло́вица	*proverb*
реставри́ровать	*to restore*
свято́й	*saint*
се́рдце	*heart*
фре́ска	*fresco*

Read the text, then answer the questions that follow in English.

Вот одна́ ста́рая ру́сская посло́вица: «Ки́ев – мать ру́сских городо́в, Москва́ – се́рдце, Но́вгород – оте́ц». А почему́ ру́сские говоря́т, что Но́вгород «оте́ц ру́сских городо́в»? – Потому́, что э́то ста́рый го́род IX ве́ка. Но́вгород нахо́дится на реке́ Во́лхов, на автомагистра́ли Москва́ – Санкт-Петербу́рг. Сего́дня э́то кру́пный промы́шленный го́род и изве́стный туристи́ческий центр. Тури́сты лю́бят э́тот го́род, потому́ что там о́чень мно́го краси́вых и ста́рых церкве́й, а та́кже мно́го интере́сных па́мятников. В Но́вгороде есть о́чень изве́стный музе́й. Музе́й изве́стный потому́, что там есть о́чень мно́го ста́рых и интере́сных ру́сских ико́н из новгоро́дских церкве́й. Что тако́е ико́на? Ико́на – э́то религио́зная карти́на, портре́т свято́го и́ли святы́х; э́то па́мятник ру́сской культу́ры и ру́сской исто́рии. Но есть ико́ны не то́лько в музе́е. Есть одна́ це́рковь XIV ве́ка в Но́вгороде, где реставра́торы рабо́тают уже́ мно́го лет. Там не то́лько краси́вые ико́ны, но и краси́вые фре́ски. Кака́я рабо́та у э́тих худо́жников-реставра́торов? Им на́до реставри́ровать фре́ски XIV ве́ка.

a What is Novgorod's nickname, according to the old Russian proverb?

b From which century does the city date?

c On which main road is it situated?

d Why do tourists particularly like this city?

e What is an icon?

f What sort of work is being carried out by the restorers in the 14th-century church?

g How long have they already been at work?

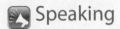 Speaking

 1 **07.04 You are in a post office. Play your part, then listen to the complete conversation on the audio.**

Вы	*a Say 'excuse me, please'.*
Дéвушка	Да?
Вы	*b Ask how much it costs to send a postcard to England.*
Дéвушка	15 рублéй.
Вы	*c Ask for five stamps at 15 roubles.*
Дéвушка	Вот, пожáлуйста. Это всё?
Вы	*d Say 'yes, thank you, that is all'.*
Дéвушка	Пожáлуйста. До свидáния.

 2 **07.05 Can you remember how to say the following in Russian? Listen to the audio and practise saying each phrase.**

a What do you need?

b At my house.

c Do you need anything?

d I want to send an e-mail.

e Is that all?

Test yourself

1 How would you say *at the post office*? Why is this unusual?

2 If you hear the word по and then a number and some form of the word rouble, what is someone telling you?

3 What is the difference in meaning between дóма and в дóме?

4 How would you say *I am going home* in Russian?

5 What is the Russian word for *why?* and *because?*

6 Why will the Russian word for *ticket* be spelled differently if you want to buy one ticket, two tickets or five tickets?

7 What is different about plural animate nouns and their adjectives if they are the object of a sentence?

8 How many different endings are there for genitive plural adjectives?

9 How would you form the genitive plural for the following nouns: конвéрты, мáрки, посы́лки, пи́сьма, имéйлы?

10 Why do we need to be careful with the letter о after ж, ц, ч, ш, щ?

SELF CHECK

I CAN...

⬤ . . . request information about cost, availability and necessity.

⬤ . . . give information about cost, availability and necessity.

⬤ . . . give instructions.

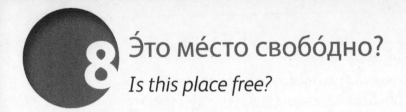

8 Это место свободно?

Is this place free?

In this unit you will learn how to:

▶ *obtain information about availability, variety and cost.*
▶ *place an order.*
▶ *indicate that a mistake has been made.*
▶ *apologize for a mistake.*

CEFR: (A2) *Can order a meal; can understand short, simple texts containing the highest frequency vocabulary, including a portion of shared international vocabulary items.*

🔘 Ресторан *Restaurant*

The choice of restaurants in modern Russia is very wide, with both international fast-food and restaurant chains as well as traditional Russian and former Soviet Union cuisine. Most restaurants now cater for varying dietary needs, though it is still the case that meat dominates most menus.

Since the Western fast-food invasion, Russian alternatives have very quickly been launched and offer reasonably priced, authentic local dishes with good service and a lovely atmosphere. Chains like **Ёлки-палки** are well worth a visit, especially if you have never tried any Russian food before, and the 'Swedish table' (**шведский стол**) option enables you to choose exactly what and how much you want.

In restaurants with table service, you will be served by a *waiter* (**официант**) or *waitress* (**официантка**). At the end of the meal you will need to ask for the *bill* (**счёт**). In the country that invented the multi-course meal, the menu is usually divided into: **закуски** *starters*; **первое (блюдо)** *first course (soup)*; **второе (блюдо)** *second course*; **сладкое** *dessert*; **напитки** *drinks*.

 All of the following dishes are commonly available in restaurants in Russia. What are they?

бефстроганов	суп	гамбургер	пицца
котлеты по-киевски	блины	сандвич	русский салат

Vocabulary builder

08.01 Complete the missing English expressions. Then listen to the audio and repeat the Russian until you can say all the words with confidence.

НА́ДО ЗНАТЬ! *ESSENTIALS*

как жаль	*what a pity/shame*
ка́жется	*it seems*
закры́т	*closed*
по-мо́ему	*in _____ opinion*
откры́т	*open*
мно́го наро́ду	*a _____ of people*
непра́вильно	*_____ right, _____ correct*
извини́те за оши́бку	*sorry about the mistake / excuse the mistake*
ско́лько сто́ит?	*how much does it cost?*
ско́лько с меня́?	*_____ do I owe you?*
да́йте, пожа́луйста, счёт.	*can I have the bill, _____?*
у вас есть …?	*do _____ have …?*
каки́е … у вас есть?	*what sort of … do _____ have?*

В РЕСТОРА́НЕ *FOOD ESSENTIALS*

все места́	*all the places*
за́няты	*occupied*
сади́тесь, пожа́луйста	*sit down, _____*
меню́	*_____*
заказа́ть	*to order*
огурцы́ со смета́ной	*cucumbers _____ soured cream*
вку́сный	*tasty*
грибы́	*mushrooms*
мы не о́чень го́лодны	*we're _____ hungry*
шашлы́к	*kebab*
котле́ты с ри́сом	*homemade burgers with _____*
моро́женое	*ice cream*
по́рция	*_____*
чай с лимо́ном	*tea with _____*
чай с са́харом	*_____ with sugar*
прия́тного аппети́та	*'bon appétit', enjoy your meal*

Dialogue

 08.02 *Anna and Sasha decide to have a meal together in a restaurant.*

1 What do they order?

А́нна	Ой, как жаль. Ресторáн, кáжется, закрыт.
Сáша	Нет, нет, А́нна, что ты! Дверь закры́та, а ресторáн, по-мóему, откры́т. *(Go into restaurant.)*
А́нна	Здесь мнóго нарóду! Кáжется, свобóдных мест нет.
Сáша	Какáя ты сегóдня пессими́стка! У вхóда все местá зáняты, а по-мóему вон там … есть свобóдные местá … *(Approaches table and asks a passing waiter.)* … Извини́те, пожáлуйста, здесь свобóдно?
Официант	Да, свобóдно. Сади́тесь, пожáлуйста.
Сáша	Спаси́бо. А где меню́?
А́нна	Вот онó … *(Waitress approaches.)* А вот официáнтка, мы мóжем заказáть.
Официáнтка	Пожáлуйста, что вы хоти́те заказáть?
Сáша	Скажи́те, пожáлуйста, каки́е у вас закýски?
Официáнтка	У нас огурцы́ со сметáной, … и грибы́ есть … А суп хоти́те?
Сáша	Спаси́бо, нет. Мы не óчень гóлодны. А что есть на вторóе? Шашлы́к есть? Я óчень люблю́ шашлыки́!
Официáнтка	Да, у нас есть шашлык. Также у нас очень вкусные котлéты с ри́сом. Я рекомендýю!
Сáша	А скóлько стóят котлéты с ри́сом?
Официáнтка	Двести пятьдесят рублéй.
Сáша	Хорошó. Дáйте нам, пожáлуйста, огурцы́ со сметáной, котлéты с ри́сом, а на слáдкое … морóженое … да, А́нна?
А́нна	Да … и чай с лимóном, пожáлуйста.
Официáнтка	Так … вам огурцы́ – две пóрции, котлéты … тóже две пóрции, морóженое и чай с сáхаром, да?
А́нна	Нет, э́то непрáвильно … мне чай с лимóном, пожáлуйста, не с сáхаром.
Официáнтка	Ах, да! Извини́те за оши́бку! Прия́тного аппети́та!

2 True or false?

  a Anna thinks that the restaurant is closed.

  b There are lots of free tables.

  c Sasha wants to order soup.

  d Sasha likes kebabs.

  e Anna orders tea with lemon.

3 Answer the following questions.

  a Где Áнна и Cáша?

  b Какúе есть закýски?

  c Áнна и Cáша голоднЫ сегóдня?

  d Что онú хотЯт на слáдкое?

  e Что Áнна хóчет пить?

Language discovery

REFLEXIVE VERBS

We have in fact already come across a reflexive verb – **находúться** *to be situated* – literally, this verb means *to find itself*; a reflexive verb in Russian corresponds to the sort of verb which in English is followed by *self* or where *self* can be understood: e.g. *to get washed* (*to wash oneself*), *to dress* (*to dress oneself*).

YOUR TURN (Давáйте)

1 Complete the English translations.

я нахожýсь	_____ find _____ self
ты нахóдишься	_____ find _____ self
он/онá нахóдится	_____ finds _____ self
мы нахóдимся	_____ find _____ selves
вы нахóдитесь	_____ find _____ selves
они нахóдятся	_____ find _____ selves

2 How is this reflexive verb different from all the other verbs we have met so far? What is the method for forming a reflexive verb?

The good news is that this method applies to all Russian reflexive verbs.

So, what happens to the present tense of **садúться**?

3 Complete the missing reflexive endings.

я сажу́ _____   мы сади́м_____

ты сади́шь _____   вы сади́те_____

он сади́т_____   они садя́т_____

SHORT ADJECTIVES

In Unit 4 we learned how to form adjectives in Russian: e.g. **свобо́дное вре́мя** *spare/free time* – these are called long adjectives and will be the form of adjectives that you see most often. However, a different ending does exist and this is called a short adjective.

4 Look at the first row of the table to spot the pattern that will enable you to complete this table of adjectives. These are some of the words which, during a trip to Russia, you are most likely to meet in the short form.

Long form	Short form, masc.	Short form, fem.	Short form, neut.	Short form, pl.	Meaning
закры́тый	закры́т	закры́та	закры́то	закры́ты	*closed*
за́нятый	за́нят	_____	_____	_____	*occupied*
откры́тый	_____	откры́та	_____	_____	*open*
вку́сный	вку́сен	вкусна́	_____	_____	*tasty*
дово́льный	дово́лен	дово́льна	_____	_____	*content*
свобо́дный	свобо́ден	свобо́дна	_____	_____	*free*
согла́сный	согла́сен	согла́сна	_____	_____	*in agreement*

The short adjective exists only in the nominative (when you are talking about the subject of a sentence) and is usually found when the adjective comes last in a phrase or sentence – i.e. when you are saying:

ме́сто свобо́дно   *the/a place is free*

rather than:

свобо́дное ме́сто   *the/a free place*

Not all Russian adjectives have a short form, for example adjectives of colour (e.g. **кра́сный** *red*) and nationality (e.g. **ру́сский** *Russian*) have no short form. In modern conversational Russian, the long form is almost always used and the short form hardly at all. The only common Russian adjective that does not have a long form is the word for *glad/happy*:

рад   **ра́да**   **ра́ды**

Have you noticed that the short form neuter adjective is also the adverb? e.g. бы́стрый means *quick,* **бы́стро means** *quickly.*

INSTRUMENTAL CASE

The instrumental is the sixth and last Russian case to meet. It is most often used with the preposition **с** *with/accompanied by.*

> **LANGUAGE TIP**
>
> Note that **со**, not **с**, often needs to be used before words starting with two consonants to ease pronunciation; this also applies to the preposition **в** (e.g. **во Фра́нции** *in France*).

The instrumental is also used after some other prepositions:

пе́ред	*in front of*
за	*behind*
ме́жду	*between*
над	*over*
под	*under*
ря́дом с	*next to*

> **LANGUAGE TIP**
>
> Notice that **с** + instrumental means *accompanied by*, whereas the instrumental without **с** means *by means of*. In the sentence *I am going to London by train with my sister*, you are going *by means of* the train (instrumental) and *in the company of* your sister (**с** + instrumental): **Я е́ду в Ло́ндон по́ездом с сестро́й**. (See Unit 9 for the verb **е́хать** *to go, travel*.)

The instrumental case is used without a preposition for:

▶ the instrument with which an action is performed:

я пишу́ ру́чкой	*I write with a pen*

▶ your job or profession:

я рабо́таю инжене́ром	*I work as an engineer*

5 Complete the table.

	Nom.	Remove	Add	Instr.
Masc.	**брат** *brother*	–	**-ом**	**братом**
	учи́тель *teacher*	-ь	**-ем**	_____
	Алексе́й *Aleksei*	-й	**-ем**	_____
Fem.	**сестра́** *sister*	-а	**-ой**	**сестро́й**
	крова́ть *bed*	–	**-ю**	_____
	тётя *aunt*	-я	**-ей**	_____
	Мария *Maria*	-я	_____	**Марией**
Neut.	**окно́** *window*	-о	**-ом**	**окном**
	мо́ре *sea*	-е	_____	**морем**
	зда́ние *building*	-е	**-ем**	_____

The following table shows the instrumental plural endings. Note that these are very straightforward and there are only three possible endings.

6 Complete the table.

	Nom. pl.	Remove	Add	Instr. pl.
Masc.	**грибы́** *mushrooms*	-ы	**-ами**	**грибами**
Fem.	**я́годы** *berries*	-ы	**-ами**	_____
Neut.	**я́йца** *eggs*	-а	_____	**я́йцами**
Soft (all genders)	**пельмени** *pelmeni* (like ravioli)	-и	**-ями**	**пельменями**
Irregular	**друзья́** *friends*	-я	**-ями**	**друзья́ми**
Irregular	**де́ти** *children*	-и	**-ьми**	**детьми́**
Irregular	**лю́ди** *people*	-и	**-ьми**	**людьми́**

The instrumental singular and plural of adjectives are also very straightforward.

Nominative	**Instrumental**
вку́сный	**вку́сным**
вку́сная	**вку́сной**
вку́сное	**вку́сным**
вку́сные	**вку́сными**

LANGUAGE TIP

For the instrumental case, as always, remember the spelling rules:

▶ After **г, к, х, ж, ч, ш** and **щ** add **-им** (not **-ым**) – this applies to the instrumental plural of adjectives.

▶ You cannot write an unstressed **-о** after **ж, ц, ч, ш** or **щ**, so you have to put an **-е** instead – this applies to the instrumental singular of nouns and adjectives.

See the Appendix for the instrumental case of personal pronouns.

КТО? *WHO?* AND ЧТО? *WHAT?*

Now that we have met all six cases, it would be useful to learn the following questions off by heart, as they will help you to remember the main function of each case.

Nom.	**Кто э́то?** *Who is it?*	**Что э́то?** *What is it?*
Acc.	**Кого́ вы зна́ете?** *Whom do you know?*	**Что вы зна́ете?** *What do you know?*
Gen.	**Без кого́?** *Without whom?*	**Без чего́?** *Without what?*
Dat.	**Кому́ э́то помога́ет?** *Whom does this help?*	**Чему́ э́то помога́ет?** *What does this help?*
Instr.	**С кем он живёт?** *With whom does he live?*	**С чем чай?** *What is the tea with?*
Prep.	**О ком он говори́т?** *Whom is he talking about?*	**О чём он говори́т?** *What is he talking about?*

Practice

ры́ба	*fish*
гарни́р	*garnish; vegetables*
жа́реная карто́шка	*chips*
бифште́кс	*steak (burger)*
карто́шка	*potato(es)*

1 Look at the table showing Sasha's preferences and explain what he prefers. The first one is done for you as an example; make up similar dialogues about each of the others.

a	чай	молоко́ ☺	лимо́н
b	суп	помидо́ры	грибы́ ☺
c	котле́ты	рис ☺	карто́шка
d	ры́ба	гарни́р	жа́реная карто́шка ☺
e	бифште́кс	рис	гарни́р ☺

A   Са́ша предпочита́ет чай с молоко́м и́ли с лимо́ном?

B   Он предпочита́ет чай с молоко́м.

2 Match the questions with the answers.

a Áнна хо́чет чай с молоко́м?

b Здесь свобо́дно?

c Да́йте, пожа́луйста, счёт.

d Са́ша любит ры́бу?

e Ско́лько сто́ит сала́т
   с помидо́рами?

f Что вы хоти́те пить?

1 Да, сади́тесь, пожа́луйста.

2 Нет, он предпочита́ет мя́со
   (*meat*).

3 Нет, с лимо́ном.

4 Да́йте, пожа́луйста, вино́.

5 Пожа́луйста, вот он.

6 150 рубле́й.

3 Complete the sentences by choosing the appropriate words from the box. (NB: Choose carefully – you don't need all of them).

> вку́сно вку́сны дово́льна
> дово́льны закры́т за́нят
> за́няты откры́т рад ра́ды
> свобо́дно согла́сен согла́сна

a Ой, как жаль, рестора́н уже́ _____.

b Скажи́те, пожа́луйста, э́то ме́сто _____?

c Са́ша о́чень _____, потому́ что сего́дня есть огурцы́ со
   смета́ной!

d Áнна ду́мает, что все места́ в рестора́не уже́ _____.

e Да, спаси́бо, мы о́чень _____. Котле́ты о́чень _____.

f Я ду́маю, что на́до заказа́ть вино́. Ты _____, Áнна?

4 Considering Galya's preferences, help her order from the menu.

a Каки́е заку́ски?

b Что на пе́рвое?

c Что на второ́е?

d Что на сла́дкое?

e Каки́е напи́тки?

> **LANGUAGE TIP**
> **о́вощи** means
> *vegetables*

Га́ля не о́чень любит мя́со, но она́ о́чень любит о́вощи и фру́кты. Она́ не о́чень любит вино́, но она́ о́чень любит сок и чай с лимо́ном. Вот меню́ в рестора́не «Кали́нка».

Закуски	**Второе**
салат с помидорами	омлет с сыром
салат мясной	котлеты с рисом
	шашлык
Первое	**Сладкое**
суп с грибами	мороженое
суп с мясом	фрукты

Напитки: Вино, шампанское, сок, минеральная вода, чай, кофе

Listen and understand

пиво	*beer*
тогда	*then, in that case*
бутерброд	*sandwich*
ветчина	*ham*
сыр	*cheese*
апельсин	*orange*
минуточку	*just a moment*
ведь	*you know/realize*

08.03 *Vadim sits down at a table in a snack bar, and Viktor prepares to go to the counter to get something to eat and drink.*

1   What does Viktor get wrong in the order?

Виктор	Садись, Вадим! Там у входа есть свободные места.
Вадим	Хорошо.
Виктор	Что ты хочешь пить, Вадим?
Вадим	А что здесь есть?
Виктор	Ну, есть чай, кофе, минеральная вода … и сок.
Вадим	А пива здесь нет?
Виктор	Ну что ты, Вадим! Конечно нет.

Вади́м	Тогда́ мне ко́фе, пожа́луйста.
Ви́ктор	А что ты хо́чешь есть?
Вади́м	Каки́е у них бутербро́ды?
Ви́ктор	С ветчино́й и с сы́ром.
Вади́м	Оди́н бутербро́д с сы́ром, пожа́луйста.
Ви́ктор	Это всё?
Вади́м	Да … а шокола́д и́ли фру́кты есть?
Ви́ктор	Шокола́да, ка́жется, нет, … а апельси́ны есть.
Вади́м	Тогда́ мне, пожа́луйста, ко́фе, бутербро́д с сы́ром и апельси́н.
Ви́ктор	Всё поня́тно. Мину́точку … (*Viktor returns with the tray of sandwiches, coffee, etc.*)
Вади́м	Ну что ты, Ви́ктор! … Ведь э́то бутербро́д с ветчино́й!
Ви́ктор	Извини́ за оши́бку, Вади́м!

2 Choose the correct answers.

a Есть свобо́дные места́
  1 у вхо́да
  2 о́коло окна́
  3 на у́лице
  4 в теа́тре

b Вади́м хо́чет
  1 вино́
  2 во́дку
  3 сок
  4 пи́во

c Вади́м хо́чет бутербро́д
  1 с помидо́рами
  2 с ветчино́й
  3 с сы́ром
  4 со смета́ной

d Вади́м хо́чет
  1 моро́женое
  2 котле́ты с ри́сом
  3 щи
  4 апельси́н

Reading and writing

всеми́рно изве́стный	*world famous*
горя́чий	*hot (to touch, taste)*
занима́ть	*to occupy*
капу́ста	*cabbage*
ка́ша	*porridge; buckwheat*
компоне́нт	*component*
ку́хня	*cuisine; kitchen*
мука́	*flour*

основно́й	basic
осо́бенно	especially
пиро́г	pie
пирожки́	pasties, small pies
соль (f.)	salt
те́сто	pastry, dough
филе́ ка́мбалы	fillet of plaice
холо́дный	cold
чесно́к	garlic

Read the text, then answer the questions that follow in English.

Ру́сская ку́хня – всеми́рно изве́стная. Наприме́р, есть таки́е изве́стные национа́льные блю́да, как щи, блины́, пироги́.

Ка́ша, грибы́ и супы́ то́же занима́ют большо́е ме́сто в ру́сском национа́льном меню́. В ру́сской национа́льной ку́хне есть мно́го супо́в: наприме́р, есть и холо́дные и горя́чие супы́, ры́бные супы́, супы́ с мя́сом и с овоща́ми.

Щи – горя́чий суп; основно́й компоне́нт – капу́ста. Ру́сские о́чень лю́бят грибы́, осо́бенно грибы́ со смета́ной и с чесноко́м. Пироги́ то́же о́чень популя́рны. Пиро́г и пирожки́ с ры́бой о́чень вку́сны; основны́е компоне́нты – ры́ба (наприме́р, филе́ ка́мбалы) и те́сто (основны́е компоне́нты – мука́, ма́сло, яйцо́, соль).

a What different kinds of soup feature prominently in Russian cooking?
b What is the main ingredient of щи?
c What are the popular ways of serving mushrooms?
d What particular kind of pie is recommended here?
e What ingredients are needed for the pastry?

Speaking

помидо́р	tomato
щи	cabbage soup
сок	fruit juice
вино́	wine

1 **08.04** You are in a restaurant, ordering a meal. Play your part in the conversation by choosing items from the accompanying menu, then listen to the complete conversation on the audio.

Официа́нт	Пожа́луйста, что вы хоти́те заказа́ть?
Вы	**a** *Order a starter.*
Официа́нт	Вы хоти́те суп?
Вы	**b** *Say 'no thanks', you're not very hungry.*
Официа́нт	Что вы хоти́те на второ́е?
Вы	**c** *Ask how much the beef stroganoff costs.*
Официа́нт	Три́ста пятьдеся́т рубле́й.
Вы	**d** *Order the beef stroganoff.*
Официа́нт	А что вы хоти́те на сла́дкое?
Вы	**e** *Order ice cream.*
Официа́нт	Что вы хоти́те пить?
Вы	**f** *Order fruit juice and tea with lemon.*
Официа́нт	Хорошо́. Спаси́бо.

МЕНЮ

Заку́ски
огурцы́ со смета́ной ◦ сала́т с помидо́рами

Пе́рвое
суп с гриба́ми ◦ щи

Второ́е
котле́ты с ри́сом ◦ бефстро́ганов

Сла́дкое
моро́женое ◦ фру́кты

Напи́тки
сок ◦ вино́ ◦ чай ◦ ко́фе

2 **08.05** Can you remember how to say the following in Russian? Listen to the audio and practise saying each phrase.

a Is this place/seat free?

b Could I have the bill, please? (lit. Give, please, bill)

c Could I order, please? (lit. Is it possible to order?)

d What would you like to drink? (lit. What do you want to drink?)

e Sorry about the mistake.

Test yourself

1 If *Sorry about the mistake* is извините за ошибку, how would you apologize for a problem? (проблéма *problem*).

2 How would you ask *Who wants what?*

3 At what stage of a meal would you say to the waiter/waitress: Дáйте, пожáлуйста, счёт?

4 At what stage of a meal would you be eating закýски?

5 How do you say *tea with lemon*? What case do need to use for *with lemon*?

6 What would you say to the waiter if you want to order a steak (burger) with mushrooms?

7 Your friend is a vegetarian – will she prefer мя́со or óвощи?

8 How would you ask the waiter what sort of sandwiches are available?

9 What sign are you likely to see on a restaurant door if it is closed?

10 You want to say *I prefer the new restaurant*. Would you use a long or a short adjective?

9 Во ско́лько отхо́дит по́езд?

When does the train leave?

In this unit you will learn how to:
▶ *ask and tell the time.*
▶ *ask and answer questions about particular times.*
▶ *request and give information about travel.*

CEFR: (A2) *Can get simple information about travel and use of public transport; can indicate and handle time.*

По́езд *The train*

Действителен в течение 30 дней с момента первого прохода			
04.01.09	60	150	003359192
НАЧАТЬ ИСПОЛЬЗОВАТЬ ДО	НЕ БОЛЕЕ ПОЕЗДОК	СТОИМОСТЬ РУБЛЕЙ	№ БИЛЕТА
● ⬅	Билет для проезда в Московском Метрополитене		Ⓜ

Просьба сохранить билет до конца поездки.
Подделка проездных документов преследуется по закону.

Train travel is a key part of Russian life. There are various types of train: **ско́рый по́езд** *express train*, **электри́чка** *local electric train*, **фи́рменный по́езд** *long-distance train* (run by a private company).

On long-distance trains each carriage is looked after by a *train attendant* (**проводни́к** or **проводни́ца**), who checks tickets, makes sure each compartment has the correct supply of bedding and supplies tea to the passengers (refreshments may also be available in a **ваго́н-рестора́н**).

Public transport within towns (**городско́й тра́нспорт**) includes *buses* (**авто́бусы**), *trams* (**трамва́и**), *trolleybuses* (**тролле́йбусы**) and *minibus 'taxis'* (**ма́ршрутки**). In some cities, there is also an *underground* (**метро́**). Bus/tram/trolleybus tickets can be bought from kiosks and the driver, and each ticket must be punched when it is used (**компости́ровать** *to punch*); access to the Moscow metro is by tickets purchased at the **ка́сса**. A **еди́ный биле́т** is an all-in-one ticket, which covers transport by bus, tram, trolleybus and underground.

Match the ticket prices to the figures.

1	семьсо́т соро́к один рубль	**a**	2,657 roubles
2	ты́сяча восемьсо́т соро́к четы́ре рубля́	**b**	6,239 roubles
3	две ты́сячи шестьсо́т пятьдеся́т семь рубле́й	**c**	741 roubles
4	шесть ты́сяч две́сти три́дцать де́вять рубле́й	**d**	1,844 roubles

---

Vocabulary builder

09.01 **Complete the missing English expressions. Then listen to the audio and repeat the Russian until you can say all the words with confidence.**

НА́ДО ЗНАТЬ! *ESSENTIALS*

вся гру́ппа	*the whole _____*
ско́лько сейча́с вре́мени?	*what time is it now?*
два́дцать мину́т двена́дцатого	*_____ past eleven*
во ско́лько?	*at what time?*
в по́лночь	*at midnight*
че́рез со́рок мину́т	*in _____ minutes' time*
за́втра у́тром	*tomorrow morning*
ты бу́дешь	*you will be*
(в) семь часо́в	*(at) _____ o'clock*
день (m.)	*day*
всего́	*in all, only*
тебе́ везёт	*you're lucky*
тако́й	*such a, so*
всегда́	*always*
удо́бно (удо́бный)	*convenient, comfortable*
тепло́	*it is warm*
спать	*to sleep*

мы все е́дем	_____ are all going
отхо́дит (отходи́ть)	*leaves (to leave)*
по́езд	*train*
е́здить	*to travel*
биле́т на по́езд (в Санкт-Петербу́рг)	*a _____ for the train (to _____)*
в оди́н коне́ц	*one way*
обра́тный биле́т	*a return _____*
шесто́й ваго́н	*sixth carriage*
четвёртое купе́	*fourth compartment*
платфо́рма	*platform*
От како́й платфо́рмы отхо́дит по́езд?	*from which _____ does the train depart?*
го́лос	*voice*
объявля́ться	*to be announced*
поса́дка	*boarding*
счастли́вого пути́!	*bon voyage! have a _____ journey!*

Dialogue

 09.02 *Anna is at the railway station waiting with her fellow tourists for the train to St Petersburg. Ira has come to see her off.*

1 Which carriage, compartment and berth is Anna in?

И́ра	*(Arriving in a hurry.)* А́нна, вот ты где! Вся твоя́ гру́ппа здесь?
А́нна	Да, мы все е́дем в Санкт-Петербу́рг.
И́ра	Ско́лько сейча́с вре́мени?
А́нна	Два́дцать мину́т двена́дцатого.
И́ра	А во ско́лько отхо́дит по́езд?
А́нна	В по́лночь. Зна́чит, че́рез со́рок мину́т.
И́ра	Ага́, поня́тно. Зна́чит, за́втра у́тром ты уже́ бу́дешь в Санкт-Петербу́рге.
А́нна	Да, в семь часо́в.
И́ра	Ско́лько дней ты там бу́дешь?
А́нна	Всего́ три дня.
И́ра	Тебе́ везёт, А́нна! Санкт-Петербу́рг тако́й краси́вый го́род. И всегда́ удо́бно, коне́чно, е́здить по́ездом.

Áнна	Почему́?
Йра	Потому́ что в по́езде тепло́, прия́тно. Мо́жно спать, пить чай. Я о́чень люблю́ е́здить по́ездом. А у тебя́ како́й биле́т на по́езд? В оди́н коне́ц, да?
Áнна	Нет, обра́тный биле́т … вот он.
Йра	Ага́ … шесто́й ваго́н, четвёртое купе́, два́дцать четвёртое ме́сто. С како́й платфо́рмы?
Áнна	С пя́той платфо́рмы.
Го́лос	Объявля́ется поса́дка на по́езд Москва́ – Санкт-Петербу́рг.
Йра	Зна́чит, тебе́ уже́ пора́, Áнна. Счастли́вого пути́!

2 True or false?

a Anna gets to the railway station at 12.20 a.m.

b Tomorrow morning, Anna will be in St Petersburg.

c Anna will be in St Petersburg for four days.

d Anna is planning to have a coffee on the train.

e The train leaves from platform number 5.

3 Answer the questions.

a Во ско́лько отхо́дит по́езд?

b Во ско́лько Áнна бу́дет в Санкт-Петербу́рге?

c Что Йра говори́т о Санкт-Петербу́рге?

d Почему́ Йра ду́мает, что всегда́ удо́бно е́здить по́ездом?

e Како́й биле́т у Áнны?

Language discovery

ВСЯ ГРУ́ППА   *THE WHOLE GROUP*

In Russian, the word for *all* has several forms.

1 Looking at the following, can you work out why the word changes? Complete the left-hand column with a grammatical explanation for the change.

_____	**весь день**	*the whole day*
_____	**вся гру́ппа**	*the whole group*
_____	**всё письмо́**	*the whole letter*
_____	**все тури́сты**	*all the tourists*

The full declension (i.e. all the case endings) of **весь** is given in the Appendix.

2 When making a purchase in a shop, or an order in a restaurant, you will often hear the question: Это всё? and you might answer Да, спасибо, это всё. What do these two phrases mean?

INSTRUMENTAL CASE

In Unit 8 we learned that this case is used for the means by which an action is performed, so it is commonly used when describing means of transport.

YOUR TURN (Давайте)

3 What do the following words in the instrumental case mean?

поездом by _____; **автобусом** by _____; **самолётом** by _____

The instrumental is also used in time phrases, of which the following are very common:

у́тром	*in the morning*
днём	*during the day*
ве́чером	*in the evening*
но́чью	*at night*
зимо́й	*in winter*
весно́й	*in spring*
ле́том	*in summer*
о́сенью	*in autumn*

> **LANGUAGE TIP**
>
> It is important to remember that, unlike English, Russian does not use a preposition for these eight time phrases (i.e. when saying *in the morning, in the afternoon, in the evening, at night, in spring, in summer, in autumn, in winter*); simply use the instrumental case with no preposition.

ТЫ БУ́ДЕШЬ *YOU WILL BE*

Although there is no present tense of the verb *to be* (**быть**) in Russian, there is a future tense (*I will be, you will be,* etc.). Even though this is a different tense, the endings should be reassuringly familiar.

4 **Given the stem for the future of** *to be* **(буд-), you should find it easy to complete this new tense.**

я бу́ду		*I will be*
_____ бу́дешь		_____
он/она́ бу́д____		_____
_____ бу́дем		_____
вы бу́д____		_____
_____ бу́дут		_____

TIME

In order to tell the time in Russian we need to know two sets of numbers, cardinal (the ones we have already met – 1, 2, 3, etc.) and ordinal (the ones which tell us the order – 1st, 2nd, 3rd, etc.).

5 **Complete the lists for these two sets of numbers. Do you notice anything about the endings of the ordinals?**

Cardinal		Ordinal	
оди́н	1	пе́рвый	_____
_____	2	второ́й	_____
_____	3	тре́тий	_____
_____	4	четвёртый	_____
_____	5	пя́тый	_____
_____	6	шесто́й	_____
_____	7	седьмо́й	_____
_____	8	восьмо́й	_____
_____	9	девя́тый	_____
_____	10	деся́тый	_____
_____	11	оди́ннадцатый	_____
_____	12	двена́дцатый	_____

Telling the time on the hour is quite straightforward: simply state the appropriate cardinal number and follow it by a form of the word **час** *hour*.

Ско́лько сейча́с вре́мени?	Час	*one o'clock*
Ско́лько сейча́с вре́мени?	Три часа́	*three o'clock*
Ско́лько сейча́с вре́мени?	Де́вять часо́в	*nine o'clock*

6 Why do you think the word **час** is spelled differently in these three examples?

Unfortunately, telling the time between hours is not quite so straightforward.

 7 Complete the following and see if you can work out the pattern for minutes past, minutes to, half past and quarter past/to before reading the explanation that follows.

четыре часа	_____ o'clock
пять минут пятого	_____ past four
десять минут пятого	_____ past four
четверть пятого	quarter past _____
двадцать минут пятого	_____ past four
двадцать пять минут пятого	_____ past four
полпятого	half past _____
без двадцати пяти пять	25 to _____
без двадцати пять	_____ to five
без четверти пять	_____ to five
без десяти пять	_____ to five
без пяти пять	_____ to five
пять часов	_____

▶ *Minutes past the hour are said in Russian to be x minutes of the following hour:*

five minutes past four = five minutes of the fifth hour = **пять минут пятого**

▶ *Quarter past and half past are said to be quarter/half of the following hour:*

quarter past four = quarter of the fifth hour = **четверть пятого**

half past four = half of the fifth hour = **полпятого**

▶ *Minutes to the hour are said to be without x minutes (next) hour:*

five minutes to five = without five five = **без пяти пять**

▶ *Quarter to is said to be without quarter (next) hour:*

quarter to five = without quarter five = **без четверти пять**

8 What do you think по́лдень and по́лночь mean?

The question *At what time?* is usually **Во ско́лько?**

9 Look at some possible answers to the question Во ско́лько отхо́дит по́езд? *At what time does the train leave?* Try to work out how you say *at* a time in Russian.

В три часа́	*At three o'clock*
В два́дцать мину́т второ́го	*At 20 past one*
Полшесто́го	*At half past five*
Без че́тверти три	*At quarter to three*

Good news! Although telling the time in everyday life in Russian is not straightforward, times that you hear being announced officially (for example: at airports, on TV) will usually use the 24-hour clock. This is a direct translation of English, e.g. **восемна́дцать три́дцать** – *18:30*.

> **LANGUAGE TIP**
> Try learning a few specific times to help you remember the different ways of dealing with them, e.g. hours: **три часа́** *3:00*, **пять часо́в** *5:00*; half hours: **полчетвёртого** *3:30*; minutes to: **без пяти́ три** *2:45*; minutes past: **че́тверть пя́того** *4:15*

ЧЕ́РЕЗ *ACROSS*

Че́рез literally means *across*, and it is always followed by the accusative case.

10 Can you work out what Че́рез means when it is used with a time expression?

По́езд в Санкт-Петербу́рг *The St Petersburg train leaves*
**отхо́дит че́рез со́рок мину́т.* _____.

Че́рез is also useful when giving information about the number of stops to be travelled.

YOUR TURN (Дава́йте)

11 Complete the translation of the following dialogue.

Когда́ мне выходи́ть?	*When should _____ get off?*
Че́рез три остано́вки	*After _____ stops.*

TO GO

The Russian verbs meaning *to go*, at first sight, might seem bewildering. However, if you follow a few logical steps, you will always choose the right verb. Look at the following, which summarizes these logical steps.

TO GO

By Foot		By Transport	
often	*once*	*often*	*once*
ходить	идти	ездить	ехать
я хожу́	я иду́	я е́зжу	я е́ду
ты хо́дишь	ты идёшь	ты е́здишь	ты е́дешь
он/она́ хо́дит	он/она́ идёт	он/она е́здит	он/она е́дет
мы хо́дим	мы идём	мы е́здим	мы е́дем
вы хо́дите	вы идёте	вы е́здите	вы е́дете
они хо́дят	они иду́т	они е́здят	они е́дут

So when deciding how to say *to go* in Russian, first decide if it is on foot or by transport, and then decide if you are going on more than one occasion or just once, and then choose the appropriate verb ending.

YOUR TURN (Дава́йте)

12 Complete the sentences.

Она́ всегда́ хо́дит в _____   *She always _____ into town*

Сейча́с она́ идёт в _____   *She _____ into town now*

Я обы́чно е́зжу на рабо́ту _____   *I usually go to _____ by bus*

Сего́дня _____ е́дет в Санкт-Петербу́рг   *Anna is going to _____ today*

> **LANGUAGE TIP**
>
> Note that while people *travel* (**е́здить/е́хать**) on vehicles, the movement of certain vehicles is described by **ходи́ть/идти́** – thus trains and trams, for example, *walk*:
> **Поезда́ хо́дят бы́стро и ча́сто** *The trains run quickly and frequently.*

СЧАСТЛИВОГО ПУТИ! *HAVE A GOOD JOURNEY!*

Wishes of this kind are expressed in the genitive case; this is because the verb **желать** *to wish* must be followed by the genitive case – even if the verb itself is not stated, it is always understood.

YOUR TURN (Давайте)

13 What are we being wished in the following two expressions?

(Я желаю вам) приятного аппетита!

(Я желаю вам) всего хорошего!

Practice

1 Replace the time given in the dialogue with the times indicated on the clocks. Say it out loud!

A	Извините, пожалуйста, сколько сейчас времени?
B	Два часа.
A	Спасибо.
B	Пожалуйста.

Четыре часа
It's four o'clock

Четверть восьмого
It's quarter past seven

Полчетвёртого
It's half past three

Без десяти пять
It's ten to five

Now look at the time and answer: Сколько сейчас времени?

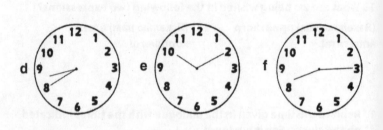

2 When does the train leave? Give the times in Russian. The first one has been done for you.

Во сколько отходит поезд?

Куда?	Когда?		
В Москву	11 a.m.	**a**	<u>**В одиннадцать часов утра.**</u>
В Обнинск	6 p.m.	**b**	
В Ялту	8:30 a.m.	**c**	
В Киев	11:30 p.m.	**d**	

деловая поездка	*business trip*
длительный	*long, lengthy*
железная дорога	*railway*
путешествие	*travel*

3 **Look at the advertisement for railway travel, and then answer the questions. (NB: You don't need to understand all the words in the advert to be able to answer them.)**

ЖЕЛЕЗНЫЕ ДОРОГИ

ЖЕЛЕЗНЫЕ ДОРОГИ ПРЕДЛАГАЮТ:

- для деловой поездки
- для туристского путешествия

Поезда и беспересадочные спальные вагоны

Спальные вагоны прекрасно

приспособлены для длительных

путешествий

Прямое сообщение с 24 странами Европы и Азии

ЖЕЛАЕМ ПРИЯТНОЙ ПОЕЗДКИ!

---

a What different types of journey can the railways cater for?
b What sort of carriages are especially designed for long journeys?
c Which continents do the railways connect?
d What wish is expressed at the end of the advert?

Listen and understand

сло́жный	complicated
ближа́йший	nearest
сади́ться на автобус	to catch a bus
выходи́ть	to get out
остано́вка	stop
прое́хать	to travel to
переса́дка	change (buses, trains, etc.)
снача́ла	at first
ходьба́	walking
пое́здка	journey, trip
занима́ть	to occupy

09.03 *Alla is talking to her new neighbour, Boris.*

1   What is Alla talking to Boris about?

Бори́с	Как вы обы́чно е́здите на рабо́ту, А́лла?
А́лла	Зна́ете, э́то немно́жко сло́жно …
Бори́с	Почему́?
А́лла	Потому́, что ближа́йшая ста́нция метро́ далеко́ отсю́да.
Бори́с	Зна́чит, на́до сади́ться на трамва́й?
А́лла	Нет. На́до сади́ться на сто два́дцать второ́й автобус.
Бори́с	А когда́ на́до выходи́ть?
А́лла	Че́рез шесть остано́вок.
Бори́с	Ста́нция метро́ далеко́ от остано́вки автобуса?
А́лла	Нет. Отту́да ста́нция метро́ «Беля́ево» недалеко́.
Бори́с	А отту́да мо́жно прое́хать в центр?
А́лла	Да, мо́жно.
Бори́с	Без переса́док?
А́лла	Да, без переса́док.
Бори́с	Зна́чит, снача́ла автобусом до метро́, а пото́м в метро́, без переса́док. Ну, пото́м что?
А́лла	Пото́м де́сять мину́т ходьбы́ до институ́та.
Бори́с	Да … сло́жно. Пое́здка на рабо́ту занима́ет мно́го вре́мени?
А́лла	Ну, пятьдеся́т мину́т, час.

2 Choose the correct answers.

a Áлла живёт

1 недалекó от стáнции метрó
2 налéво от стáнции метрó
3 далекó от стáнции метрó
4 напрáво от стáнции метрó

b Áлла обы́чно éздит на стáнцию метрó

1 велосипéдом
2 автомоби́лем
3 автóбусом
4 трамвáем

c Стáнция метрó

1 далекó от останóвки автóбуса
2 hедалекó от останóвки автóбуса
3 За останóвкой автóбуса
4 рядом с дóмом Áллы

d От стáнции метрó

1 Áлла éздит на рабóту трамвáем
2 Áлла хóдит на рабóту
3 Áлла éздит на рабóту автомоби́лем
4 Áлла éздит на рабóту троллéйбусом

Reading and writing

бýква	*letter* (of the alphabet)
достигáть	*to reach*
как прáвило	*as a rule*
крáсный	*red*
срéдний	*average*
считáть	*to consider*
час пик	*rush hour*

Read the text, then answer the questions in English.

Если вы идёте по у́лице и ви́дите большу́ю кра́сную бу́кву «М» – зна́чит э́то ста́нция метро́. Метро́– о́чень бы́стрый, удо́бный и популя́рный вид городско́го тра́нспорта. Моско́вский метрополите́н всеми́рно изве́стен и москвичи́, как пра́вило, предпочита́ют е́здить на метро́. А почему́? Они́ счита́ют, что моско́вское метро́ хорошо́ организо́вано, поезда́ хо́дят и бы́стро и ча́сто. Сре́дний интерва́л ме́жду поезда́ми – 2,5 мину́ты. Минима́льный интерва́л в «часы́ пик» – 90 секу́нд. Максима́льный интерва́л мо́жет достига́ть 10 мину́т.

a What sign indicates the presence of a metro station?

b Why do Muscovites prefer to travel by metro?

c How long might you have to wait for a train?

 ## Speaking

 1 09.04 You are buying a train ticket. Play your part, then listen to the complete conversation on the audio.

Вы	**a** *Ask how much a ticket to Yalta costs.*
Де́вушка	150 рубле́й.
Вы	**b** *Ask for two tickets to Yalta.*
Де́вушка	Пожа́луйста. С вас 300 рубле́й.
Вы	**c** *Say 'here is 500 roubles'.*
Де́вушка	У вас нет ме́лочи?
Вы	**d** *Apologize that you have no change.*
Де́вушка	Ничего́.
Вы	**e** *Ask what time the train leaves.*
Де́вушка	Че́рез час.
Вы	**f** *Ask what platform the train leaves from.*
Де́вушка	от четвёртой платфо́рмы.

> **LANGUAGE TIP**
> Remember that the accusative is needed with **в** for direction/ motion towards (see Unit 3), so you should say **биле́т в Я́лту**; if you say **в Я́лте**, it means you are there already.

 2 09.05 Can you remember how to say the following in Russian? Listen to the audio and practise saying each phrase.

a What time is it?

b What time does the train leave?

c What platform does the train leave from?

d The train leaves in ten minutes.

e How many days will you be there for?

Test yourself

1 Which case do you need to remember to use when you want to wish someone all the best?

2 To make the future of the verb *to be* (*I will*, *you will*, etc.) you need to know its stem. Can you remember the stem, and how to say *I will* and *you* (ты) *will*?

3 Two key words when you are travelling on public transport: остановка and пересадка. Can you remember what they mean?

4 Дайте, пожалуйста, билет в Москву. Which case has been used here for Moscow and why?

5 Девять часов *It is nine o'clock*. What would you need to add to make this mean *9.00 a.m.*?

6 The words сначала and потом are often used when you're giving directions or explaining your route to work, for example. Can you remember what they mean?

7 What would you be wanting to find out if you asked the question Сколько сейчас времени? or Который час?

8 The verb ездить/ехать *to go* (by transport), like many verbs of motion, has two forms of the present tense. Can you explain why *She often travels* will be Она часто ездит and not едет?

9 There are lots of useful time phrases in Unit 9. If you were invited to a concert завтра вечером, when would you expect to go?

10 If someone asked you a question beginning Почему …?, how would your reply be likely to start?

10 По средам я обычно…

On Wednesdays
I usually…

In this unit you will learn how to:

▶ *talk about daily and weekly routine.*
▶ *ask for and give information about age.*
▶ *talk about days of the week.*
▶ *express approximation with regard to time.*

CEFR: (A2) *Can describe habits and routines; can understand sentences and frequently used expressions related to areas of most immediate relevance (basic personal or family info).*

Russian meals: завтрак, обед, ужин

In Russia, **завтрак** *breakfast* might consist of virtually any dish, and sometimes it can be difficult to distinguish it from **обед** *lunch* or **ужин** *supper*. Modern Russian breakfast menus, both in hotels and at home, have in recent years increasingly been influenced by Western breakfast habits. However, in Soviet times, a traditional breakfast typically consisted of things like **каша** *porridge*, cooked cereal, meat, fish or eggs of some kind – e.g. **яичница** *fried eggs* – perhaps a glass of **кефир** (a sort of liquid, sour yoghurt), sweet buns, tea, coffee and *bread* (**хлеб**). Bread (typically a light rye bread) still accompanies every meal.

If the main meal of the day is to be late, then in the late morning there can be a second breakfast, perhaps of a savoury dish, bread and a sweet fruit or cottage cheese dish – e.g. **кисель** *sweet fruit jelly*. The main meal of the day, **обед**, is a moveable feast – it may be at midday, in the afternoon or in the evening; it may start off with **закуски**, usually includes a rich soup such as **щи**, followed by a meat dish such as **котлеты**. **Ужин** is a lighter meal – a typical dish would be **блины** *pancakes* served with *sour cream* (**сметана**).

Can you match the Russian for these common foods and drinks to the English?

1 суп	**2** борщ	**3** ку́рица	**4** майоне́з	**5** шокола́д
6 соль	**7** пе́рец	**8** чай	**9** ко́фе	**10** молоко́
a mayonnaise	**b** chocolate	**c** soup	**d** beetroot soup	**e** chicken
f pepper	**g** tea	**h** milk	**i** salt	**j** coffee

Vocabulary builder

10.01 Complete the missing English expressions. Then listen to the audio and repeat the Russian until you can say all the words with confidence.

НА́ДО ЗНАТЬ! *ESSENTIALS*

я пишу́	*I write*
то есть	*that is (i.e.)*
сове́товаться с (instr.)	*to consult, get advice from*
ти́хо (ти́хий)	*quiet*
я могу́	*_____ can*
споко́йно (споко́йный)	*peaceful, calm*
тогда́	*then, in that case*
ско́лько ему́ лет?	*how old is he?*
я встаю́ (встава́ть)	*I get up (to get up)*
за́втракаю (за́втракать)	*I have breakfast (to have breakfast)*
начина́ть	*to begin*
часо́в в де́вять	*at about _____ o'clock*
ра́но у́тром	*early in the morning*
зави́сит от (зави́сеть от gen.)	*it depends on*
обе́даю (обе́дать)	*I have _____ (to have _____)*
гуля́ть (гуля́ю, гуля́ешь)	*to stroll*
по́сле у́жина	*after _____*
туда́	*to there*
моего́ сы́на нет до́ма	*my son is not at home (lit. There is not of my son at home)*
кем вы рабо́таете?	*what is your job? (lit. as whom do you _____?)*
занима́юсь	*I do (lit. busy myself with)*
администрати́вной рабо́той	*_____ work*
отвеча́ть на пи́сьма	*to reply to letters*

КОГДА? *FREQUENCY WORDS*

всегда́	*always*
иногда́	*sometimes*
обы́чно	*usually*
ча́сто	*often*
ка́ждый	*every*
по понеде́льникам	*on Mondays*
по сре́дам	*on Wednesdays*
по утра́м	*in the mornings*
по вечера́м	*in the evenings*

> **LANGUAGE TIP**
> Frequency words are usually placed at the beginning of sentences, or just before the verb.

Dialogue

учи́тельница	*(female) teacher*
сценари́ст	*scriptwriter*
киносту́дия	*film studio*
колле́га	*colleague*

10.02 *Ira has introduced Anna to her friend Anatoly, who works at a film studio in Moscow.*

1 What does Anatoly's work involve on Mondays? And on Wednesdays?

Анато́лий	О́чень прия́тно, А́нна. Вы рабо́таете учи́тельницей, да?
А́нна	Пра́вда. А кем вы рабо́таете?
Анато́лий	Я сценари́ст … э́то зна́чит, что я пишу́ сцена́рии для кинофи́льмов.
А́нна	Ой, как интере́сно! Зна́чит, вы ка́ждый день рабо́таете в киносту́дии?
Анато́лий	Нет, не ка́ждый день. Обы́чно по понеде́льникам я рабо́таю в киносту́дии, то есть я занима́юсь администрати́вной рабо́той – ча́сто мне на́до отвеча́ть на пи́сьма, сове́товаться с колле́гами.
А́нна	Поня́тно.
Анато́лий	А по сре́дам, наприме́р, я обы́чно рабо́таю до́ма, пишу́ сцена́рии. До́ма ти́хо, я могу́ споко́йно рабо́тать … то есть э́то тогда́, когда́ моего́ сы́на нет до́ма!

Áнна	А ско́лько ему́ лет?
Анато́лий	Ему́ шесть лет.
Áнна	Всё поня́тно! … Скажи́те, а киносту́дия далеко́ от до́ма?
Анато́лий	К сожале́нию, да. Я всегда́ е́зжу туда́ на маши́не.
Áнна	Во ско́лько вы обы́чно начина́ете рабо́тать?
Анато́лий	По понеде́льникам, когда́ я рабо́таю в киносту́дии, я встаю́ полседьмо́го, за́втракаю и начина́ю рабо́тать часо́в в де́вять.
Áнна	А е́сли вы рабо́таете до́ма, когда́ вы начина́ете?
Анато́лий	Тогда́ я начина́ю рабо́тать часо́в в семь … я предпочита́ю писа́ть сцена́рии ра́но у́тром.
Áнна	Ско́лько часо́в вы рабо́таете ка́ждый день?
Анато́лий	Понима́ете, э́то зави́сит от рабо́ты. Обы́чно я рабо́таю часо́в семь в день.
Áнна	А по вечера́м вы отдыха́ете, да?
Анато́лий	Да, … и не то́лько по вечера́м! В киносту́дии я обы́чно обе́даю с друзья́ми, часа́ в три, пото́м мы гуля́ем в па́рке.
Áнна	А что вы де́лаете по́сле у́жина?
Анато́лий	Обы́чно я сижу́ до́ма. Иногда́ слу́шаю ра́дио, смотрю́ телеви́зор и́ли чита́ю интере́сную кни́гу.

> **LANGUAGE TIP**
>
> Anatoly and Anna use the instrumental case to talk/ask about jobs (**учи́тельницей** – *as a teacher*) and the instrumental of **кто** *who* in the phrase **кем вы рабо́таете?** NB: You can either say *I am a journalist* (**я журнали́ст**) or *I work as a journalist* (**я рабо́таю журнали́стом**).

2 True or false?

a Anna is a teacher.

b On Mondays, Anatoly works at home.

c Anatoly doesn't live far from the film studio.

d Anatoly gets up at half past six.

e Anatoly works about seven hours a day.

3 Answer the following questions.

a Кем рабо́тает Анато́лий?

b Что он де́лает по сре́дам?

c Как он е́здит на рабо́ту?

d Когда́ Анато́лий предпочита́ет писа́ть сцена́рии?

e Как он отдыха́ет по вечера́м?

Language discovery

VERBS

Note that two of the verbs you've just met in the dialogue are common irregular verbs – **писа́ть** *to write* and **мочь** *to be able*.

YOUR TURN (Дава́йте)

1 Can you complete the present tense endings for these two verbs?

писа́ть: я пишу́ *I write*; **ты пи́шешь** *you write*; **он/она́ пиш_____** *he/she writes*; **мы пиш_____** *we write*; **вы пиш_____** *you write*; **они́ пи́шут** *they write*

мочь: я могу́ *I am able*; **ты мо́жешь** *you are able*; **он/она́ мож_____** *he/she is able*; **мы мож_____** *we are able*; **вы мож_____** *you are able*; **они́ мо́гут** *they are able*

> **LANGUAGE TIP**
> Remember all you need to learn for the present tense of verbs like these two is: the **я** and **ты** forms (because the **я** form shows you what the **они́** form will be, and the **ты** form shows you what the **он, она́, оно́, мы** and **вы** forms will be).

DATIVE CASE

In Unit 6 we met some of the uses of the dative case and learned how to form the dative singular of nouns. The following tables give all the dative endings for nouns and adjectives, singular and plural.

2 Try to complete the dative singular noun endings from memory.

	Nom. sing	Dat. sing.	Dat. pl.
Masc.	студе́нт	студент _____	студе́нтам
	учи́тель	учител _____	учителя́м
Fem.	соба́ка	собак _____	соба́кам
	дверь	двер _____	дверя́м
Neut.	окно́	окн _____	о́кнам
	мо́ре	мор _____	моря́м

The next table include two adjectives which have slightly different endings because of two spelling rules.

3 Can you remember what these spelling rules are?

	Nom. sing	Dat. sing.	Dat. pl.
Masc.	интере́сный	интере́сному	интере́сным
	хоро́ший	хоро́шему	хоро́шим
Fem.	интере́сная	интере́сной	интере́сным
	хоро́шая	хоро́шей	хоро́шим
Neut.	интере́сное	интере́сному	интере́сным
	хоро́шее	хоро́шему	хоро́шим

> **LANGUAGE TIP**
>
> A useful expression using the dative is *in my/your*, etc. *opinion*: **по моему/ва́ш/ему мне́нию**. Often, this is shortened to: **по-мо́ему** *in my opinion*, **по-ва́шему** *in your opinion*.

TALKING ABOUT YOUR AGE

Another common use of the dative case is when asking and giving information about your age:

Ско́лько ему́ лет? *How old is he?*
(lit. *How many years to him?*)

> **LANGUAGE TIP**
>
> See the Appendix for the dative of **я, ты, он, она́, оно́, мы, вы** and **они́**.

YOUR TURN (Дава́йте)

4 How old are the following people?

Ива́ну два́дцать оди́н год *Ivan is _____*

О́льге со́рок два го́да *Olga is _____*

Ему́ шесть лет *He is _____*

Giving ages usually involves compound numbers, which affects how you spell the Russian for *of age* (lit. *years*):

▶ Whenever the final digit is 1, use **год**: **Мне два́дцать оди́н год**
   I am 21
▶ Whenever the final digit is 2, 3 or 4, use **года**: **Ему́ со́рок два го́да**
   He is 42
▶ For everything else, use **лет**: **Ей три́дцать лет?** *Is she 30?*

TIME PHRASES

The dative and accusative cases are very useful when dealing with time phrases that involve days of the week.

Note that days of the week are written with a small letter in Russian, unless at the beginning of a sentence. Saying *on a (single) day* is easy – you just use **в** (apart from *on Tuesday*, when you use **во**). Saying *on -days* is also easy – you just use the ending **-ам** (apart from *on Sundays*, which ends in **-ям**).

	Day	on (a) -day (acc.)	on -days (dat.)
Monday	понеде́льник	в понеде́льник	по понеде́льникам
Tuesday	вто́рник	во вто́рник	по вто́рникам
Wednesday	среда́	в сре́ду	по сре́дам
Thursday	четве́рг	в четве́рг	по четвергам
Friday	пя́тница	в пя́тницу	по пя́тницам
Saturday	суббо́та	в суббо́ту	по суббо́там
Sunday	воскресе́нье	в воскресе́нье	по воскресе́ньям

So, if you're talking about a specific Saturday, you will use the accusative singular:

В суббо́ту я бу́ду в Ло́ндоне   *On Saturday I will be in London*

But for Saturdays in general, use the dative plural:

По суббо́там я ча́сто де́лаю   *On Saturdays I often do the*
поку́пки   *shopping*

The accusative is also useful in the phrases *per day*, *per week*, etc.:

семь часо́в в день   *seven hours a day*

со́рок часо́в в неде́лю   *40 hours a week*

If you want to give an approximate time, simply invert the numeral and the number of hours:

часо́в семь в день   *about seven hours a day*

Во ско́лько вы за́втракаете?   *At what time do you have breakfast?*

Часо́в в семь   *At about seven o'clock*

ACCUSATIVE CASE

The only form of the accusative we have not yet met is for feminine singular adjectives – in other words, if you want to say *I am reading an interesting book* (**интере́сная кни́га**), you say: **Я чита́ю интере́сную кни́гу**.

 5 Can you work out what the rule is?

124

Practice

1 **Look at this shopping list. Based on the example answer to a, make up sentences to say that you want to buy the other items.**

a кра́сная ру́чка *(pen)*

b чёрная ю́бка *(skirt)*

c деревя́нный стул

d интере́сная кни́га

e ру́сский журна́л

f но́вая ка́рта

a Я хочу́ купи́ть кра́сную ру́чку.

приглаша́ть	*to invite*
преподава́тель (m.)	*teacher*
для спра́вок	*for information*
ко́нкурс	(here) *vacancy*
до́лжность (f.)	*job, position*

2 **Look at these advertisements for jobs, then answer the questions that follow.**

ЕЛАБУЖСКИЙ ЗАВОД АВТОМОБИЛЕЙ ПРИГЛАШАЕТ

преподавателей итальянского языка для обучения

специалистов по месту работы.

Телефоны для справок: 2-11-00, 7-19-29

МОРДОВСКИЙ ПЕДАГОГИЧЕСКИЙ ИНСТИТУТ ОБЪЯВЛЯЕТ КОНКУРС

по вакантным должностям:

- преподавателей русского языка
- преподавателей математики
- преподавателей английского языка

телефоны для справок: 4-40-30, 4-60-39

a What sort of teachers are needed at the car factory?

b What sort of teachers are needed at the pedagogical institute?

3 Complete this paragraph with the correct form of the verb in brackets.

Игорь _____ (жить) в Москве. Он _____ (работать) переводчиком и очень хорошо _____ (говорить) по-итальянски. Он часто _____ (ходить) в театр с группами туристов, вот почему по вечерам он часто не _____ (мочь) отдыхать дома. В свободное время он очень _____ (любить) смотреть телевизор и он часто _____ (играть) в шахматы с друзьями. Иногда он _____ (писать) письма и по воскресеньям он обычно _____ (плавать) в бассейне или _____ (гулять) в парке.

4 Answer these questions about yourself.

a Где вы живёте?

b Вы живёте в доме или в квартире?

c Кем вы работаете?

d Сколько вам лет?

e Во сколько вы обычно встаёте по утрам?

f Как вы ездите на работу?

g Во сколько вы начинаете работать?

h Во сколько вы обедаете?

i Что вы обычно делаете по вечерам?

j Что вы обычно делаете по субботам и по воскресеньям?

Listen and understand

официа́нт	*waiter*
до полу́ночи	*until midnight*
ложи́ться спать	*to go to bed*
ведь	*you realize/know, after all*
конча́ться	*to finish*

10.03 *A journalist interviews a waiter from the restaurant 'Kalinka'.*

1 For how many years has Vadim worked as a waiter?

Журнали́ст	Здра́вствуйте. Как вас зову́т?
Официа́нт	Меня́ зову́т Вади́м.
Журнали́ст	Вади́м, ско́лько вам лет?
Официа́нт	Мне два́дцать во́семь лет.
Журнали́ст	И ско́лько лет вы рабо́таете официа́нтом?
Официа́нт	Уже́ шесть лет.
Журнали́ст	И э́то интере́сная рабо́та?
Официа́нт	И да, и нет! Иногда́ о́чень ску́чная, а иногда́ интере́сная. Вот, наприме́р, когда́ у нас в рестора́не англи́йские тури́сты.
Журнали́ст	Почему́?
Официа́нт	Потому́, что я немно́жко говорю́ по-англи́йски.
Журнали́ст	Ско́лько часо́в в день вы рабо́таете?
Официа́нт	Часо́в де́вять. Начина́ю в два часа́ дня, рабо́таю иногда́ до оди́ннадцати, а иногда́ и до полу́ночи.
Журнали́ст	Вы далеко́ живёте от рестора́на?
Официа́нт	Не о́чень далеко́.
Журнали́ст	Как вы е́здите на рабо́ту?
Официа́нт	На трамва́е.
Журнали́ст	Что вы де́лаете по́сле рабо́ты?
Официа́нт	Ложу́сь спать! … Ведь рабо́та конча́ется о́чень по́здно!

2 Choose the correct answers.

a Вади́му
  1 26 лет
  2 35 лет
  3 28 лет
  4 38 лет

b Рабо́та Вади́ма
  1 всегда́ интере́сная
  2 всегда́ ску́чная
  3 ча́сто интере́сная
  4 иногда́ интере́сная

c Вади́м лю́бит, когда́ в рестора́не
  1 нет тури́стов
  2 англи́йские тури́сты
  3 италья́нские тури́сты
  4 журнали́сты

d По́сле рабо́ты Вади́м
  1 игра́ет в ша́хматы
  2 пла́вает в бассе́йне
  3 гуля́ет в па́рке
  4 ложи́тся спать

Reading and writing

везде́	*everywhere*
в на́ши дни	*nowadays*
да́же	*even*
дома́шняя рабо́та	*housework*
досу́г	*leisure*
заня́тие	*activity, occupation*
кроссво́рд	*crossword*
ма́ло (gen.)	*little*
ме́жду (instr.)	*between*
мир	*world*
мно́жество	*multitude*
обы́чный	*usual*
проходи́ть	*to pass*
разде́л	*section*
ра́зный	*different, various*
рассчи́танный на	*intended for*
США	*USA*
телепереда́ча	*television programme*
уходи́ть	(here) *to be spent*

 Read the text, then answer the questions that follow in English.

Как прохо́дит ваш обы́чный день? Ско́лько часо́в у вас ухо́дит на а) рабо́ту? б) дома́шнюю рабо́ту? в) заня́тия с детьми́ г) досу́г? (то есть ра́дио и телепереда́чи, кино́, теа́тр, чте́ние, спорт, тури́зм …) К сожале́нию, о́чень ма́ло вре́мени ухо́дит на досу́г! Но когда́ вре́мя есть, ру́сские о́чень лю́бят чита́ть – у них мно́жество ра́зных газе́т и журна́лов. Интере́сно, что о́чень ча́сто в газе́тах и журна́лах есть таки́е разде́лы как, наприме́р, «кроссво́рды, ю́мор, ша́хматы» – то есть разде́лы, рассчи́танные на «досу́г». Ру́сские, коне́чно, о́чень лю́бят ша́хматы … они́ игра́ют в ша́хматы везде́– и до́ма, и в па́рке, да́же в шко́ле … в на́ши дни ша́хматы преподаю́тся в шко́лах Росси́и, Герма́нии, Кана́ды, Ме́ксики, Фра́нции и США. Ру́сские шахмати́сты всеми́рно изве́стны, наприме́р, все зна́ют и́мя и фами́лию Га́рри Каспа́рова, экс-чемпио́на ми́ра.

a What sort of leisure activities are mentioned?
b What choice of newspapers and magazines do Russians have?
c How do newspapers and magazines cater for leisure?
d Where do Russians play chess?
e In which countries is chess taught in schools?

Speaking

1 **10.04 You are explaining your daily routine to a friend. Play your part, then listen to the complete conversation on the audio.**

Друг	Во ско́лько вы встаёте?
Вы	**a** *Say you get up at 7 a.m.*
Друг	Как вы е́здите на рабо́ту?
Вы	**b** *Say 'by tram'.*
Друг	Во ско́лько вы начина́ете рабо́тать?
Вы	**c** *Say you start work at 9 a.m.*
Друг	Ско́лько часо́в вы рабо́таете ка́ждый день?
Вы	**d** *Say 'about nine hours'.*

2 **10.05 Can you remember how to say the following in Russian? Listen to the audio and practise saying each phrase.**

a I get up at eight o'clock.
b I usually have lunch at one.
c I always travel by metro.
d How old is he?
e What time do you start work?

? Test yourself

1 How can you give an approximate time?

2 When talking about age, how do you decide whether to use год, года or лет?

3 What does the following phrase mean and, in particular, what is the meaning of в in this context: он смотрит телевизор три часа в день

4 What case is this person's name in and why: Виктора нет дома

5 How do you ask someone's age in Russian?

6 What is the difference in meaning between в пятницу and по пятницам?

7 Why would you say новая книга but я хочу новую книгу?

8 If you follow the verbs *to begin/start* and *to finish/end* with a second verb, what form will this verb be in?

9 Why do you need to be careful with the *I* form of the verb вставать *to get up*?

10 For the irregular verbs писать and мочь, how would you say *I write* and *I am able*?

SELF CHECK

	I CAN...
○	... talk about daily and weekly routine.
○	... ask for and give information about age.
○	... talk about days of the week.
○	... express approximation with regard to time.

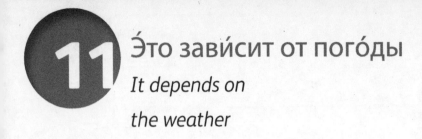

11 Это зави́сит от пого́ды

It depends on

the weather

In this unit you will learn how to:

▶ *talk about future actions and intentions.*
▶ *give and seek information about the weather.*

CEFR: (A2) *Can make arrangements to meet, decide where to go and what to do; can agree and disagree; can make and respond to suggestions.*

🔲 Пого́да *Weather*

In an enormous country like the Russian Federation, it is no surprise that there is considerable variation in the climate. Moscow has a humid continental climate; winter temperatures rarely drop below –15°C and summer temperatures sometimes reach 30°. In Yakutia (in the far east of Siberia) winter temperatures dip to as low as –65°, and it has relatively short and hot summers (with July temperatures in excess of 30°). This temperature range contrasts with the mountainous southern republic of Altai, which has a temperate continental climate with winter temperatures dropping to –30° and summer highs of 19°.

Due to the huge range of possible temperatures at various times of the year, Russians have to have an equally varied range of clothing and are very aware of dressing appropriately for the season.

Based on the information given and the following sentences, work out the meaning of these four Russian words:

жа́рко   **хо́лодно**   **тепло́**   **прохла́дно**

В Москве́ в а́вгусте – жа́рко: +30°C

В Яку́тии в Сиби́ри в декабре́ – холодно́: –65°C

В Со́чи в апре́ле – тепло́: +20°C

В Смоле́нске в октябре́ – прохла́дно: то́лько +8°C

Vocabulary builder

11.01 Complete the missing English expressions. Then listen to the audio and repeat the Russian until you can say all the words with confidence.

НА́ДО ЗНАТЬ! *ESSENTIALS*

свобо́дный (свобо́ден, свобо́дна, свобо́дно)	*free*
я пойду́ по магази́нам	*I'll do the shopping (go to the shops)*
выходно́й день	_____ *off*
дава́й пое́дем	*let's go*
за́ город	*into the country*
го́стья	*(_____) guest*
подру́га	*(_____) friend*
тем лу́чше	*so much the better*
собира́ть	*to gather, collect*
по ра́дио	*on the _____*
дава́й послу́шаем	*let's listen*
тогда́	*then, in that case*
я позвоню́ тебе́	*I'll ring you, I'll telephone _____*
дере́вня	*village, countryside*
ма́сса	*mass*
е́сли и пое́дем	*if we do go*
где встре́тимся?	*_____ shall we meet each other?*
посереди́не платфо́рмы	*in the middle of the _____*
договори́лись	*agreed*
объясню́	*I will explain*
за́втра	*tomorrow*
план	*plan*

ПОГО́ДА *WEATHER ESSENTIALS*

кака́я сего́дня пого́да?	*what is the _____ like today?*
кака́я за́втра бу́дет пого́да?	*what will the _____ be like tomorrow?*
хо́лодно	*(it is) _____*
дождь (m.) идёт	*it's raining*
в таку́ю пого́ду	*in such _____*

прогно́з пого́ды	weather _____
тепло́	(it is) _____
жарко́	(it is) _____
прохла́дно	(it is) _____

 Do the Russian words for *warm* **and** *cold* **remind you of English at all?**

Dialogue

 11.02 *Sasha is trying to persuade Ira to come mushroom picking in the country with him on his day off.*

1   Why is Ira not keen to go at first, and how does Sasha persuade her to go?

Cа́ша	И́ра, каки́е у тебя́ пла́ны на за́втра?
И́ра	На за́втра?
Cа́ша	Да, что ты бу́дешь де́лать за́втра?
И́ра	За́втра я бу́ду свобо́дна, я пойду́ по магази́нам и …
Cа́ша	Хорошо́! За́втра у меня́ выходно́й день. Дава́й пое́дем за́город!
И́ра	Слу́шай, Cа́ша, и у меня́ бу́дет го́стья, англи́йская подру́га, А́нна.
Cа́ша	Тем лу́чше! В лесу́ бу́дет о́чень прия́тно … зна́ешь, там бу́дут грибы́ …
И́ра	*(Uncertainly.)* … Да … но слу́шай, Cа́ша … мне ка́жется, что э́то зави́сит от пого́ды. Кака́я сего́дня пого́да? – хо́лодно, идёт до́ждь. Собира́ть грибы́ в таку́ю пого́ду я не о́чень хочу́ …
Cа́ша	*(Thoughtfully.)* … Да, сего́дня пого́да плоха́я. А когда́ прогно́з пого́ды по ра́дио? … Сейча́с? … Нет? … Ну, дава́й послу́шаем прогно́з пого́ды сего́дня ве́чером – е́сли бу́дет хоро́ший прогно́з, тогда́ пое́дем за́город!
И́ра	Ла́дно, е́сли бу́дет тепло́ и дождя́ не бу́дет, пое́дем.
Cа́ша	Хорошо́. Я позвоню́ тебе́ сего́дня ве́чером часо́в в во́семь. Е́сли бу́дет хоро́шая пого́да, пое́дем на авто́бусе в дере́вню.
И́ра	В каку́ю дере́вню? В Тарака́новку, да?
Cа́ша	Да. Недалеко́ отту́да большо́й, краси́вый лес. Там всегда́ ма́сса грибо́в.

И́ра	Ну, е́сли и пое́дем, где встре́тимся?
Cа́ша	По-мо́ему, А́нна не зна́ет, где остано́вка авто́буса … но она́ зна́ет, где ста́нция метро́ «Беля́ево», да?
И́ра	Ду́маю, да.
Cа́ша	Хорошо́, встре́тимся в метро́, посереди́не платфо́рмы, в семь часо́в.
И́ра	Договори́лись. Ты позвони́шь мне сего́дня ве́чером, пото́м я позвоню́ А́нне и всё объясню́ ей.
Cа́ша	Ну, всё! До ско́рого!

> **LANGUAGE TIP**
>
> Sasha uses the phrase **пла́ны на за́втра** *plans for tomorrow*. We first met **на** + accusative, meaning *intended for / planned for* in Unit 5, and it is very useful in time phrases: e.g. **пла́ны на суббо́ту** *plans for Saturday*.

2 True or false?

a Ira plans to go shopping tomorrow.
b The weather is good today.
c Sasha wants to go mushroom picking today.
d They plan to leave the city at seven o'clock.

3 Answer the following questions.

a Почему́ Cа́ша ду́мает, что в лесу́ бу́дет прия́тно?
b Как они́ пое́дут за́город?
c Где они́ встре́тятся?
d Во ско́лько они встре́тятся?

Language discovery

TALKING ABOUT THE WEATHER

Answers to the question **Кака́я сего́дня пого́да?** fall into four different categories:

▶ **идёт дождь**	*it's raining*
▶ **идёт снег**	*it's snowing*
▶ **идёт град**	*it's hailing*

1 Which word is used in all of the above phrases and what does it usually mean?

b | светит со́лнце | *it's sunny* (lit. *the sun is _____*)
| ду́ет ве́тер | *it's windy* (lit. *the wind is _____*)

2   What exactly do the verbs mean in the above phrases?

c | хо́лодно | *(it is) cold* | прохла́дно | *(it is) chilly*
| па́смурно | *(it is) overcast* | тепло́ | *(it is) warm*
| ду́шно | *(it is) close/muggy* | жа́рко | *(it is) hot*

3   What kind of words are these? Why will they be spelled slightly differently if you mention the word for weather as well, e.g.

Сего́дня жа́рко | *It's hot today*

Сего́дня пого́да жа́ркая | *The weather's hot today*

d   Сего́дня тума́н | *It's foggy today*

Сего́дня мете́ль | *There is a blizzard today*

4   Why is there no verb in Russian in the phrases above?

THE FUTURE TENSE

There are two kinds of future tense in Russian but one is used much more often than the other. More often than not, to express the future tense in Russian you will use a construction that is very similar to the English *I will* (*watch*).

The verb used for *I will* is **быть**, with the *I* form being **я бу́ду**.

5 Can you remember all the forms of the verb быть?

я бýду I will; **ты бýдешь** you will; **он/онá буд____** he/she will; **мы буд____** we will; **вы буд____** you will; **они будýт** they will

So, *I will watch* would be **я бýду** followed by the infinitive of the verb *to watch* (**смотреть**): **я бýду смотрéть**. The good news is that there are no exceptions to this rule.

> **LANGUAGE TIP**
>
> Many of the expressions used to describe weather do not have a verb in the present tense, but in the future, they use **будет**.
>
> | | | | |
> |---|---|---|---|
> | **хóлодно** | *it is cold* | **бýдет хóлодно** | *it will be cold* |
> | **теплó** | *it is warm* | **бýдет теплó** | *it will be warm* |
> | **тýман** | *it is foggy* | **бýдет туман** | *it will be foggy* |

ASPECTS OF VERBS

The tense system for verbs in Russian is very simple: there is a present tense, a past tense and a future tense. In English, there are over 20 different tenses! The way that you can express all these different English tenses in Russian is with the help of aspects of verbs. In Russian, verbs usually have two aspects, called the imperfective and the perfective. The convention is to list the imperfective first:

	Imperfective	Perfective
to read	**читáть**	**прочитáть**
to ring	**звонúть**	**позвонúть**
to discuss	**обсуждáть**	**обсудúть**
to agree	**договáрываться**	**договорúться**

> **LANGUAGE TIP**
>
> As you will notice, there is no single way of forming a perfective from an imperfective: sometimes you add a prefix, such as **по-**, sometimes you change the ending slightly (as for *to discuss*), sometimes you shorten the verb (as for *to agree*). Using these different methods will not be a problem as, from now on, we will learn new verbs in pairs.

The present tense always uses the imperfective:

Imperfective: **слу́шать** *to listen to*

Present tense: **я слу́шаю**, **ты слу́шаешь**, etc.

The kind of future tense that we have already met (**я бу́ду** + infinitive) always uses the imperfective. This future tense always describes actions in the future that are incomplete, repeated or continuing, e.g.:

▶ incomplete – *Tomorrow, I will be reading the novel* War and Peace
▶ repeated – *I will ring you every day*
▶ continuing – *Tomorrow, we will be discussing the project*

All of the these sentences use the imperfective future:

▶ **За́втра я бу́ду чита́ть рома́н 'Война́ и мир'**
▶ **Я бу́ду звони́ть тебе́/вам ка́ждый день**
▶ **За́втра мы бу́дем обсужда́ть прое́кт**

There is a second kind of future tense: used for actions that will be single and completed – e.g. *I will ring at nine o'clock*. This kind of future tense always uses the perfective aspect with what appear to be present tense endings. So, if *to ring* is **звони́ть/позвони́ть**, then *I will ring at nine o'clock* is **я позвоню́ в 9 часо́в**.

Note that **дава́й(те)** *let's* is always followed by the perfective future:

Дава́йте пое́дем за́город   *Let's go into the country*

Remember that the future tense of **быть** is needed if you want to use **мо́жно**, **на́до**, **нельзя́** or **пора́** in a future sense, e.g.:

**За́втра мне на́до бу́дет   *Tomorrow I will have to work*
рабо́тать**

Note too that, just as **нет** + genitive is used to express *do not have any*, **не бу́дет** is used to express *will not have any*:

У меня́ не бу́дет вре́мени   *I won't have any time*

Usually it is quite clear when you need to use the future tense – *will* is the clearest indicator and there are often other clues as well (*tomorrow*, *next week*, etc.). However, English sometimes implies the future tense, but doesn't use it, e.g. *When you are in Moscow, I will ring you every day*. In Russian the future tense must be used whenever it is implied:

Когда́ ты бу́дешь в Москве́, я бу́ду звони́ть тебе́ ка́ждый день

When you are (i.e. *will be*) *in Moscow, I will ring you every day*

ЗВОНИ́ТЬ/ПОЗВОНИ́ТЬ *TO TELEPHONE*

This verb means *to ring, to telephone*. If you are ringing someone, you have to use the dative case for the person you are ringing:

Я позвоню́ тебе́ сего́дня ве́чером	*I'll ring you this evening*
И́ра позвони́т А́нне за́втра	*Ira will ring Anna tomorrow*

If you're ringing a place, use **в** + accusative:

Он позвони́т в больни́цу	*He'll ring the hospital*

ЗА́ГОРОД *INTO THE COUNTRY*

This literally means *beyond the town* – here the preposition **за** (*beyond*, *behind*), which is normally used with the instrumental case, is used with the accusative case to express motion; *in the country* is **за́городом** (i.e. with the instrumental case).

EMPHATIC И

The principal meaning of **и** is *and*, but it is also used to give extra emphasis; on such occasions it can be translated by English emphatic terms, such as *do*, *indeed*, *even*, e.g. **е́сли и пое́дем** *if we do go*.

Practice

1 **Choose the correct form of the future tense. Remember that verbs are always listed in the order imperfective/perfective.**

   a Когда́ она́ бу́дет в Аме́рике, она́ ча́сто (бу́дет игра́ть/сыгра́ет) в те́ннис.

   b За́втра я (бу́ду писа́ть/напишу́) письмо́ Ви́ктору.

   c Я всегда́ (бу́ду де́лать/сде́лаю) поку́пки в универса́ме.

   d Я (бу́ду звони́ть/позвоню́) вам за́втра в пять часо́в.

   e Когда́ они́ бу́дут в Москве́, они́ ча́сто (бу́дут обе́дать/пообе́дают) в рестора́не «Кали́нка».

2 Look at the pictures and answer the questions.

a Какáя сегóдня погóда?

b Какáя сегóдня погóда?

c Какáя сегóдня погóда?

d Какáя сегóдня погóда?

3 Look at the list and make up sentences about where each person lives and what the weather is like there, as in the example.

	Кто?	Где?	Далеко от Москвы?	Какая сегодня погода?
a	Ольга	Обнинск	не очень	солнце, не холодно
b	Серёжа	Архангельск	очень	снег, очень холодно
c	Елена	Киев	далеко	туман, тепло
d	Юрий	Ташкент	очень далеко	солнце, душно
e	Галя	Екатеринбург	далеко	ветер, пасмурно

a <u>Ольга живёт в Обнинске, недалеко от Москвы. Сегодня светит солнце, не холодно.</u>

4 Look at the following extract about television programmes and answer the questions that follow.

СПРАВКИ: ТВ

Понедельник – 28 мая

18.30 Документальный фильм «Суздаль»

20.15 Испанский язык

21.00 Новости

23.00 Конкурсы

Среда – 30 мая

18.00 «Музыкальный киоск»

20.00 Мультфильм (cartoon)

21.00 Новости

22.05 «Что, где, когда?»

Вторник – 29 мая

18.30 Теннис

19.30 Итальянский язык

20.00 «Здравствуй, музыка!»

21.00 Новости

Четверг – 31 мая

18.45 Фильм – для детей

19.15 Хоккей

21.00 Новости

22.00 «Музыкальный телефон»

---

a Which programme is on at nine o'clock every evening?

b What is on at 18:30 on a Monday?

c When are there sports programmes?

d What are the names of the various music programmes?

e Which programmes would interest language students?

Listen and understand

как же?	*how on earth?*
е́здить/е́хать/пое́хать в го́сти (**к** + dative)	*to visit* (lit. *to go as a guest*)
до́брый	*good, kind*

11.03 *Misha and Lena are trying to agree about how to spend the weekend.*

1 Who's keen to get out of the city – Misha or Lena?

Ми́ша	Что мы бу́дем де́лать в суббо́ту?
Ле́на	Как, что? Мы пое́дем в го́род, ведь нам на́до сде́лать поку́пки.
Ми́ша	Ой, как ску́чно! Ка́жется, в суббо́ту бу́дет хоро́шая пого́да. Ты не хо́чешь пое́хать за́город?
Ле́на	А как же мы мо́жем? В суббо́ту ве́чером мы пое́дем в го́сти к Мари́не.
Ми́ша	Пра́вда? *(Sighs.)* Ой, как ску́чно!
Ле́на	Ми́ша, что ты! Мари́на о́чень до́брый, интере́сный челове́к.
Ми́ша	Тогда́, что мы бу́дем де́лать в воскресе́нье?
Ле́на	Ве́чером мы пое́дем в теа́тр: у нас биле́ты на пье́су.
Ми́ша	А днём что бу́дем де́лать?
Ле́на	Что ты хо́чешь де́лать?
Ми́ша	Я хочу́ пое́хать за́город.
Ле́на	Вре́мени не бу́дет, ведь ве́чером мы пойдём в теа́тр.
Ми́ша	Зна́ю, зна́ю. Тогда́ дава́й погуля́ем в па́рке …
Ле́на	Хорошо́, е́сли бу́дет хоро́шая пого́да.
Ми́ша	… пото́м пообе́даем в рестора́не.
Ле́на	Хорошо́ … а по́сле обе́да ты напи́шешь письмо́ ма́ме, да?
Ми́ша	*(Sighs.)* Напишу́, напишу́ …

2 Choose the correct answers.

a В суббо́ту Ле́на хо́чет
1 сиде́ть до́ма
2 пое́хать за́город
3 сде́лать поку́пки
4 погуля́ть в па́рке

b Ми́ша ду́мает, что у Мари́ны
1 не бу́дет ску́чно
2 бу́дет ску́чно
3 бу́дет интере́сно
4 бу́дет прия́тно

c У них биле́ты
1 на о́перу
2 на фи́льм
3 на бале́т
4 на пье́су

d Когда́ Ми́ша напи́шет письмо́ ма́ме?
1 в суббо́ту по́сле обе́да
2 в воскресе́нье у́тром
3 в воскресе́нье по́сле обе́да
4 в воскресе́нье ве́чером

Reading and writing

в дальне́йшем	*later on, subsequently*
вода́	*water*
12 гра́дусов тепла́	*12 degrees above zero*
гроза́	*(thunder)storm*
кратковре́менные дожди́	*showers*
места́ми	*in places*
моро́з	*frost*
нача́ло	*beginning*
ожида́ться	*to be expected*
опа́сность (f.)	*danger*
оса́дки	*precipitation*
отде́льный	*separate*
си́льный	*strong*
Сре́дняя А́зия	*Central Asia*
сухо́й	*dry*
тепло́	*warmth*
Ура́л	*Urals*

11.04 Read and listen to the text, then answer the questions that follow in English.

А

В Крыму́ в нача́ле неде́ли без оса́дков, но́чью 12–17 гра́дусов тепла́, днём 22–27. В дальне́йшем кратковре́менные дожди́, гро́зы, но́чью 9–14, днём 18–24 гра́дуса. Температу́ра воды́ у берего́в Кры́ма 16–18 гра́дусов.

В Санкт-Петербу́рге в отде́льные дни кратковре́менные дожди́, но́чью 4–9, днём 13–18 гра́дусов.

В Москве́ и Подмоско́вье кратковре́менные дожди́, но́чью 7–12, днём 14–19, в отде́льные дни до 22 гра́дусов.

В Сре́дней А́зии бу́дет суха́я и жа́ркая пого́да, без оса́дков – там ожида́ется высо́кая пожа́рная опа́сность в леса́х.

Б

В Арха́нгельске в нача́ле неде́ли температу́ра днём бу́дет 2–6 гра́дусов моро́за.

На восто́ке Украи́ны 2–7, места́ми 9 гра́дусов моро́за.

Снег и мете́ли на се́вере Ура́ла. Днём от 1–6 до 7–12 гра́дусов моро́за.

В Санкт-Петербу́рге в нача́ле неде́ли оса́дки; днём 1–5 гра́дусов моро́за, си́льный ве́тер.

В Москве и Подмоско́вье днём 3–7 гра́дусов моро́за.

a How much rain will there be in the Crimea this week?
b What news is there for swimmers?
c Will it be colder in Moscow or St Petersburg during the night according to forecast А?
d Which is the only place in forecast А to be unaffected by rain?
e Where is there a risk of fire?
f Where will there be snow according to forecast Б?
g Which place will be affected by strong wind according to forecast Б?

Speaking

1   11.05 You're not keen on taking up Petya's invitations! Play your part, then listen to the complete conversation on the audio.

Петя	У меня два билета на оперу. Вы хотите пойти со мной?
Вы	**a** *Thank him, but say you can't because you've got to work (i.e. it will be necessary for you to work) this evening.*
Петя	Ой, как жаль. Ничего. У меня тоже два билета в кино на завтра. Хотите пойти?
Вы	**b** *Say 'sorry', you're going (i.e. will go) to Olga's tomorrow.*
Петя	Ничего. В четверг будет хоккейный матч – у меня уже есть два билета. Хотите пойти со мной?
Вы	**c** *Thank him, but say it's very cold today. If it will be cold on Thursday you will be watching TV at home.*
Петя	Тогда давайте послушаем прогноз погоды в среду.
Вы	**d** *Say OK, you'll ring him on Wednesday at about eight o'clock.*
Петя	А какие у вас планы на субботу?
Вы	**e** *Say you don't know, it depends on the weather.*

2   11.06 Can you remember how to say the following in Russian? Listen to the audio and practise saying each phrase.

    a What are your plans for tomorrow?
    b What's the weather like today?
    c Tomorrow it will be hot.
    d I will ring you this evening / I will telephone you this evening.
    e Where shall we meet?

1 If you were told that the temperature tomorrow was expected to reach три́дцать гра́дусов моро́за, would you opt for your fur hat or your sun hat?

2 What question would you ask to find out what the weather is like today?

3 What question would you ask to find out your friend's plans for Tuesday?

4 If э́то зави́сит от пого́ды means *it depends on the weather,* how would you say *it depends on Anna*?

5 What sort of action requires the imperfective future?

6 What sort of action requires the perfective future?

7 What is the difference in meaning between Я бу́ду чита́ть рома́н «Война́ и мир» за́втра and Я прочита́ю роман «Война́ и мир» за́втра?

8 What would you need to change and add to make the following phrase refer to tomorrow, instead of today? Сего́дня мо́жно смо́треть телеви́зор.

9 If you wanted to say *I will ring you tomorrow*, which case would you need for the word *you*?

10 What would you need to change and add to make the following weather phrase refer to tomorrow, instead of today? Сего́дня хо́лодно и я сижу́ до́ма.

SELF CHECK

	I CAN...
●	. . . talk about future actions and intentions.
●	. . . give and seek information about the weather.

Ира дóма?

Is Ira at home?

In this unit you will learn how to:

▶ *hold a conversation on the telephone (identify yourself, ask for the person you want to speak to and deal with wrong numbers).*

▶ *talk about past events and actions.*

CEFR: (A2) *Can describe plans, arrangements, habits and routines, past activities and personal experiences.*

Телефóн *Telephone*

When answering the telephone, it is usual to say **Аллó! Слýшаю вас** (or just **слýшаю**) or **Кто э́то говори́т?** If you are ringing a person's home telephone number you can ask for the person you want to speak to by asking if they are at home (**Ири́на дóма?**); in more formal situations you might say **Мóжно Ири́ну Николáевну к телефóну?** (lit. *Is it possible (to call) Irina Nikolaevna to the telephone?*) or **Позови́те Ири́ну Николáевну к телефóну, пожáлуйста** (lit. *Call Irina Nikolaevna to the telephone please*). To identify yourself say **С вáми говори́т …** or just **Говори́т …**; if someone asks for you and you want to say speaking, simply say **Э́то я** or **Я у телефóна**. When you are dealing with wrong numbers, use **Э́то не тот** (lit. *It is not that one/that number*), **Вы не тудá попáли** (lit. *You have got not to there*) or **Вы непрáвильно набрáли нóмер** (lit. *You have dialled wrongly*). Mobile phones are as much a part of life in modern Russia as they are anywhere in the world. The Russian for *mobile phone* is either **моби́льный телефóн** or **сóтовый телефóн**, but there are also a range of colloquial terms as well, such as **моби́льник** or **трýбка**.

Russian telephone numbers are often seven digits long and will usually be split up and spoken as follows:

336-32-25 три́ста три́дцать шесть – три́дцать два – двáдцать пять

(i.e. *three hundred and thirty six, thirty-two, twenty-five*)

However, if you find it easier to say each digit separately, you would be understood.

How would you say the following phone numbers if giving them to a Russian?

a 555-12-24   **b** 389-66-78   **c** 812-33-45
d 495-06-62   **e** 499-90-03   **f** 963-22-56

Vocabulary builder

12.01 Complete the missing English expressions. Then listen to the audio and repeat the Russian until you can say all the words with confidence.

НА́ДО ЗНАТЬ! *ESSENTIALS*

прости́те	*sorry, forgive me*
Де́тский мир	*Children's World* (name of a store)
опя́ть	*again*
благодари́ть/поблагодари́ть	*to thank (for)* (за + accusative)
всё бы́ло	*everything was*
пое́здка мне о́чень понра́вилась	*_____ really enjoyed the trip*
обяза́тельно скажу́	*I'll tell him without fail / I'll be sure to tell him*
послеза́втра	*the day after _____*
уви́димся	*_____ will see one another*
всего́ до́брого	*all the best*
всё бы́ло о́чень интере́сно	*It _____ all very interesting*
нам то́же о́чень понра́вилось	*_____ also really enjoyed it*

ПО ТЕЛЕФО́НУ *TELEPHONE ESSENTIALS*

како́й но́мер вы набра́ли?	*what _____ did you dial?*
э́то не тот	*it's _____ the right one*
я не туда́ попа́л(а)	*_____ got the wrong number*
отку́да ты звони́шь?	*where are _____ ringing from?*
кто э́то говори́т?	*who is speaking?*

Dialogue

 12.02 *Anna decides to ring Ira to thank her for the recent trip with Sasha, but she has some trouble getting through …*

1   Anna and Ira agree to meet. Where, at what time and why?

Áнна	Алло́! Йра, э́то ты?
Го́лос 1	А? … Како́й но́мер вы набра́ли?
Áнна	428-39-56.
Го́лос 1	Нет, э́то не тот.
Áнна	Прости́те. *(Dials again.)* … Алло́!
Го́лос 2	Магази́н «Де́тский мир». Слу́шаю вас.
Áнна	Извини́те. Опя́ть я не туда́ попа́ла! *(Dials again.)* … Алло́! Йра до́ма?
Йра	Кто э́то говори́т?
Áнна	Говори́т Áнна … Áнна Принс.
Йра	Áнна, приве́т! Отку́да ты звони́шь?
Áнна	Я в гости́нице. Йра, я о́чень хочу́ тебя́ поблагодари́ть за на́шу пое́здку за́город!
Йра	Интере́сно бы́ло, да?
Áнна	Да, всё бы́ло о́чень интере́сно! Спаси́бо большо́е!
Йра	Ну, что ты, Áнна. Нам то́же бы́ло о́чень прия́тно.
Áнна	Скажи́ Са́ше, пожа́луйста, что пое́здка мне о́чень понра́вилась.
Йра	Обяза́тельно скажу́. Он бу́дет о́чень рад … Áнна, у меня́ два биле́та в Большо́й теа́тр на послеза́втра. Ты хо́чешь пойти́ со мной на о́перу?
Áнна	Коне́чно, о́чень хочу́!
Йра	Хорошо́, уви́димся послеза́втра на о́пере в Большо́м теа́тре, да?
Áнна	Как хорошо́!
Йра	Встре́тимся у вхо́да в теа́тр, полседьмо́го. Поня́тно?
Áнна	Да, всё поня́тно. Ещё раз спаси́бо! До ско́рого.
Йра	Всего́ до́брого, Áнна. До свида́ния.

2 True or false?

a Anna dials the wrong number twice.

b Anna rings from the hotel.

c Anna enjoyed the trip to the shopping centre.

d Ira will buy two tickets.

3 Answer the following questions.

a Áнна хóчет позвони́ть в магази́н «Дéтский мир»?

b Как Áнне понрáвилась поéздка зáгород?

c Когдá Йра и Áнна опя́ть уви́дятся?

d Где они́ встрéтятся?

Language discovery

БЛАГОДАРИ́ТЬ/ПОБЛАГОДАРИ́ТЬ *TO THANK*

Note that this verb is followed by **за** + accusative: **благодарю́ тебя́ за экску́рсию.** Note also **Спаси́бо за** + accusative (**Спаси́бо за подáрок** *thank you for the present*) and **плати́ть/заплати́ть за** + accusative *to pay for.*

YOUR TURN (Давáйте)

1 What do the following phrases mean?

Благодари́м вас за письмó

Спаси́бо за нóвую кни́гу!

Надó плати́ть за нáши театрáльные биле́ты

PAST TENSE

In English we have various forms of the past tense:

I was reading, I used to read, I have read, I read, I had read

In Russian there is only one form of the past tense, but its meaning is slightly different if you use the imperfective aspect or the perfective aspect.

2 Before reading the explanation, can you work out what the difference in meaning will be?

The imperfective past tense is used for actions which are repeated, continuing or incomplete:

I used to read the newspaper every day.

I was reading the newspaper when the telephone rang.

I was reading/read the newspaper yesterday (but I didn't finish it).

I read for two hours yesterday.

Note that in a sentence such as *I read for two hours yesterday*, there is a sense of continuation – we are not informed whether the reading was finished or not, but that it went on for two hours – so we need to use the imperfective past tense.

The perfective past tense is used for single, completed actions:

I read the newspaper all the way through yesterday morning.

I had already read the newspaper when the telephone rang.

Just as for the future tense, you have a choice in Russian for the past tense: use the imperfective if you are talking about the process of an action (habitual, repeated, continuing, general, unspecific), and the perfective for the result of an action (single, specific, completed).

Formation of the past tense is the same for both the imperfective and the perfective. Take the infinitive, remove **-ть** and add the following:

Subject of verb	Add	Example	Meaning
Masc. sing. (verb: **читáть/ прочитáть**)	-л	**Вúктор читáл ромáн**	*Viktor was reading a novel*
Fem. sing. (verb: **писáть/ написáть**)	-ла	**Óля написáла письмó**	*Olya has written the letter*
Neut. sing. (verb: **светúть/** (no perf.))	-ло	**Сóлнце светúло**	*The sun was shining*
Pl. (verb: **слýшать/ послýшать**)	-ли	**Мы слýшали мýзыку**	*We were listening to music*

In other words, past tense endings are rather like adjective endings – they have to agree with the number (singular or plural?) and gender (masculine, feminine, neuter?) of the subject. (Note that when you are forming the past tense to agree with **вы**, the ending will always be **-ли**, whether **вы** is referring to a group of people or whether it is being used as the polite form to one person only.) Most irregular verbs form their past tenses in this way too, e.g.: **жить** (**жил, жилá**, etc.), **хотéть** (**хотéл, хотéла**, etc.). The only exceptions among the verbs we have met so far are:

есть	*to eat*	**ел, éла, éло, éли**
идтú	*to go on foot, to walk*	**шёл, шла, шло, шли**
мочь	*to be able*	**мог, моглá, моглó, моглú**

Verbs of motion have three possible past tenses (since they have three infinitives – two imperfectives and one perfective). The past tense of the first imperfective can imply a habit or a return journey. The past tense of the second imperfective indicates an action which was in progress. The past tense of the perfective implies one single action in the past; this form often also means *to set off*:

Imperfective	Imperfective	Perfective
ходи́ть	**идти́**	**пойти́**
он ходи́л *he used to go* (habit)	**он шёл** *he was going* (action in progress)	**он пошёл** *he has gone, he has set off*
он ходи́л *he has been* (return journey)		

Note that the past tense of **быть** *to be* is required if you want to give **мо́жно, на́до, нельзя́, пора́**, a past meaning: **Вчера́ мне на́до бы́ло рабо́тать** *Yesterday I had to work*. Similarly the past tense of **быть** is required if you need to use phrases like **У меня́ нет де́нег** *I have no money* in the past tense: **У меня́ не бы́ло де́нег** *I had no money*.

PREPOSITIONAL CASE

We have already met some of the uses of the prepositional case and learned how to form the prepositional singular of nouns; in **в Большо́м теа́тре** *at the Bolshoi Theatre* the prepositional singular of the adjective **большо́й** is used. To form the prepositional of masculine and neuter singular adjectives add **-ом** (unless the rule about the unstressed **о** applies, in which case add **-ем**). Feminine singular adjectives add **-ой** (unless the rule about the unstressed **о** applies, in which case add **-ей**).

YOUR TURN (Дава́йте)

3 Can you complete the prepositional case noun endings?

masc.   **в но́вом дом_____**   *in the new house*

fem.   **в новой кни́г_____**   *in a new book*

neuter   **в новом зда́ни_____**   *in the new building*

We have now covered all six singular case endings for adjectives. Have you noticed that there aren't many different feminine ones to learn? Just -ая for nominative and -ую for accusative; -ой or -ей for all the rest (genitive, dative, instrumental and prepositional).

Practice

1 Match the questions with the answers.

a Кому́ она́ звони́т?

b Когда́ он обы́чно де́лает поку́пки?

c Когда́ он позвони́л тебе́?

d Где он обы́чно покупа́ет проду́кты?

e Вам понра́вилась экску́рсия?

1 По сре́дам.

2 Нет, не о́чень.

3 В универса́ме.

4 И́ре.

5 В сре́ду.

2 Which is the correct alternative (imperfective past or perfective past)?

a Когда́ он жил в Герма́нии, он ча́сто (игра́л/сыгра́л) в футбо́л.

b Вчера́ она́ (писа́ла/написа́ла) письмо́ Ви́ктору.

c Ра́ньше Ни́на всегда́ (де́лала/сде́лала) поку́пки в це́нтре го́рода.

d Вчера́ мы (смотре́ли/посмотре́ли) телеви́зор, когда́ вдруг кто́- то (звони́л/позвони́л) в дверь.

e Снача́ла я (чита́ла/прочита́ла) газе́ту, пото́м я (обе́дала/ пообе́дала).

 3 What sort of career would you be interested in if you applied for a place on the course outlined in this extract from an advertisement?

Факультет административного менеджмента предлагает ...

Курсы МЕНЕДЖЕРОВ – МАРКЕТОЛОГОВ

В программе обучения – информационные ресурсы ИНТЕРНЕТ для маркетинга

---

4 **You made a lot of phone calls yesterday. Describe them using the following information. The first one has been done for you.**

Кому?	О чём?
a Са́ша	его́ но́вая маши́на
b И́ра	пое́здка в Се́ргиев Поса́д
c Макси́м	францу́зский фильм
d А́лла	но́вый уче́бник *(textbook)*
e Воло́дя	плоха́я пого́да

a <u>**Вчера́ я позвони́л(а) Са́ше. Мы говори́ли о его́ но́вой маши́не.**</u>

Listen and understand

она́ сейча́с подойдёт	*she's just coming*
совеща́ние	*meeting*
дире́ктор	*director*
ва́жный	*important*
забыва́ть/забы́ть	*to forget*
по́мнить/вспо́мнить	*to remember*
догово́р	*agreement, contract*
автомоби́льная компа́ния	*car company*

12.03 *Maxim is very absent-minded and has forgotten what is in his diary for the following day. He rings Lena for help.*

1 **Why is Maxim anxious to find out what is happening tomorrow?**

Го́лос	Алло́.
Макси́м	Алло́. Мо́жно Ле́ну к телефо́ну, пожа́луйста?
Го́лос	Мину́точку … она́ сейча́с подойдёт.
Макси́м	Алло́. Ле́на?
Ле́на	Да, э́то я. Кто э́то говори́т?
Макси́м	Э́то Макси́м.
Ле́на	Здра́вствуй, Макси́м. Как дела́?
Макси́м	Ничего́, спаси́бо … Скажи́, Ле́на, ты за́втра бу́дешь на совеща́нии у дире́ктора?
Ле́на	Коне́чно, ведь э́то о́чень ва́жное совеща́ние.
Макси́м	Зна́ю, зна́ю … то́лько я забы́л … во ско́лько э́то бу́дет?

Ле́на	Полоди́ннадцатого утра́.
Макси́м	Ах, да, коне́чно …
Ле́на	Э́то всё? … Я сейча́с о́чень занята́, Макси́м.
Макси́м	Извини́, Ле́на … а я не о́чень хорошо́ по́мню, о чём мы бу́дем говори́ть на совеща́нии.
Ле́на	Что ты, Макси́м! Мы коне́чно бу́дем говори́ть о но́вом догово́ре с францу́зской автомоби́льной компа́нией.
Макси́м	Ах, да, коне́чно … Спаси́бо, Лена … э́то всё! До за́втра.
Ле́на	Всего́ до́брого, Макси́м. До свида́ния.

2 Choose the correct answers.

a Ва́жное совеща́нии будет
1 сего́дня в 10ч30 утра́
2 за́втра в 10ч30 утра́
3 за́втра в 11 часо́в
4 сего́дня у́тром

b Ле́на сейча́с
1 отдыха́ет
2 свобо́дна
3 о́чень занята́
4 не о́чень занята́

c На совеща́нин они́ бу́дут говори́ть о
1 но́вом догово́ре с италья́нской компа́нией
2 ста́ром догово́ре с францу́зской компа́нией
3 но́вом догово́ре с французской компа́нией
4 нева́жном догово́ре с французской компа́нией

Reading and writing

во́зраст	age
жизнь (f.)	life
ли́чный	personal
не́которые молоды́е лю́ди	some young people
обще́ние	communication
опро́с	questionnaire, survey
опро́шенный	person who answers a questionnaire
пока́зывать/показа́ть	to show
по́мнить	to remember
проводи́ть/провести́	to spend (time)
совреме́нный	modern
социа́льные се́ти	social networking sites

1 Read the text, then answer the questions that follow in English.

Что такóе мобúльный телефóн для совремéнного человéка? Результáты опрóса покáзывают, что 46% опрóшенных в вóзрасте от 25 до 34 лет сказáли, что не мóгут жить без мобúльных телефóнов. Молодыé, конéчно, не пóмнят жизнь без мобúльников для организáции лúчной и социáльной жúзни. Нéкоторые молодыé люди сказáли, что онú провóдят в общéнии со своúм мобúльным часá три в день. Для 40% респондéнтов сáмые популярные услуги – мобúльный шóппинг и социáльные сéти.

a What did 46% of people between the ages of 25 and 34 say they could not do?

b What do young people not remember?

c What does the mobile phone help them to organize?

d How much time do young people say their spend on their mobiles per day?

e What are the two most popular mobile services?

| вставáть/встать | to get up |
| готóвить/приготóвить | to prepare, cook |

2 Read what Nina did yesterday, then answer the questions that follow in Russian.

Вчерá я былá óчень занятá. Я встáла в семь часóв и позáвтракала на кýхне. Утром я рабóтала два часá в библиотéке, потóм я пообéдала в буфéте. Пóсле обéда я сдéлала покýпки в универсáме. Вéчером я приготóвила ýжин, позвонúла мáме, потóм смотрéла телевúзор.

a Во скóлько Нúна встáла?

b Где онá позáвтракала?

c Что онá дéлала ýтром?

d Где онá пообéдала?

e Что онá дéлала вéчером?

3 The following information tells you what Vadim did yesterday. Use it to write a paragraph following the model about Nina.

Ýтром	Пóсле обéда	Вéчером
Встать: полшестóго	рабóтать: 3 часá/	игрáть: футбóл
позáвтракать: кухня	завóд	смотрéть: телевúзор
рабóтать: 5 часóв/завóд	читáть: газéта	пообéдать: ресторáн

4 Now answer these questions about yourself.

a Во ско́лько вы вста́ли вчера́?

b Где вы поза́втракали?

c Что вы де́лали у́тром?

d Где вы пообе́дали?

e Что вы де́лали ве́чером?

 ## Speaking

12.04 Can you remember how to say the following in Russian? Listen to the audio and practise saying each phrase.

a Who's speaking?

b Is Viktor at home?

c Everything was very interesting.

d Thanks again!

e All the best.

Test yourself

1 When might you use the phrase Всего́ до́брого and why is it in the genitive case?

2 What do the following mean: до за́втра, до понеде́льника, до свида́ния?

3 Which case do you need after за when you are thanking someone for something? How would you say *Thank you for the delicious supper*?

4 Why is it important when forming the past tense to choose whether to make it from the imperfective or the perfective?

5 What is strange about the past tense of идти́ *to go*?

6 Which past tense ending would you use if you were addressing a colleague using the polite pronoun вы?

7 Now that we have met all the Russian cases, can you give the correct endings for но́вый дом for the nominative, accusative, genitive, dative, instrumental and prepositional singular?

8 Can you give the correct endings for но́вая маши́на for the nominative, accusative, genitive, dative, instrumental and prepositional singular?

9 And can you give the correct endings for но́вое письмо́ for the nominative, accusative, genitive, dative, instrumental and prepositional singular?

10 How would you read aloud the following phone number in Russian? 317-28-45

SELF CHECK

I CAN...

○ ... hold a conversation on the telephone (identify myself, ask for the person I want to speak to and deal with wrong numbers).

○ ... talk about past events and actions.

13 Мне ну́жно к врачу́!

I must go to the doctor's!

In this unit you will learn how to:

▶ *say how you feel.*
▶ *ask others how they feel.*
▶ *seek and give advice.*
▶ *talk about necessity.*

CEFR: (B1) *Can express and respond to feelings such as happiness, sadness and interest; can write accounts describing feelings and reactions in simple connected text.*

🔘 Врач *The doctor*

The Russian healthcare system continues to work extremely well since the fall of the Soviet Union. As a visitor to Russia, if you need to see a doctor, reception in your hotel will be able to help you, probably directing you to an English-speaking doctor. Russians do not pay for healthcare and, provided that you have the usual adequate travel insurance, you should be able to pay for any treatment you need.

Russian citizens would normally ring a *polyclinic* (similar to a health centre) – **поликли́ника** – to arrange for the doctor to make a home visit or they might go to the polyclinic themselves.

The doctor may give a Russian patient a **реце́пт** *prescription*, to be bought at the **апте́ка** *chemist's*, though visitors to Russia can normally buy medicines without a prescription. Note that there are two words for *doctor* – **врач** (to denote the profession) and **до́ктор** (for when you're talking to one). In the event of an emergency, an ambulance can be summoned by dialling 03 (**ноль три**). For some, a stay in **больни́ца** *hospital* may be necessary, where standards of diagnosis, care and hygiene are still the envy of the world.

Match these Russian healthcare terms to their English equivalent:

1 аспири́н **2** медсестра́ **3** шприц **4** медбра́т

5 крем **6** парацетамо́л **7** лека́рство **8** термо́метр

a nurse (f.) **b** syringe **c** aspirin **d** nurse (m.)

e medicine **f** cream **g** thermometer **h** paracetamol

Vocabulary builder

13.01 Complete the missing English expressions. Then listen to the audio and repeat the Russian until you can say all the words with confidence.

НА́ДО ЗНАТЬ! *ESSENTIALS*

что ты сове́туешь (вы сове́туете)?	*what do _____ advise?*
сове́товать (я сове́тую)	*to advise (_____)*
не беспоко́йся (беспоко́йтесь) об э́том!	*don't worry about it*
ты до́лжен/должна́/вы должны́	*you must*
ты о́чень добра́	*you're _____ kind*
не́ за что!	*think nothing of it!*
тебе́ хо́чется пить?	*are _____ thirsty? (lit. do you _____ to drink?)*
я закажу́ (зака́зывать/заказа́ть)	*I order (_____)*
помога́ть/помо́чь	*to help*
что мне де́лать?	*what should _____ do?*
что тебе́ ну́жно?	*what do _____ need?*

ЗДОРО́ВЬЕ *HEALTH ESSENTIALS*

ты не ва́жно вы́глядишь	*_____ don't look too well*
что с тобо́й (с ва́ми)?	*what's wrong with _____ ?*
ты бо́лен/ты больна́/вы больны́?	*_____ ill?*
я заболе́л(а)	*I'm ill (lit. I have fallen ill)*
мне пло́хо	*_____ feel unwell*
у меня́ боли́т го́рло	*I have a _____ throat*
голова́	*head*
грипп	*flu*

мне нужно к врачу?	must _____ go to the _____?
тебе (вам) лучше лежать в постели	you'd better stay in bed
врач скоро придёт	the _____ will soon be here
тебе скоро будет лучше	you'll _____ feel better

> **LANGUAGE TIP**
>
> **Нам сегодня нельзя** *for us today it is not possible.* Remember that you need to use the dative case to explain who can't/must do something: **Тебе надо отдыхать!** *You must rest!*

Dialogue

 13.02 *Ira has called for Anna at her hotel room but finds Anna is not well.*

1 What advice does Ira give Anna?

Ира	Анна, ты сегодня неважно выглядишь. Что с тобой? Ты больна?
Анна	Да, мне кажется, я заболела. Мне плохо. У меня болит горло.
Ира	И голова болит?
Анна	Кажется, да.
Ира	Гм! Может быть у тебя начинается грипп.
Анна	Что мне делать? Что ты советуешь? Мне нужно к врачу?
Ира	Нет, тебе лучше лежать в постели. Я сейчас позвоню в бюро обслуживания. Врач скоро придёт.
Анна	Значит, нам сегодня нельзя в Сергиев Посад?
Ира	Да, Анна, я думаю, что сегодня нельзя.
Анна	Ой, как жаль. Извини, Ира.
Ира	Ничего, Анна. Не беспокойся об этом. Сегодня ты должна отдыхать.
Анна	Спасибо, Ира, ты очень добра.
Ира	Не за что! Скажи, Анна, что тебе нужно? Тебе хочется пить?
Анна	Да, очень хочу.
Ира	Хорошо … я закажу чай с лимоном. Это всегда помогает. Тебе скоро будет лучше.

2 True or false?

a Anna has a headache.

b Ira thinks that Anna should go to the doctor's.

c Ira phones the polyclinic.

d Anna and Ira had planned to go to Red Square.

3 Answer the following questions.

a Как Áнна сегóдня вы́глядит?

b Что у Áнны боли́т?

c Áнне óчень хóчется есть?

d Куда́ Áнна хотéла сегóдня поéхать?

Language discovery

DATIVE CASE

1 Look at the following phrases. Which words are in the dative case, and what do the phrases have in common?

Мне жáрко	*I feel hot* (lit. *it is hot for me*)
Вам не хóлодно?	*Are you cold?*
Емý бы́ло плóхо	*He felt ill*

We already know that the dative case is used to mean *to, for* and is used after verbs such as *to give, to say*. The dative case is also very useful when describing how you feel. It is used in impersonal expressions made up of the dative case and the short form of the neuter adjective.

YOUR TURN (Давáйте)

2 Complete the English expressions.

Мне хорошó	*I feel* _____
Вам жáрко?	*Are you* _____?
Ей бы́ло неудóбно	_____ *felt uncomfortable*

This construction is not only useful when you are describing physical feelings – you can also use it to talk about boredom and interest:

YOUR TURN (Дава́йте)

3 Complete the English expressions.

Мне бы́ло о́чень ску́чно на ле́кции	I found it very _____ at the _____
Ему́ о́чень интере́сно чита́ть ру́сские газе́ты	He finds it very _____ to read _____ newspapers

The dative case is also used after several other verbs, some of which we have already met. Here is a list of the most common:

звони́ть/позвони́ть	to ring
Óля позвони́ла врачу́	Olya rang the doctor
каза́ться/показа́ться	to seem
Мне ка́жется, что у тебя́ грипп	I think (it seems to me) you've got the flu
нра́виться/понра́виться	to please
Ей не нра́вятся э́ти табле́тки	She doesn't like these tablets
помога́ть/помо́чь	to help
Э́ти табле́тки помо́гут вам	These tablets will help you
рекомендова́ть/ порекомендова́ть	to recommend
Что вы рекоменду́ете мне?	What do you recommend for me?
сове́товать/посове́товать	to advise
Врач посове́товал ей отдыха́ть	The doctor advised her to rest
хоте́ться/захоте́ться	to want, feel like
Мне хо́чется спать	I want to sleep

Note that the dative case is also found in time expressions with the preposition **к**:

к ча́су	at about one o'clock, towards one o'clock
к шести́ часа́м	at about six o'clock, towards six o'clock

Finally, the dative case is very useful when you are talking about necessity:

Что мне де́лать? *What should I do? (lit. what to me to do?)*

Когда́ мне принима́ть табле́тки? *When should I take the tablets?*

You have now met various ways of stating how you think/feel:

Я ду́маю, что здесь интересно *I think it's interesting here*

Мне ка́жется, что здесь интересно *It seems to me that it's interesting here*

Мне здесь интересно *I feel interested here*

По-мо́ему, здесь интере́сно *In my opinion it's interesting here*

SHORT ADJECTIVES

We already know that most Russian adjectives have a long and a short form, and we have met some commonly used short forms. Note the following further examples of short form adjectives:

Meaning	Masc.	Fem.	Neut.	Pl.
ill	**бо́лен**	**больна́**	**бо́льно**	**больны́**
duty-bound (must, have to, should)	**до́лжен**	**должна́**	**должно́**	**должны́**
necessary	**ну́жен**	**нужна́**	**ну́жно**	**ну́жны**

До́лжен agrees with the person who must do something, e.g.:

Сего́дня А́нна должна́ отдыха́ть *Anna must rest today*

Вчера́ Алексе́й до́лжен был отдыха́ть *Yesterday Alexei had to rest*

За́втра мы должны́ бу́дем отдыха́ть *We must/will have to rest tomorrow*

Ну́жен must agree with the thing that is needed, e.g.:

Тебе́ нужна́ э́та кни́га? *Do you need this book? (lit. is this book necessary to you?)*

The neuter form **ну́жно** is identical in meaning to **на́до**.

In English, verbs express the idea of *must* and *need*, but Russian uses short adjectives:

▶ **До́лжен** agrees with the person who must do something – **Они́ должны́ рабо́тать** *They must work*

▶ **Ну́жен** agrees with the item which is necessary: **Мне нужна́ ва́ша кни́га** *I need your book*

Note that for once there is a significant difference in meaning between the short form adjective **бóлен** and the long form adjective **больнóй**:

бóлен (больнá, больны́)	*sick, ill* (temporarily)
больнóй	*chronically ill; an invalid, a patient*

Note also:

прав	*right, correct*	**жив**	*alive*
прáвый	*right wing*	**живóй**	*lively*

VERBS ENDING IN -ОВАТЬ AND -ЕВАТЬ

 4 **The infinitive of these verbs looks like the infinitive of a regular first conjugation verb. However, look at the following verb. Why isn't it 'regular'?**

рекомендовáть *to recommend*

рекомендýю	**рекомендýем**
рекомендýешь	**рекомендýете**
рекомендýет	**рекомендýют**

Many of these verbs are imported from other languages, e.g.:

танцевáть	*to dance* (from German)
интересовáться	*to be interested*
организовáть	*to organize*

In the context of health, the following are very common:

жáловаться (**на** + accusative)	*to complain (of, about)*
На что вы жáлуетесь?	*What's the problem?* (lit. What are you complaining of?)

> **LANGUAGE TIP**
> Note that with the verb *to feel* the **себя́** never changes.

чýвствовать себя́	*to feel*
Как вы себя́ чýвствуете?	*How are you feeling?*

TO BE ILL, TO HURT AND TO BE SORE

The verb **болéть** (present tense **болéю, болéешь**) means *to be ill (with)*, e.g.:

Áнна болéет грúппом	*Anna is ill with the flu*

The verb **заболева́ть/заболе́ть** means *to fall ill with*, *catch*, e.g.:

А́нна заболе́ла гри́ппом   *Anna has caught the flu*

(NB: **Заболева́ть** is a regular first conjugation verb because it doesn't come from a foreign word – i.e. **заболева́ю**, **заболева́ешь**).

Note how you say that you have an *ache*:

У меня́ боли́т голова́   *My head aches*

У меня́ боля́т но́ги   *My legs/feet ache*

The perfective form **заболе́ть** has the meaning *to begin to hurt*:

Когда́ у вас заболе́л зуб?   *When did your tooth begin to hurt?*

VERBS ENDING IN -КАЗАТЬ

This ending is found in the verb *to seem* (**каза́ться/показа́ться**) and also in the perfective infinitive of a number of common verbs:

говори́ть/сказа́ть	*to say, tell*
зака́зывать/заказа́ть	*to order, book, reserve*
пока́зывать/показа́ть	*to show*

Note that verbs which end in this way have the following pattern:

я скажу́	*I will say*	**мы ска́жем**	*we will say*
ты ска́жешь	*you will say*	**вы ска́жете**	*you will say*
он/она ска́жет	*he/she will say*	**они ска́жут**	*they will say*

Practice

1 How do they feel?

Как они́ себя́ чу́вствуют?

a Ива́н

hot

Ива́ну жа́рко

b О́ля

cold

c Макси́м

bad/unwell

d Ви́ктор

bored

2 Look at the doctor's question and the patient's answer.

Зуб

– На что вы жа́луетесь?

– У меня́ боли́т зуб.

Now answer in a similar way, using the words given.

  a голова́

  b го́рло

  c ру́ки (hands/arms)

  d живо́т (stomach)

  e спина́ (back)

3 Look at the pictures and decide what the doctor is advising.

  a Что рекоменду́ет врач?

    <u>Врач рекоменду́ет мне не кури́ть.</u>

петь (пою́, поёшь)	to sing
дискоте́ка	disco
«Война́ и мир»	War and Peace

4 Choose the most appropriate 'prescription' for each of the following.

a Арка́дий чу́вствует себя́ нехорошо́. У него́ боли́т зуб. Что ему́ на́до де́лать?

1 купи́ть моро́женое **2** пойти́ в бассе́йн **3** принима́ть табле́тки

b У Све́ты боли́т го́рло. Что ей на́до де́лать?

1 смотре́ть футбо́льный матч **2** отды́хать до́ма **3** петь на конце́рте

c У Бори́са голова́ боли́т. Что ему́ на́до де́лать?

1 чита́ть «Войну́ и мир» **2** идти́ на дискоте́ку **3** лежа́ть в посте́ли

d У вас боли́т нога́. Что вам на́до де́лать?

1 игра́ть в хоккей **2** сиде́ть до́ма **3** гуля́ть с соба́кой

> **LANGUAGE TIP**
>
> Different ways of seeking advice:
>
> ▶ Question word + dative of the person needing advice + infinitive:
> **Что нам де́лать?** — *What should we do?*
> **Когда́ ему́ принима́ть табле́тки?** — *When should he take the tablets?*
>
> ▶ Use the verbs to recommend, to advise:
> **Что вы рекоменду́ете/сове́туете, до́ктор?** — *What do you recommend/ advise, doctor?*

Listen and understand

си́льно	strongly
бо́льно	painful
ничего не ел	I ate nothing
ни в ко́ем слу́чае	on no account
неме́дленно	immediately

13.03 *Sasha is at the doctor's.*

1 Why has Sasha gone to the doctor's?

Врач	На что вы жа́луетесь?
Са́ша	У меня́ о́чень боли́т живо́т.
Врач	Когда́ э́то начало́сь?
Са́ша	Вчера́ то́лько.
Врач	Покажи́те мне, где у вас боли́т?
Са́ша	Вот здесь, с пра́вой стороны́.
Врач	Си́льно боли́т?
Са́ша	Да, до́ктор, о́чень бо́льно.
Врач	Гм. Аппети́т есть?
Са́ша	Нет. Вчера́ я ничего́ не ел. Сего́дня то́же не хочу́ есть. Что де́лать, до́ктор? Табле́тки мне помо́гут?
Врач	Я не ду́маю. У вас, ка́жется, аппендици́т.
Са́ша	За́втра мне ну́жно пое́хать в Новосиби́рск!
Врач	Ни в ко́ем слу́чае! Вам ну́жно неме́дленно в больни́цу.

2 True or false?

a У Са́ши боли́т рука́.

b Он бо́лен уже́ четы́ре дня.

c У него́ си́льные бо́ли (*pains*) в живо́те.

d Са́ше не хо́чется есть.

e Са́ша до́лжен принима́ть табле́тки.

f Са́ше нельзя́ за́втра пое́хать в Новосиби́рск.

Reading and writing

 Read the symptoms, advice and conclusions in the list, then write a sentence about each following the model.

	Кто?	Что боли́т?	Что де́лать?	Зна́чит, нельзя́ …
a	О́ля	живо́т	позвони́ть в поликли́нику	обе́дать в рестора́не
b	Та́ня	нога́	сиде́ть до́ма	игра́ть в те́ннис
c	Вы	спина́	лежа́ть в посте́ли	рабо́тать в саду́
d	А́лла	го́рло	пить чай с лимо́ном	петь на конце́рте
e	Он	глаз	отдыха́ть	смотре́ть телеви́зор

a <u>У Óли боли́т живо́т. Она́ должна́ позвони́ть в поликли́нику. Зна́чит ей нельзя́ обе́дать в рестора́не.</u>

Speaking

температу́ра	*temperature*
высо́кий	*high*
откро́йте!	*open!*
рот	*mouth*
анги́на	*tonsillitis*
принима́ть	*to take*
по табле́тке два ра́за в день	*one tablet twice a day*
заходи́ть/зайти́	*to call in/pop in*

> **LANGUAGE TIP**
>
> A reminder about two really useful expressions if you are feeling ill:
> ▸ **y** + genitive + **боли́т/боля́т** (for plural) + part of the body: **У меня́ боли́т го́рло и боля́т глаза́** *I have a sore throat and my eyes hurt*
> ▸ dative of the person + adverb to describe the feeling: **мне пло́хо** *I feel ill*

1 **13.04 You are on holiday in Yalta. You are feeling unwell and the doctor has come to visit you. Play your part, then listen to the complete conversation on the audio.**

Врач	Здра́вствуйте! Сади́тесь, пожа́луйста. На что вы жа́луетесь?
Вы	**a** *Say 'hello' to the doctor. Explain that you have a sore throat.*
Врач	А кака́я у вас температу́ра?
Вы	**b** *Say you think you have a high temperature.*
Врач	Ну, откро́йте, пожа́луйста, рот … да, го́рло кра́сное. У вас анги́на.
Вы	**c** *Ask what you should do.*
Врач	Вы должны́ отдыха́ть. Вот вам табле́тки.
Вы	**d** *Ask when you should take the tablets.*
Врач	Принима́йте по табле́тке два ра́за в день. Заходи́те ко мне за́вρτа в медпу́нкт.

2 **13.05 Can you remember how to say the following in Russian? Listen to the audio and practise saying each phrase.**

   a What's wrong with you?

   b I feel ill.

   c Do you feel better?

   d Don't worry.

   e Are you thirsty?

Test yourself

1 How would you tell someone that you feel cold?

2 If someone says спаси́бо to you, you could reply пожа́луйста. What else could you say? Have another look at the dialogue at the beginning of this unit if you can't remember.

3 Your head aches. How will you explain this to the doctor?

4 The verb боле́ть/заболе́ть can be followed by the instrumental case. How would you explain to someone that you have fallen ill with the flu?

5 The verb жа́ловаться is followed by на and the accusative case. How would you complain about a bad back?

6 Мне ну́жны табле́тки! *I need some tablets!* Can you explain the ending of ну́жны?

7 Which word will you need to put into this sentence to explain that you can't go to the theatre today? Извини́те, мне сего́дня _____ в теа́тр.

8 You have a sore throat. How will you ask for lemon tea?

9 Не беспоко́йтесь! What advice is being given here?

10 Good news! You feel better. How will you explain this to the doctor?

SELF CHECK

I CAN. . .
. . . say how I feel.
. . . ask others how they feel.
. . . seek and give advice.
. . . talk about necessity.

14 Э́то тебе́ о́чень идёт

It really suits you

In this unit you will learn how to:

▶ *talk about clothes and appearance.*
▶ *ask for and give advice about size and colour.*
▶ *express simple comparisons and negatives.*

CEFR: (A2) *Can use simple descriptive language to make brief statements about and compare objects and possessions; can explain what he likes or dislikes.*

Универма́г *Department store*

As with many aspects of life in post-Soviet Russia, the consumer society has developed in recent years to now be very similar to what is on offer throughout the developed world. Shops are unrecognizable from their pre-1991 counterparts, with the most startling example being the most famous of all Russian department stores, **ГУМ (Гла́вный универса́льный магази́н)**. Situated just off Red Square in Moscow, this lavish shopping centre is now bursting with designer label boutiques from around the world. Long gone are the dark days of the 1990s when virtually everything in the shops was rationed, there was very limited choice and frequent shortages led to empty shelves. Customer service has also improved dramatically as private enterprise has flourished. However, smaller Russian shops still tend to have names describing their *goods* (**това́ры**) rather than brand names: **о́бувь** *footwear*, **оде́жда** *clothes*, **това́ры для дете́й** *children's goods*, **хозтова́ры** *household goods*.

Which sign would you look out for if you wanted to buy the following items?

1 T-shirt	**2** mug	**3** camera batteries	**4** toy	**5** slippers
a О́бувь	**b** Оде́жда	**c** Това́ры для дете́й	**d** Хозтова́ры	**e** Электротова́ры

Vocabulary builder

14.01 Complete the missing English expressions. Then listen to the audio and repeat the Russian until you can say all the words with confidence.

В МАГАЗИНЕ *SHOPPING ESSENTIALS*

универма́г	*department store*
оде́жда (sing. only)	*clothes*
сви́тер мне идёт	*the jumper suits* _____
я́ркий	_____
цвет (pl. цвета́)	*colour(s)*
мал	*too small*
на разме́р бо́льше	*a size bigger*
примеря́ть/приме́рить	*to try on*
вели́к	*too big*
како́го цве́та твоя́ ю́бка?	*what _____ is your skirt?*
подойдёт (подходи́ть/подойти́)	*(here) will go with*
я обы́чно ношу́ (носи́ть)	_____ *wear*
тёмный	*dark*
во́лосы	*hair*
шика́рно вы́глядишь	*you look smart*
возьму́ (брать/взять)	*to take*
мехова́я ша́пка	*fur hat*
продавщи́ца нам помо́жет (помога́ть/помо́чь)	*the shop assistant will help* _____
како́й у тебя́ (у вас) разме́р?	*what size are you?*

ЦВЕТА *COLOURS*

бе́лый	*white*	**ора́нжевый**	*orange*
голубо́й	*light blue*	**ро́зовый**	*pink*
жёлтый	*yellow*	**седо́й**	*grey* (hair)
зелёный	*green*	**се́рый**	*grey*
ка́рий	*brown* (eyes)	**си́ний**	*dark blue*
кори́чневый	*brown*	**чёрный**	*black*
кра́сный	*red*	**како́го цве́та ...**	*(of) what colour is ...*

To qualify shades of colour, use the following prefixes:

бле́дно-	*pale-*
све́тло-	*light-*
тёмно-	*dark-*
я́рко-	*bright-*

Dialogue

ничего́	*nothing; never mind*
найду́ (находи́ть/найти́)	*I will find (to find)*
уста́ла (устава́ть/уста́ть)	*tired (to get tired)*
лу́чше	*better*
уве́рен(а) (уве́ренный)	*certain, sure*
бо́лее	*more*
зачем	*why (more emphatic than* **почем***)*
весёлый	*cheerful*
мо́жет быть	*perhaps*

14.02 *Ira and Anna are shopping.*

1   What do they want to buy?

А́нна	Что ты хо́чешь купи́ть, И́ра? Куда́ мы идём?
И́ра	Я хочу́ купи́ть сви́тер. Зна́чит, мы пойдём снача́ла в универма́г, а е́сли там ничего́ не найду́, пойдём в магази́н «Оде́жда», а пото́м в «Твоё».
А́нна	А до магази́на «Твоё» далеко́?
И́ра	Нет, не о́чень – э́тот магази́н нахо́дится недалеко́ от ста́нции метро́ Академи́ческая … ты не уста́ла?
А́нна	Нет, что ты!
И́ра	*(Looking at jumpers in* «Твоё».*)* Ты ду́маешь, что э́тот сви́тер мне идёт, А́нна? Тако́й краси́вый, я́рко-кра́сный цвет!
А́нна	*(Uncertainly.)* Да, о́чень я́ркий … то́лько немно́жко мал, по-мо́ему.

Йра	(Sighs.) Да, ты права …
Анна	А посмотри на э́тот свитер, он на разме́р бо́льше. Ты не хо́чешь его́ приме́рить?
Йра	Да … (Tries it on.) Ты не ду́маешь, что э́тот свитер вели́к?
Анна	Нет, нет. Это лу́чше. Свитер тебе́ о́чень идёт. Како́го цве́та твоя́ ю́бка? Зелёная, да?
Йра	Да, све́тло-зелёная.
Анна	Я уве́рена, что э́тот чёрный свитер о́чень хорошо́ подойдёт твое́й ю́бке.
Йра	Ну, а я хоте́ла купи́ть свитер бо́лее весёлого цве́та.
Анна	Я сове́тую тебе́ купи́ть вот э́тот чёрный свитер.
Йра	Но я обы́чно ношу́ бо́лее я́ркие цвета́ …
Анна	Заче́м? Чёрный цвет так хорошо́ тебе́ идёт – ведь у тебя́ тёмные глаза́, тёмные во́лосы. Ты в нём о́чень шика́рно вы́глядишь.
Йра	Пра́вда? Да, мо́жет быть ты и права́. Хорошо́, я возьму́ вот э́тот.
Анна	О́чень хорошо́ … Скажи́, Йра, у нас вре́мя ещё есть? … Я о́чень хочу́ приме́рить мехову́ю ша́пку …
Йра	Коне́чно! Како́й у тебя́ разме́р?
Анна	Не зна́ю.
Йра	Ничего́. Продавщи́ца нам помо́жет.

> **LANGUAGE TIP**
>
> **Ты не уста́ла?** means *Are you tired?* Ira used the perfective past tense (literally, *have not you got tired?*). To say *I'm tired*, use **я уста́л** if you are a man, or **я уста́ла** if you are a woman (and *we are tired* would be **мы уста́ли**).

2 True or false?

  a First they go to a shop called 'Tvoyo'.
  b The shop they go into is near a metro station.
  c Ira likes the bright red jumper.
  d Anna thinks that the black jumper suits Ira better.
  e Anna wants to try on a black jumper.

3 Answer the following questions

a Где нахо́дится магази́н «Твоё»?

b Почему́ А́нна ду́мает, что И́ре не на́до покупа́ть я́рко-кра́сный сви́тер?

c Почему́ А́нна ду́мает, что И́ре на́до купи́ть чёрный сви́тер?

d Каки́е цвета́ И́ра обы́чно предпочита́ет?

e Како́й сви́тер И́ра покупа́ет наконе́ц *(finally, in the end)*?

Language discovery

NEGATIVE EXPRESSIONS

1 Look at the following Russian phrases, all of which are in the negative. How does the Russian negative differ from its English equivalent?

Я ничего́ не понима́ю	*I understand nothing / I don't understand anything*
Я никогда́ не смотрю́ телеви́зор	*I never watch television*
Она́ нигде́ не рабо́тает	*She doesn't work anywhere*
Мы никуда́ не идём	*We're not going anywhere*
Никто́ не зна́ет об э́том	*No one knows about this*

The words **ничто́** *nothing* and **никто́** *no one* decline (i.e. change according to case) in the same way as **кто** and **что**. Note that **ничего́** is the accusative of **ничто́**:

Он ничего́ не сказа́л об э́том	*He didn't say anything about this*
Она́ никого́ не зна́ет в э́том го́роде	*She doesn't know anyone in this town*

If you need to use a preposition with *nothing* and *no one*, it splits them up and the two parts are written separately.

YOUR TURN (Дава́йте)

2 Complete the English.

Он ни о чём не говори́л	*He didn't speak about _____*
Она́ ни с кем не говори́ла об э́том	*She didn't speak with _____ about this*

DATIVE CASE

Note the use of the dative case in the expression *to suit*:

Э́тот сви́тер Ви́ктору (dative) **о́чень идёт**   *This jumper really suits Viktor*

COLOURS

The Russian for *what colour is …?*, for example *What colour is your skirt?*, is: **Како́го цве́та твоя́ ю́бка?**

3 A case is being used here for *what colour*. Can you recognize which case it is?

Another useful question involving colours is: **Вы предпочита́ете я́рко-кра́сное пла́тье и́ли бле́дно-ро́зовое?**

4 What does this question mean?

SHORT ADJECTIVES

The short form of one group of adjectives is used to suggest *too big*, *too small*, etc.:

вели́к, велика́, велико́, велики́	*(too big)*
дли́нен, длинна́, дли́нно, дли́нны	*(too long)*
ко́роток, коротка́, ко́ротко, коротки́	*(too short)*
мал, мала́, мало́, малы́	*(too small)*
у́зок, узка́, у́зко, узки́	*(too narrow)*
широ́к, широка́, широко́, широки́	*(too wide)*

5 Complete these sentences:

Это плáтье (мне) великó	The dress is _____ (for me)
Это плáтье (мне) длúнно	_____
Эти брю́ки (мне) короткú	These trousers _____
Эта ю́бка (мне) малá	This skirt _____
Эти брю́ки (мне) узкú	_____
Эта рубáшка (мне) широкá	This shirt _____

БРАТЬ/ВЗЯТЬ *TO TAKE*

This is a very common verb, meaning *to take*, and both the imperfective and perfective are irregular.

6 Complete the following:

брать	*to take*	**взять**	*to take*
я берý	*I take*	**я возьмý**	*I will take*
ты берёшь	*you take*	**ты возьмёшь**	*you will take*
он/она бер_____	*he/she takes*	**он/она возьм_____**	*he/she will take*
мы бер_____	*we take*	**мы возьм_____**	*we will take*
вы бер_____	*you take*	**вы возьм_____**	*you will take*
они бер_____	*they take*	**они возьм_____**	*they will take*

> **LANGUAGE TIP**
>
> The future of the verb *to take* is very often used in the context of shopping: **Я возьмý голубýю рубáшку** *I'll take the pale blue shirt.*
>
> The command form of **взять** is also commonly used: **Возьмúте!**

COMPARISON

7 From the following six sentences, choose which two sentences include a comparative adjective:

a This is a big shirt.

b This is a bigger shirt.

c This is the biggest shirt.

d This is a fashionable shirt.

e This is a more fashionable shirt.

f This is the most fashionable shirt.

In English, the comparative is formed either by adding *-er* to an adjective or by using *more*:

a bigger book   *a more interesting book*

In Russian, however, the comparative is usually formed by using the word **бо́лее** in front of an adjective where English uses *more*:

Я хочу́ купи́ть бо́лее   *I want to buy a more fashionable*
мо́дную руба́шку   *shirt*

The word **ме́нее** *less* is used in the same way:

Я хочу́ купи́ть ме́нее я́ркую   *I want to buy a less bright skirt*
ю́бку

These forms of the comparative must be used when you are using an adjective before the noun (called an attributive adjective).

There are a few, usually very common, adjectives in Russian which are exceptions and cannot form the comparative with **бо́лее**:

бо́льший/ме́ньший	*bigger/lesser*
лу́чший/ху́дший	*better/worse*
ста́рший/мла́дший	*older/younger; senior/junior*
Я хочу́ купи́ть лу́чшую	*I want to buy a better shirt*
руба́шку	

Also, note that a short form of the comparative adjective exists. This is used after the noun (called a predicative adjective) and is formed by adding **-ее** to the stem of the adjective.

YOUR TURN (Дава́йте)

8 What therefore does this phrase mean? Эта руба́шка модне́е.

> **LANGUAGE TIP**
> The short form of the comparative adjective is also the comparative adverb, so, for example, **быстре́е** means both *quicker* and *more quickly*.

There are a number of common short comparative adjectives which are irregular (a full list is given in the Appendix).

большо́й	big	бо́льше	bigger/more
дешёвый	cheap	деше́вле	cheaper
дорого́й	dear, expensive	доро́же	dearer/more expensive
ма́ленький	small	ме́ньше	smaller/less
плохо́й	bad	ху́же	worse
по́здний	late	по́зже/поздне́е	later
просто́й	simple, easy	про́ще	simpler/easier
ра́нний	early	ра́ньше	earlier/previously
хоро́ший	good	лу́чше	better

You can always use **чем** to mean *than* when comparing two items:

Э́то бо́лее мо́дная ю́бка, чем её ю́бка — *This is a more modern skirt than hers*

Э́то пла́тье модне́е, чем твоё — *This dress is more modern than yours*

> **LANGUAGE TIP**
> With short comparatives, you will sometimes hear Russians put the second part of the comparative into the genitive case, as an alternative to using **чем**: **Э́то пла́тье модне́е твоего́** *This dress is more modern than yours*.

Practice

1 Complete the negative answers of the pessimist:

a Оптими́ст: Вы всё понима́ете? Пессими́ст: (*nothing*) Нет, я _____ понима́ю.

b Оптими́ст: Вы уже́ зна́ете дире́ктора заво́да? Пессими́ст: (*no one*) Нет, я здесь _____ зна́ю.

c Оптими́ст: Он уже́ рабо́тает в больни́це? Пессими́ст: (*nowhere*) Нет, он _____ рабо́тает.

d Оптими́ст: Вы ча́сто хо́дите в теа́тр? Пессими́ст: (*never*) Нет, мы _____ хо́дим в теа́тр.

e Оптими́ст: Вы бу́дете на ве́чере (*party*)? Пессими́ст: (*nowhere*) Нет, мы _____ идём.

| де́тский (adj.) | children's |
| мужско́й (adj.) | men's |

2 Look at the following information about shops situated near the
stations of Moscow's Circle Line and answer the questions:

МОСКВА – СПРАВКА
МЕТРОПОЛИТЕН
МАГАЗИНЫ

Кольцевая линия

Станция метро Краснопресненская	–	«Олимп» (спорттовары), «Товары для детей», «Универмаг Краснопресненская »
Станция метро Киевская	–	«Русский сувенир», «Обувь», «Товары для дома»
Станция метро Таганская	–	«Цветы », «Обувь», «Товары для детей», «Мужская одежда»
Станция метро Новослободская	–	«Молодость» (детская одежда), «Обувь», «Универмаг»

a How many department stores are accessible from the Circle Line?
b Which different clothes shops are mentioned?
c At which metro station would you have to get off if you wanted to
buy household items?
d How many shoe shops are mentioned?

3 Which question word should go at the beginning of each of
these phrases?

a	вы идёте сейча́с?	**1** Как
b	вам нра́вится э́тот костю́м?	**2** Ско́лько
c	вы обы́чно де́лаете поку́пки?	**3** Куда́
d	у вас разме́р?	**4** Како́й
e	сто́ит э́тот сви́тер?	**5** Где

> **LANGUAGE TIP**
>
> **де́лать/сде́лать
> поку́пки** = *to do the
> shopping*

4 Read the information about each person, then make up
sentences to describe their preferences. Which case will you
need to use after the verb *to prefer*?

a Ви́ктор–голуба́я руба́шка–мо́дный–бе́лая руба́шка

b Ма́ша–чёрная ю́бка–краси́вый–кра́сная ю́бка

c Вади́м–зелёный сви́тер–дешёвый–чёрный сви́тер

d И́ра–кра́сное пла́тье–я́ркий–се́рое пла́тье

e Серге́й–но́вый га́лстук *(tie)*–весёлый–ста́рый га́лстук

a **Ви́ктор предпочита́ет голубу́ю руба́шку, потому́ что она́
модне́е чем бе́лая руба́шка.**

биогра́фия	*biography*
кни́жный магази́н	*bookshop*
рома́н	*novel*

5 Read this passage about Alla, then answer the questions that
follow.

В свобо́дное вре́мя А́лла о́чень лю́бит чита́ть рома́ны. Она́ ду́мает,
что э́то интере́снее, чем смотре́ть телеви́зор. Обы́чно она́ чита́ет
романти́ческие кни́ги, но вчера́ в кни́жном магази́не она́ купи́ла бо́лее
серьёзную кни́гу – биогра́фию. На́до сказа́ть, что ей не о́чень нра́вится
э́та кни́га. Она́ ду́мает, что э́то ску́чнее, чем рома́ны. Она́ ча́сто хо́дит
в кни́жный магази́н – иногда́ два ра́за в неде́лю. За́втра она́ ещё
раз пойдёт в кни́жный магази́н, потому́ что она́ хо́чет купи́ть бо́лее
интере́сную кни́гу.

a Что А́лла лю́бит де́лать в свобо́дное вре́мя?

b Каки́е кни́ги она́ предпочита́ет?

c Что она́ купи́ла вчера́?

d В како́м магази́не мо́жно купи́ть кни́ги?

Listen and understand

я ищу́ (иска́ть: ищу́, и́щешь ... и́щут)	*to look for*
восьмо́й	*eighth*
вы́бор	*choice*
намно́го	*a lot*

наоборо́т	on the contrary
зато́	on the other hand
шестидеся́тый	sixtieth

14.03 *Vadim has gone to the department store.*

1 What does Vadim buy? Give as many details as possible.

Продавщи́ца	Вам помо́чь?
Вади́м	Я ищу́ футбо́лку.
Продавщи́ца	Како́го цве́та?
Вади́м	У вас есть тёмно-си́ние?
Продавщи́ца	Есть … то́лько вы́бор не о́чень большо́й. Како́й у вас разме́р?
Вади́м	Я не уве́рен. Сре́дний, ка́жется.
Продавщи́ца	Гм, посмо́трим … Есть чёрный сре́днего разме́ра, и́ли тёмно-си́ний большо́го разме́ра. Вы хоти́те приме́рить их?
Вади́м	Да, пожа́луйста … *(Tries them on.)* … Вам не ка́жется, что тёмно-си́няя футбо́лка мне велика́?
Продавщи́ца	Нет, наоборо́т, тёмно-си́няя намно́го лу́чше , а чёрная, по-мо́ему, мала́.
Вади́м	Ско́лько сто́ит тёмно-си́няя футбо́лка?
Продавщи́ца	Пятьсо́т рубле́й.
Вади́м	Ой, о́чень до́рого!
Продавщи́ца	Да, до́рого. Но зато́ о́чень мо́дная …
Вади́м	Да, вы пра́вы … хорошо́, я возьму́ тёмно-си́нюю футбо́лку.
Продавщи́ца	Э́то всё?
Вади́м	Нет. У вас есть тёмные ша́пки?
Продавщи́ца	Да, … вот тёмные ша́пки. Како́й разме́р?
Вади́м	Пятьдеся́т восьмо́й, шестидеся́тый– я не уве́рен … что вы посове́туете?
Продавщи́ца	Я вам рекоменду́ю пятьдеся́т восьмо́й.
Вади́м	Хорошо́ … Я возьму́. Ско́лько с меня́?
Продавщи́ца	С вас две ты́сячи рубле́й.

2 Choose the correct answer.

a Вади́м хо́чет купи́ть
1 тёмно-си́нюю руба́шку
2 чёрную руба́шку
3 се́рую футбо́лку
4 тёмно-си́нюю футбо́лку

b Продавщи́ца говори́т, что
1 чёрная футбо́лка широка́
2 чёрная футбо́лка велика́
3 чёрная футбо́лка мала́
4 чёрная футбо́лка узка́

c Вади́м покупа́ет футбо́лку, потому́ что
1 она́ до́рого сто́ит
2 э́то краси́вая футбо́лка
3 э́то мо́дная футбо́лка

d Вади́м покупа́ет та́кже
1 тёмную ша́пку
2 бе́лую ша́пку
3 бе́лую руба́шку

Reading and writing

аванга́рд	*avant garde*
вме́сте с (+ instr.)	*together with*
дина́стия	*dynasty*
жи́вопись (f.)	*painting*
клие́нт	*customer*
колле́кция	*collection*
мо́да	*fashion*
моде́ль (f.)	*model*
модельер	*modeller, fashion designer*
молодёжный	*young people's* (adjective)
оконча́ние	*finishing, graduation*
осно́ва	*basis, foundation*
посети́тель (m.)	*visitor*
постоя́нный	*constant*
приме́р	*example*
прове́рен	*tested, checked*
стиль (m.)	*style*
тексти́льный	*textile* (adjective)

Read the text, then answer the questions that follow in English.

В Москве́ есть я́ркая, тала́нтливая дина́стия модельеров – широко́изве́стный Вячесла́в За́йцев и его́ сын, Его́р. По́сле оконча́ния Моско́вского тексти́льного институ́та Его́р пошёл рабо́тать к отцу́.

Клие́нты и посети́тели Моско́вского до́ма мо́ды на проспе́кте Ми́ра уже́ хорошо́ зна́ют его́ моде́ли. Зна́ют его́ моде́ли та́кже и в Япо́нии, Австра́лии, И́ндии … везде́, где моде́ли мла́дшего За́йцева бы́ли вме́сте с колле́кциями отца́.

Вя́чеслав За́йцев бо́льше всего́ лю́бит кла́ссику: «Класси́ческий костю́м прове́рен вре́менем, э́то не мо́да, а стиль».

Его́р счита́ет, что мо́да – э́то иску́сство, как му́зыка и́ли жи́вопись. Он занима́ется молодёжной мо́дой. Если осно́ва моделе́й ста́ршего За́йцева – англи́йский костю́м, то мла́дший предпочита́ет аванга́рд. Одна́ко, отец́ для Его́ра – учи́тель и постоя́нный пример́.

(«Огонёк»)

a What is the relationship between Viacheslav and Egor Zaitsev?
b Where did Egor study?
c In which countries is Egor Zaitsev already famous?
d What is Viacheslav's preference in fashion?
e To what does Egor compare fashion?
f What does Egor consider Viacheslav to be?

Speaking

1 14.04 You are buying a fur hat. Play your part in the conversation with the shop assistant, then listen to the complete conversation on the audio.

Вы	**a** *Say 'excuse me, please, do you have any fur hats?'*
Продавщи́ца	Коне́чно. Вот они́.
Вы	**b** *Ask the assistant to show you that fur hat … over there, on the left.*
Продавщи́ца	Пожа́луйста.
Вы	**c** *Ask if you can try it on.*
Продавщи́ца	Пожа́луйста.
Вы	**d** *Say you think it's too big.*
Продавщи́ца	Да, мо́жет быть вы пра́вы. Хоти́те приме́рить э́ту ша́пку?
Вы	**e** *Say 'yes, please'.*
Продавщи́ца	Да, по-мо́ему э́то лу́чше.
Вы	**f** *Say 'yes, you're right'. Say you'll take this one.*
Продавщи́ца	Пожа́луйста.

2 **14.05 Can you remember how to say the following in Russian? Listen to the audio and practise saying each phrase.**

a I never watch television.

b Yes, perhaps you're right.

c Would you like (do you want) to try this fur hat on?

d The green jumper really suits you.

e This skirt is a lot better.

Test yourself

1 You've seen a fur hat that you like. How would you ask to try it on?

2 If you were asking for a grey jumper, would you use седо́й or се́рый?

3 What is missing from the following sentence? Я ничего́ _____ понима́ю!

4 Which word would you insert in the following sentence to make it mean *I prefer the more expensive design*? Я предпочита́ю _____ дорогу́ю моде́ль.

5 Which case of the word for *you* would you use to ask Anna if something suits her?

6 Which word is missing from the following sentence? моя́ футбо́лка модне́е, _____ твоя́

7 If the reply is Я сове́тую вам взять зелёную руба́шку, what advice are you being given?

8 You decide to follow the advice in Question 7. How will you say *I'll take it*?

9 What will you add to the following sentence to make it mean *I am sure you are right*? Я _____, что ты _____.

10 How would you make this sentence negative? Я всегда́ понима́ю всё *I always understand everything.*

SELF CHECK

I CAN...
. . . talk about clothes and appearance.
. . . ask for and give advice about size and colour.
. . . express simple comparisons and negatives.

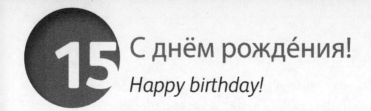

С днём рождения!

Happy birthday!

In this unit you will learn how to:
▶ *talk about dates.*
▶ *say when and where you were born and state your age.*
▶ *ask other people about their age, and place and date of birth.*
▶ *greet people on special occasions.*

CEFR: (A2) *Can use a series of phrases and sentences to describe family, other people, living conditions, daily routines, educational background and present or most recent job.*

Пра́здник *A holiday*

New Year (**Но́выи год**) is the main public holiday celebrated in Russia, and this occasion is marked in a very similar way to Christmas in the West. Although the majority of ethnic Russians are Orthodox Christians, religious festivals are not official public holidays. The other thing to remember is that Christmas for an Orthodox Russian is celebrated on 6–7 January because the Russian Orthodox church calendar remains Julian rather than Gregorian. There are many other significant dates celebrated by Russians, such as International Women's Day (8 March), Day of Spring and Labour (1 May), Victory Day (9 May, marking the end of the 'Great Patriotic War', i.e. the Second World War) and Russia Day (12 June), marking the declaration of Russian sovereignty after the fall of the Soviet Union.

Russian is rich in greetings, but perhaps the most useful (to cover all occasions!) is **С пра́здником!** (literally *with the holiday* – actually a shortened form of **Поздравля́ю вас с пра́здником!** *I congratulate you on the holiday!*) Similar constructions are used for *Happy New Year!* (**С Но́вым го́дом!**), *Welcome!* – after a journey – (**С прие́здом!**) and, of course, **С днём рожде́ния!**

Can you match these Russian state holidays to their dates? Although you have not met the Russian for months yet, they are very similar to the English when you read them out loud.

1 День Побе́ды **2** День Росси́и   **3** Междунаро́дный же́нский день

4 Но́вый год **5** Пра́здник весны́ и труда́

a 1-ое января́ **b** 8-ое ма́рта   **c** 1-ое ма́я

d 9-ое ма́я **e** 12-ое ию́ня

Vocabulary builder

15.01 Complete the missing English expressions. Then listen to the audio and repeat the Russian until you can say all the words with confidence.

НА́ДО ЗНАТЬ! *ESSENTIALS*

входи́ть/войти́	*to enter, come/go in*
оригина́льно	_____
носки́ (носо́к)	*socks (_____)*
знамени́тый	*well-known*
прихо́жая	*(entrance) hall*
что ли?	*eh?, perhaps?*
проходи́ть/пройти́	*to go through, past*
секре́т	_____
ско́лько тебе́/вам лет?	_____?
ошиба́ться/ошиби́ться	*to make a mistake*
ты роди́лся (роди́ться)	*you were born (_____)*
тебе́ легко́ даётся матема́тика	*you're good at _____ (lit. _____ gives itself to you easily)*
обо мне	*about _____*
како́го числа́ (число́)	*on what date? (_____)*
же́нщина	*woman*
комплиме́нт	_____
передава́ть/переда́ть	*to pass, pass on*

С ПРА́ЗДНИКОМ! *CELEBRATIONS*

[поздравля́ю тебя́ /вас] с пра́здником!	*happy _____!*
с днём рожде́ния!	*happy _____!*
жела́ю тебе́/вам всего́ са́мого наилу́чшего!	*I wish _____, all the very best!*
сча́стье	*happiness*
успе́х	*success*
наде́яться	*to hope*
тост за (+ accusative)	_____
пра́здник	_____
дари́ть/подари́ть	*to give as a present*
шампа́нское	_____
буты́лка	_____
бока́л	*wine glass*

> **LANGUAGE TIP**
> The instrumental case is used for greetings which name the special day (**С днём учи́теля!** *Happy Teachers' Day!*)

> **LANGUAGE TIP**
> The genitive case is needed for wishes expressed on a special day (**Жела́ю вам/тебе́ успе́ха!** *I wish you success!*)

Dialogue

15.02 *Ira has taken Anna to Volodya's birthday celebrations.*

1 How old are Volodya and Ira, and when is Anna's birthday?

И́ра	Воло́дя, приве́т. С днём рожде́ния! Жела́ю тебе́ всего́ са́мого наилу́чшего, … сча́стья, здоро́вья и успе́хов во всех твои́х дела́х!
А́нна	С днём рожде́ния, Воло́дя!
Воло́дя	Спаси́бо. Пожа́луйста, входи́те!
И́ра	Вот тебе́ пода́рок … извини́, э́то не о́чень оригина́льно!

Воло́дя	Ну, что ты, И́ра … мне о́чень нужны́ носки́.
А́нна	А вот пода́рок от меня́ … наде́юсь, что он тебе́ понра́вится … э́то кни́га о знамени́тых англи́йских спортсме́нах. Я зна́ю, что ты лю́бишь спорт.
Воло́дя	Спаси́бо большо́е, А́нна. Я о́чень люблю́ чита́ть таки́е кни́ги. *(Starts leafing through book.)*
И́ра	Ну, Воло́дя, мы бу́дем весь ве́чер стоя́ть в прихо́жей, что ли? Где же шампа́нское, где заку́ски?
Воло́дя	Пожа́луйста, проходи́те в гости́ную. Там всё есть.
И́ра	*(Sips champagne.)* … Хоро́шее шампа́нское … Я предлага́ю тост за Воло́дю!
А́нна	За Воло́дю!
И́ра	Скажи́, Воло́дя, е́сли не секре́т, ско́лько тебе́ лет?
Воло́дя	Мне? Ну, лет три́дцать.
И́ра	Е́сли я не ошиба́юсь, тебе́ уже́ три́дцать во́семь лет … ведь ты на три го́да ста́рше меня́ … зна́чит ты роди́лся в како́м году́?
Воло́дя	*(Sighs.)* В се́мьдесят шесто́м.
А́нна	*(Embarrassed.)* Тебе́ легко́ даётся матема́тика, И́ра! … А где ты роди́лся, Воло́дя?
Воло́дя	На Ура́ле, в Екатеринбу́рге … Ну, всё обо мне. Како́го числа́ твой день рожде́ния, А́нна?
А́нна	Восьмо́го ма́рта.
И́ра	Восьмо́го ма́рта! … Ты ведь зна́ешь, что э́то у нас пра́здник?
А́нна	Нет, не зна́ла. Како́й э́то пра́здник?
И́ра	Э́то междунаро́дный же́нский день. В э́тот день же́нщинам де́лают мно́го комплиме́нтов, да́рят им цветы́, пода́рки.
А́нна	Пра́вда? … И́ра, ты права́, шампа́нское о́чень вку́сное …
Воло́дя	Да, в буты́лке есть ещё немно́жко … переда́й мне твой бока́л, А́нна!

2 True or false?

  a Ira gives Volodya some socks.

  b Volodya is younger than Ira.

  c Volodya was born in Moscow.

  d Anna was born on 8 March.

  e Anna likes the champagne.

3 Answer the following questions.

  a Почему́ А́нна да́рит Воло́де кни́гу об знаменитых спортсме́нах?

  b Како́й тост И́ра предлага́ет?

  c Ско́лько лет Воло́де?

  d Где он роди́лся?

  e Како́й пра́здник восьмо́го ма́рта?

Language discovery

PREPOSITIONAL CASE

In the phrase **о знамени́тых англи́йских спортсме́нах**, the prepositional plural of the adjectives (**знамени́тый** and **англи́йский**) and noun (**спортсме́н**) are used.

1 What are the prepositional plural endings for adjectives and nouns?

Adjectives: _____   Nouns: _____

2 Can you predict the prepositional plural endings for 'soft' adjectives and nouns?

Adjectives: _____   Nouns: _____

YOUR TURN (Дава́йте)

3 Complete the Russian phrases with the appropriate prepositional plural endings.

в стар _____ ру́сск _____ город _____	*in old Russian towns*
в э́т _____ больш _____ кни́г _____	*in these big books*
Он говори́л обо мне и мо _____ друзь _____	*He was talking about me and my friends*
в твои́х интере́сн _____ пи́сьм _____	*in your interesting letters*

MONTHS

4 Try to match all the Russian months of the year to their English equivalents.

> **а́вгуст   апре́ль   дека́брь**
> **ию́ль   ию́нь   май**
> **март   ноя́брь   октя́брь**
> **сентя́брь   февра́ль   янва́рь**

_____	January	_____	July
_____	February	_____	August
_____	March	_____	September
_____	April	_____	October
_____	May	_____	November
_____	June	_____	December

Note that months are written with a small letter in Russian (except at the beginning of a sentence) and that all months are masculine. To say *in* a month, simply use **в** + prepositional:

в январе́	*in January*
в ма́рте	*in March*
в а́вгусте	*in August*

DATES

5 **Look at the following phrases containing dates. What do you notice about the numbers used, the case used for months and the case used to say *on* a date?**

Какóе сегóдня числó?	*What is the date today?*
– Сегóдня восемнáдцатое октябрЯ	*Today is 18 October*
Какóго числá ваш день рождéния?	*On what date is your birthday?*
– Двáдцать седьмóго февралЯ	*On 27 February*

Ordinal numbers are used when talking about specific dates, so Russian, like English, talks about the *18th* (i.e. ordinal number) *of October* (using the genitive case for the month) – **восемнáдцатое октябрЯ**. The neuter form of the ordinal is used because the word for *date* – **числó** – is understood but not stated. To say *on* a date, you need to put the ordinal into the genitive case.

The ordinal numbers are also important if you want to talk about a particular year. For *1991*, for example, what Russian says literally is the *one thousand, nine hundred and ninety-first year*: **тЫсяча девятьсóт девянóсто пéрвый год**. If you want to say *in* what year something happened, then **в** + prepositional is used, but only the very last digit (i.e. the ordinal number) has to be put into the prepositional case:

В какóм годý Áнна познакóмилась с Úрой?	*In what year did Anna meet Ira?*
– В тЫсяча девятьсóт девянóсто пéрвом годý	*In 1991*

The year *2000* is **двухтЫсячный год**. *In 2000* is **в двухтЫсячном годý**. A simpler way of expressing the year in writing is:

1991 г	*1991*
в 2000-ом годý	*in 2000*
в апрéле 1991-ого гóда	*in April 1991* – i.e. *in April of the 1991st year*

To help remember how to express dates in Russian, try working out in Russian some birthdays which are significant for you:

Моя́ дочь родила́сь в две ты́сячи девя́том году́	*My daughter was born in 2009*
День рожде́ния моего́ му́жа тре́тьего октября́	*My husband's birthday is on 3 October*

TIME EXPRESSIONS

Note the different ways in which units of time are treated in Russian:

▶ If you are dealing with units of time from a second to a day, use **в** + accusative case:

в э́тот моме́нт	*at this/that moment*
в час	*at one o'clock*
в пя́тницу	*on Friday*

▶ If you are dealing with a week, **на** + prepositional must be used:

на э́той неде́ле	*this week*
на про́шлой неде́ле	*last week*
на бу́дущей неде́ле	*next week*

▶ As we saw above, months and years take **в** + prepositional case:

в декабре́	*in December*
в како́м ме́сяце?	*in which month?*
в э́том году́	*this year*

VERBS OF MOTION

In English, we can modify the meaning of a verb such as *to go* by using a preposition like *in* or *out*. A similar principle applies in Russian, except you add something to the beginning of the verb (a prefix) as well as often using a preposition after it.

In the dialogue we saw two verbs meaning *to go* which look very similar: **входи́ть** *to enter, go in* and **проходи́ть** *to go past, through*. Verbs like these are called prefixed verbs of motion and for them, it is important to remember both the meaning of the prefix and the preposition most likely to be used after the verb, e.g. **входи́ть/войти́** means *to go into* and this is usually followed by **в** + accusative:

6 **What does the following sentence mean?**

Он открывáет дверь и вхóдит в библиотéку.

7 **The most important prefixed verbs of motion include those in the following table. What do all the imperfective forms have in common? What do all the perfective forms have in common?**

8 **Complete the English translations.**

Meaning	Imperfective/ perfective + preposition	Example Russian sentence	English translation
to approach	подходи́ть/подойти́ к + dat.	Официáнт подошёл к нáшему сто́лику	
to arrive, come	приходи́ть/прийти́ в + acc.	Я надéюсь, что он во́время придёт!	
to cross	переходи́ть/перейти́ че́рез + acc.	Он бы́стро перехо́дит че́рез у́лицу	
to enter	входи́ть/войти́ в + acc.	Врач вошёл в ко́мнату	
to exit	выходи́ть/вы́йти из + gen.	Тури́сты сейчáс выхо́дят из музéя	
to get off	сходи́ть/сойти́ с + gen.	Все дéти сойду́т с авто́буса	
to leave	уходи́ть/уйти́ из + gen.	Воло́дя ужé ушёл	
to pass	проходи́ть/пройти́ ми́мо + gen.	Онá всегдá прохо́дит ми́мо шко́лы	
to pop into	заходи́ть/зайти́ в + acc.; к + dat.	Я обы́чно захожу́ в универсáм	

LANGUAGE TIP

Note that the perfective future and perfective past are formed like the future and past of **идти́**.

9 **There are many useful nouns related to prefixed verbs of motion. Can you match the meaning of the following?**

a вход

b вы́ход

c отхо́д

d отъéзд

e перехо́д

f приéзд

g прихо́д

1 *arrival* (on foot)

2 *arrival* (by transport)

3 *crossing*

4 *departure* (on foot)

5 *departure* (by transport)

6 *entrance*

7 *exit*

Practice

1 Match the question with the answer.

a Как вас зовут?

b Когда вы родились?

c Где вы живёте?

d Кем вы работаете?

e Какое сегодня число?

f Какая сегодня погода?

g Во сколько отходит поезд?

1 Идёт снег.

2 Двадцать первое сентября.

3 В три часа.

4 В 1964-ом году.

5 Виктор.

6 Учителем.

7 В Новосибирске.

> **LANGUAGE TIP**
>
> **Кем** (instr. of **кто**) **вы работаете?** means lit. *as whom do you work?*

2 Look at the two cards and explain what each is for.

a

С новым годом!

b

С днём рождения!

отчество   *patronymic*

местожительство   *place of residence*

3 Read this information about Валентина Сергеевна Яблокова.

Валентина Сергеевна Яблокова русская, родилась в Новгороде 15-ого января 1968-ого года. Валентина живёт в Санкт-Петербурге, где она работает врачом.

Now look at the following information and use it to write a paragraph like the one above.

Фами́лия:	Быко́в
И́мя, о́тчество:	Оле́г Петро́вич
Национа́льность:	ру́сский
Да́та рожде́ния:	12-ого апре́ля 1972-ого го́да
Ме́сто рожде́ния:	Я́лта
Местожи́тельство:	Краснода́р
Профе́ссия:	учи́тель

4 Complete the sentences with an appropriate phrase from the list which follows.

   a Англи́йские тури́сты о́чень лю́бят обе́дать в _____.
   b Анато́лию о́чень нра́вится _____.
   c Официа́нт рекоменду́ет _____ грибы́ со смета́ной.
   d В _____ есть о́чень интере́сные карти́ны.
   e Извини́те, у нас сего́дня нет _____.
   f Они живу́т в _____.

> больши́х рестора́нах
> но́вых кварти́рах
> иностра́нным тури́стам (*foreign*)
> ру́сских музе́ях
> кни́га о спортсме́нах
> све́жего (*fresh*) молока́

ждать (жду, ждёшь … ждут)	*to wait for*
де́ло в том, что	*the thing is that*
ти́хо	*quietly*
кабине́т	*office; study*

5 Complete the following description of the start of Boris's working day.

Ча́сто Бори́с по́здно _____ (*arrives*) на рабо́ту. Де́ло в том, что он далеко́ живёт от музе́я, где он рабо́тает. Обы́чно он _____ (*goes out of*) из кварти́ры в 8 ч., _____ (*approaches*) к остано́вке и ждёт трамва́я. Он _____ (*gets off*) с трамва́я недалеко́ от музе́я, _____ (*crosses*) че́рез у́лицу и _____ (*goes into*) в музе́й. Он ти́хо _____ (*passes*) ми́мо кабине́та дире́ктора и _____ (*enters*) в свой кабине́т.

Listen and understand

и́менно	*precisely*
насчёт (+ gen.)	*as regards, concerning*
духи́ (m.)	*perfume*
запи́сывать/записа́ть	*to note down*
по́мощь (f.)	*help*

15.03 *Valentina and Oleg are deciding how best to celebrate their daughter's birthday.*

1 How do Valentina and Oleg split the organizational tasks between them?

Валенти́на	Седьмо́го а́вгуста день рожде́ния Ма́ши. Ты уже́ поду́мал об э́том?
Оле́г	Я не понима́ю, почему́ на́до об э́том ду́мать! Ведь мы, коне́чно, ку́пим ей пода́рок, пригласи́м друзе́й на ве́чер. Всё о́чень про́сто.
Валенти́на	Ну что ты, Оле́г, э́то далеко́ не просто́е де́ло! Что и́менно на́до купи́ть ей? Кого́ и́менно на́до пригласи́ть на ве́чер?
Оле́г	Ты же намно́го лу́чше меня́ понима́ешь, что на́до купи́ть!
Валенти́на	Мо́жет быть, но на э́той неде́ле я так занята́! Помоги́ мне, пожа́луйста!
Оле́г	Ну, насчёт пода́рка не беспоко́йся ... я куплю́ ей духи́ и́ли джи́нсы.
Валенти́на	Спаси́бо. А кого́ пригласи́ть?
Оле́г	Са́шу, коне́чно, да ... и А́ню, и ...
Валенти́на	Мину́точку! Я запи́сываю ...
Оле́г	И Све́ту, и Бо́рю ...
Валенти́на	А почему́ Бо́рю? Он мне не о́чень нра́вится.
Оле́г	Мо́жет быть, но он тако́й ста́рый друг и с ним бу́дет веселе́е.
Валенти́на	Ла́дно ... а ещё пробле́ма: на́до купи́ть хоро́шее шампа́нское, а у меня́ так ма́ло вре́мени ...
Оле́г	Не беспоко́йся об э́том. Я куплю́ шампа́нское, а ты пригото́вишь заку́ски. Договори́лись, да?
Валенти́на	Договори́лись. Спаси́бо тебе́ за по́мощь, Оле́г.

2 Complete the following sentences.

a День рождéния Мáши _____.

b _____ считáет, что э́то не слóжное дéло.

c Олéг кýпит Мáше _____.

d Олéг хóчет приглаcи́ть Бóрю, потомý что _____.

Reading and writing

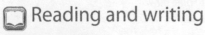

бить/проби́ть (бью, бьёшь … бьют)	*to strike* (of clock)
бородá	*beard*
важнéе всегó	*most important of all*
взрóслый	*adult*
внýчка	*granddaughter*
Дед Морóз	*Grandfather Frost* (i.e. *Father Christmas*)
друг дрýга	*one another*
игрýшка	*toy*
конéц	*end*
конфéта	*sweet*
Кремлёвские курáнты	*Kremlin chimes*
мешóк	*sack*
мнóго нарóду	*a lot of people*
нетерпéние	*impatience*
новогóдняя ёлка	*New Year (fir) tree*
по тради́ции	*according to tradition*
раздавáть/раздáть	*to distribute*
роднь́е	*relatives*
Снегýрочка	*Snow Maiden*
собирáться/собрáться	*to gather*
стари́к	*old man*
счáстье	*happiness*

украша́ть/укра́сить	to decorate
шар	ball
шу́ба	fur coat

15.04 Read and listen to the text, then answer the questions that follow in English.

Как ру́сские встреча́ют Но́вый год? К концу́ декабря́ они́ гото́вятся к э́тому пра́зднику. На́до коне́чно купи́ть пода́рки де́тям, родны́м, друзья́м, но важне́е всего́ – купи́ть нового́днюю ёлку. Вот почему́ на ёлочных база́рах всегда́ мно́го наро́ду. И де́ти и взро́слые лю́бят украша́ть ёлку шара́ми, игру́шками, конфе́тами. Де́ти с нетерпе́нием ждут прихо́да одного́ о́чень ва́жного го́стя … до́брого старика́, Де́да Моро́за. Дед Моро́з – стари́к с бе́лой бородо́й, в бе́лой шу́бе и с больши́м мешко́м. В мешке́, коне́чно, пода́рки для дете́й. Дед Моро́з обы́чно прихо́дит вме́сте со свое́й вну́чкой, Снегу́рочкой. Она́ то́же в бе́лой шу́бе и помога́ет Де́ду Моро́зу, когда́ он раздаёт пода́рки де́тям. Ве́чером 31-ого декабря́ взро́слые собира́ются за столо́м, предлага́ют то́сты … пе́рвый тост по тради́ции за ста́рый год. В 12 часо́в бьют Кремлёвские кура́нты. Лю́ди встаю́т, пьют шампа́нское, поздравля́ют друг дру́га с Но́вым го́дом, жела́ют друг дру́гу сча́стья, здоро́вья и успе́хов.

- **a** What is considered the most important purchase in preparation for New Year's Eve?
- **b** Describe Grandfather Frost.
- **c** Who usually accompanies him?
- **d** What is traditionally the first toast to be made on New Year's Eve?
- **e** What do people wish one another at midnight?

LANGUAGE TIP

One another: the ending of the second word changes depending on what is being said:

▶ accusative: **они́ понима́ют друг дру́га** they understand one another
▶ dative: **они́ пи́шут друг дру́гу** they write to one another
▶ prepositional: **они́ ду́мают друг о дру́ге** they think about one another

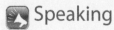 Speaking

 1 **15.05 You have gone to see the doctor, who is filling in a form with all your details. Play your part, then listen to the complete conversation on the audio.**

Врач	Как вáша фами́лия?
Вы	**a** *Say that your surname is Brown.*
Врач	Национáльность?
Вы	**b** *Say that you are English.*
Врач	Дáта рождéния?
Вы	**c** *Say that you were born on 12 April 1968.*
Врач	Где вы роди́лись?
Вы	**d** *Say that you were born in Leeds, in the north of England.*
Врач	Кем вы рабóтаете?
Вы	**e** *Say that you work as a journalist.*

 2 **15.06 Can you remember how to say the following in Russian? Listen to the audio and practise saying each phrase.**

a Happy birthday!

b Happy New Year!

c How old are you?

d I was born in 1968.

e Congratulations!

Test yourself

1 There is a word missing in the following expression – what is it?
_____ пра́здником!

2 What is the gender of all months of the year?

3 How would you ask the question *on what date*?

4 If you wanted to say *in 1997*, which words would you put in the prepositional case?

5 Which preposition would you add to complete the following sentence? Он обы́чно выхо́дит _____ музе́я в 5 часо́в *He usually leaves the museum at five o'clock.*

6 Which preposition would you add to complete the following sentence? Вчера́ она́ по́здно пришла́ _____ теа́тр *Yesterday she arrived late at the theatre.*

7 How would you say *this week*?

8 How would you ask someone what job they do?

9 How would you propose a toast to your friend, Viktor?

10 Put the correct endings on the last two words in the following sentence: Они́ хотя́т обе́дать в лу́чш _____ рестора́н _____ *They want to have lunch in the best restaurants.*

SELF CHECK

I CAN...
. . . talk about dates.
. . . say when and where I was born and state my age.
. . . ask other people about their age, and place and date of birth.
. . . greet people on special occasions.

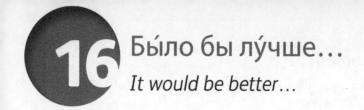

16 Бы́ло бы лу́чше…

It would be better…

In this unit you will learn how to:

▶ *express your opinion about arrangements and events.*
▶ *indicate preference in arrangements.*
▶ *express hopes and intentions about arrangements.*
▶ *make hypothetical statements.*
▶ *express statements contrary to fact.*

CEFR: (B1) *Can briefly give reasons and explanations for opinions and plans, and actions.*

Moscow's theatres

Visitors to Moscow have a huge number of theatres to choose from. The most famous Moscow theatres include the world-famous Bolshoi (for opera and ballet), the Taganka Theatre of Drama and Comedy, and the Moscow Arts Theatre (**МХАТ**), which is named after Anton Chekhov. Many theatres and concert halls are named after famous writers, composers and directors – this is indicated by the letters **им.** (an abbreviation of **и́мени**), e.g. **Моско́вский Худо́жественный Академи́ческий Теа́тр им. Чехова.**

In the last few years, musicals have become much more popular in Russia, and venues such as the Olympic stadium in Moscow have become part of the international concert circuit, attracting the biggest names in modern music. A trip to the theatre remains a popular activity and a special event worth dressing up for. On arrival at the theatre, it is always necessary to hand in your coat and any large bags at the **гардеро́б** *cloakroom* in exchange for a **тало́нчик** *token*. During the interval, it is common to have an open sandwich with your glass of champagne or tea or coffee.

What are the following venues and after whom are they named?

1 Конце́ртный зал им. П.И. Чайко́вского

2 Теа́тр и́мени Н.В. Го́голя

3 Драмати́ческий теа́тр и́мени К.С. Станисла́вского

4 Теа́тр и́мени А.С. Пу́шкина

Vocabulary builder

16.01 Complete the missing English expressions. Then listen to the audio and repeat the Russian until you can say all the words with confidence.

НА́ДО ЗНАТЬ! *ESSENTIALS*

ле́кция	_____
серьёзно (серьёзный)	_____
бе́дная (бе́дный)	*poor*
после́дний но́мер	*latest edition*
предпочла́ бы	*she would prefer*
что́-нибудь	*some* _____
поле́гче (лёгкий)	*a bit lighter (* _____ *)*
посмешне́е (смешно́й)	*a bit more amusing (* _____ *)*
она́ бы сама́ вы́брала	*she herself would choose*
кото́рая (кото́рый)	*which*
уважа́емый	*respected*
должно́ быть	*probably (lit. it must be)*
не пра́вда ли?	*isn't that* _____ *?*
пра́вильно	*right, correct*
постара́юсь (стара́ться/постара́ться)	*I'll try (* _____ *)*
и́ли … и́ли	*either … or*
действи́тельно	*really*
бы́ло бы лу́чше	*it would be* _____ */it would have been* _____
пора́ньше	*a bit sooner*
бу́дем наде́яться на лу́чшее	*let's hope for the* _____
как то́лько	*as soon as*

В ТЕАТРЕ *IN THE THEATRE*

свобо́дный	*free*
«Князь И́горь»	*'Prince _____'*
теа́тр ку́кол	*puppet _____*
«Кот в сапога́х»	*'_____ in Boots'*
коме́дия	*_____*
достава́ть/доста́ть	*to get, obtain*
(доста́ну, доста́нешь)	

Dialogue

 16.02 *The end of Anna's stay in Moscow is approaching. Ira and Sasha are trying to agree about where to take Anna on one of her last free evenings.*

1   Where do they decide to take Anna?

Са́ша	Éсли я не ошиба́юсь, А́нна бу́дет свобо́дна во вто́рник ве́чером.
И́ра	Ты ошиба́ешься. Как я уже́ сказа́ла, во вто́рник она́ должна́ пойти́ на ле́кцию о ру́сской жи́вописи.
Са́ша	Ой, как серьёзно! Бе́дная А́нна! Зна́чит, бы́ло бы лу́чше пригласи́ть её в теа́тр в четве́рг?
И́ра	Да. Дава́й посмо́трим после́дний но́мер «Театра́льно-конце́ртной Москвы́» … ага́, в Большо́м идёт о́пера Ве́рди «Оте́лло» …
Са́ша	Но она́ уже́ была́ с тобо́й в Большо́м на о́пере «Князь И́горь» – я ду́маю, что она́ бы предпочла́ что́-нибудь поле́гче, посмешне́е … посмотри́, в Центра́льном теа́тре ку́кол идёт пье́са «Кот в сапога́х».
И́ра	Я уве́рена, что она́ бы сама́ вы́брала коме́дию, кото́рая идёт в теа́тре и́мени Го́голя.
Са́ша	Кака́я э́то коме́дия?
И́ра	Михаи́л Зо́щенко: «Уважа́емый това́рищ».
Са́ша	Да, И́рочка, мо́жет быть ты права́. Смешна́я пье́са, должно́ быть. Я э́то запи́сываю. А что ещё ты предлага́ешь?
И́ра	В Большо́м за́ле консервато́рии … игра́ет симфони́ческий орке́стр, а в Музыка́льном теа́тре идёт бале́т «Снегу́рочка».

Са́ша	Гм! на конце́рте симфони́ческого орке́стра бы́ло бы немно́жко ску́чно, а бале́т, по-мо́ему, ей о́чень понра́вился бы. Э́то бале́т на му́зыку Чайко́вского, не пра́вда ли?
И́ра	Пра́вильно.
Са́ша	Хорошо́ … я постара́юсь доста́ть биле́ты и́ли на коме́дию «Уважа́емый това́рищ» и́ли на бале́т «Снегу́рочка», на четве́рг.
И́ра	Всё пра́вильно. Жела́ю тебе́ успе́ха.
Са́ша	Спаси́бо … да, действи́тельно, бы́ло бы лу́чше, е́сли бы мы об э́том поду́мали пора́ньше.
И́ра	Да, э́то пра́вда. Мы должны́ бы́ли бы доста́ть биле́ты до э́того. Ничего́. Бу́дем наде́яться на лу́чшее. Позвони́ мне, как то́лько доста́нешь биле́ты!

> **LANGUAGE TIP**
>
> Remember how to use **в** and **на** – you usually use **на** for events and **в** for places (+ accusative for motion; + prepositional for position): **пойти́ на о́перу / в теа́тр** *to go to see an opera / to the theatre*; **в Большо́м на о́пере** *at the Bolshoi theatre at the opera*.

> **LANGUAGE TIP**
>
> **Как то́лько** *As soon as*: Remember that in English this can hide a future meaning – *I will ring you as soon as I (will) get the tickets*. In such as a case, the verb must be in the future tense in Russian: **Я тебе́ позвоню́, как то́лько доста́ну биле́ты**.

2 True or false?

a Anna will be free on Tuesday evening.

b Sasha thinks that the lecture on art will be boring.

c Ira doesn't have the latest edition of 'What's on in Moscow'.

d 'Respected Colleague' is a comedy.

e 'Snow Maiden' has music by Tchaikovsky.

f Sasha thinks that it will be difficult to get tickets for Thursday.

3 Answer the following questions.

a Когда́ А́нна бу́дет свобо́дна?

b Что идёт в Большо́м теа́тре?

c В како́м теа́тре идёт «Кот в сапога́х»?

d Почему́ Са́ша не хо́чет пойти́ на конце́рт в консервато́рию?

e Когда́ Са́ша до́лжен позвони́ть И́ре?

Language discovery

DIMINUTIVE FORMS OF NAMES

When Sasha addresses Ira as **Ирочка** he is using a diminutive form of her name. Spoken Russian makes considerable use of diminutive forms. Sometimes the diminutive indicates affection or endearment: thus, for example, **мать** *mother* becomes **ма́ма**, **мам** or **ма́мочка**. The use of diminutives is frequent with first names.

 1 Can you match the following diminutives with the full form of the names? Some names have more than one form of diminutive – the number in brackets shows how many you are looking for.

Full name		Diminutives				
Алекса́ндр (5)	**1**	Бо́ренька	**8**	Ири́ша	**15**	О́ленька
Бори́с (2)	**2**	Бо́ря	**9**	И́рочка	**16**	О́ля
Влади́мир (4)	**3**	Во́ва	**10**	Ле́на	**17**	Са́ша
Еле́на (3)	**4**	Во́вочка	**11**	Ле́нка	**18**	Са́шка
Ири́на (3)	**5**	Воло́денька	**12**	Ле́ночка	**19**	Са́шенька
Ната́лья (2)	**6**	Воло́дя	**13**	Ната́ша	**20**	Шу́ра
О́льга (2)	**7**	И́ра	**14**	Ната́шенька	**21**	Шу́рочка

Requests and statements which use diminutives sound gentler, because they tend to imply that the request is only a small one or that the opinion is not too harsh. Some useful diminutives in this context are:

Да́йте, пожа́луйста, кусо́чек сы́ра	*Give me a piece of cheese, please* (**кусо́к** *a piece*)
Бы́ло немно́жко ску́чно	*It was a bit boring* (**немно́го** *a little*)

The diminutive of nouns is commonly used when talking with or about children; the most common diminutive ending for masculine nouns is **-ик** and for feminine nouns **-ка** or **-очка**.

КОТО́РЫЙ

 2 Look at the following examples and try to work out what the word который means in English.

О́льга, кото́рая рабо́тает в музе́е, на пять лет ста́рше меня́.

О́льга, кото́рую вы уже́ зна́ете, рабо́тает в музе́е.

О́льга, с кото́рой вы познако́мились на ле́кции, приласи́ла нас в теа́тр.

Музей, который находится в центре, открывается в 10 часов.

There is always a comma before **который**, and its endings work like those of an adjective.

3 **There are two things to remember when deciding on the ending for который. Again, looking at the examples, can you work out what these two things are? Translating the sentences into English will help.**

> **LANGUAGE TIP**
>
> Remember that in deciding the ending to put on который, look (1) back to decide whether it is masculine, feminine, neuter, singular or plural; (2) forward to decide on the case.

Take care not to confuse **который** and **какой** – as **какой** means *which* or *what* but is only used in questions and exclamations:

В каком театре идёт «Снегурочка»?	*At which theatre is the 'Snow Maiden' on?*
Какая интересная пьеса!	*What an interesting play!*

SOFT ADJECTIVES

We know that if the stem of an adjective ends in **г, к, х, ж, ч, ш** or **щ**, the masculine singular ending is never **-ый**, but **-ий**. However, there is also a small group of soft adjectives which have soft endings for all genders and cases. The nominative forms of a soft adjective are:

Masc. sing.	**последний номер**	*the last edition*
Fem. sing.	**последняя опера**	*the last opera*
Neut. sing.	**последнее письмо**	*the last letter*
Plural	**последние билеты**	*the last tickets*

4 **Complete the table.**

	Masc.	Fem.	Neut.	Pl.
Nom.	**синий**	**синяя**	**синее**	**синие**
Acc.	**синий/его**	**синюю**	**син _____**	**синие/их**
Gen.	**син _____**	**синей**	**син _____**	**син _____**
Dat.	**синему**	**син _____**	**син _____**	**синим**
Instr.	**синим**	**син _____**	**син _____**	**синими**
Prep.	**синем**	**син _____**	**син _____**	**синях**

Many soft adjectives are connected with time, e.g.:

весе́нний	*spring*
вече́рний	*evening*
дре́вний	*ancient*
зи́мний	*winter*
ле́тний	*summer*
осе́нний	*autumn*
по́здний	*late*
ра́нний	*early*
сего́дняшний	*today's*

A number of soft adjectives deal with location – e.g. on a long-distance train: **ве́рхняя/ни́жняя по́лка** *upper/lower bunk*, **сосе́днее купе́** *neighbouring compartment*, **дома́шний** *domestic/home.*

CONDITIONAL

 5 The following sentences contain what is known as the conditional – can you work out how this is formed in Russian and work out the meaning in English?

Бы́ло бы лу́чше пригласи́ть её в теа́тр

Она́ бы предпочла́ что́-нибудь поле́гче

Она́ сама́ вы́брала бы коме́дию

Бы́ло бы немно́жко ску́чно

In Russian, there is only one form of the conditional (i.e. the same form covers *would*, *would be*, *would have*). It is formed very simply, by adding **бы** to the past tense of the verb:

Я прочита́л[а] бы газе́ту …	*I would read the paper …*
Она́ чу́вствовала бы себя́ лу́чше …	*She would be feeling better …*
Он купи́л бы биле́ты …	*He would have bought the tickets …*

Бы usually follows the verb, but this is not a strict rule; it can follow any word in the sentence which requires special emphasis.

Note how Russian deals with conditions introduced by *if*. Where a condition is still possible, you simply use the appropriate tense and do not use **бы** at all:

Éсли + future …	+ future
If I buy (i.e. will buy) tickets,	*I will ring you*
Éсли я куплю биле́ты,	**я позвоню́ тебе́**

However, when the condition introduced by *if* is not, or is no longer, possible, then the conditional must be used both after **éсли** and in the other part of the sentence:

Éсли + conditional	+ conditional
If he had bought the tickets,	*he would have rung you*
Éсли бы он купи́л биле́ты,	**он позвони́л бы тебе́**

CAM *SELF*

The Russian for *self* is **сам/сама́/само́/са́ми** and has different case endings, in the same way as **э́тот** *this*. **Сам/сама́/само́/са́ми** is used to emphasize pronouns or nouns, stressing that one particular person is indicated and no other:

Она́ сама́ вы́брала бы …	*She herself would choose …*
Она позвони́ла самому́ дире́ктору	*She rang the director himself*

Practice

1 Choose the appropriate form of кото́рый from the list to complete the sentences.

кото́рого	кото́рой	кото́ром
кото́рую	кото́рый	кото́рыми

a Пиани́ст, _____ даёт конце́рт в большо́м за́ле консервато́рии, изве́стен во всём ми́ре.

b Пье́са, о _____ вы говори́те, не о́чень смешна́я.

c Теа́тр, в _____ идёт о́пера «Князь И́горь», о́чень ста́рый.

d Актёр, _____ мы смотре́ли вчера́, непло́хо игра́л роль кня́зя.

e Тури́стам, с _____ мы бы́ли в теа́тре, о́чень понра́вился бале́т.

f Балери́на, _____ вы о́чень лю́бите, действи́тельно тала́нтлива.

2 **Look at this extract from a theatre's calendar and complete the statements that follow.**

ПЕРМСКИЙ ТЕАТР "У МОСТА"

19-й театральный сезон

РЕПЕРТУАР НА НОЯБРЬ 2015 ГОДА

Ф.М. ДОСТОЕВСКИЙ

ПРЕМЬЕРА

ПРЕСТУПЛЕНИЕ И НАКАЗАНИЕ

15 воскресенье, начало в 14:00 и в 18:00.

16 понедельник, начало в 18:00.

17 вторник, начало в 19:00.

Версия театра "У МОСТА"

продолжительность 2.50

режиссер-постановщик С.ФЕДОТОВ

a The extract gives information about the month of _____.

b This is the theatre's _____ season.

c The play to be performed on 15th, 16th, 17th is based on a novel by _____.

d On Tuesday 17th the play begins at _____.

3 **Which activity would you choose under the following circumstances? Write a sentence for each one, as in the example.**

a Éсли бы вы бы́ли свобо́дны по́сле обе́да, что бы вы де́лали?

   1 игра́ть в футбо́л

   2 де́лать поку́пки

   3 смотре́ть телеви́зор

b Éсли бы у вас бы́ло мно́го де́нег, что бы вы сде́лали?

   1 купи́ть но́вую маши́ну

   2 купи́ть пода́рки друзья́м

   3 купи́ть но́вый дом

c Éсли бы вы плóхо чýвствовали себя, что бы вы сдéлали?

   1 пожáловаться дрýгу

   2 пойтѝ в поликлѝнику

   3 пойтѝ на хоккéйный матч

d Éсли бы вы потеряли собáку, что бы вы сдéлали?

   1 купѝть кóшку

   2 позвонѝть в полицéйский учáсток (*police station*)

   3 пойти в кино

a **<u>Éсли бы я был[á] свобóден[свобóдна] пóсле обéда, я бы смотрéл[а] телевѝзор.</u>**

4 Make up dialogues explaining which activity/entertainment you prefer.

– **Что вы лю́бите бóльше, чтéние (✓), спорт или покýпки?**

– **Бóльше всегó я люблю́ чтéние.**

Now make up similar dialogues for each set of pictures:

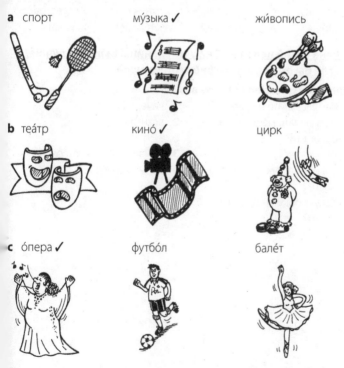

a спорт   мýзыка ✓   жѝвопись

b теáтр   кинó ✓   цирк

c óпера ✓   футбóл   балéт

совет	*advice*
библиотекарша	*librarian*
энергичный	*energetic*
гимнаст	*gymnast*
творческий	*creative*
шофёр	*driver*
техник	*technician*
адвокат	*solicitor*

 5 **Read the information given about each person and their present job. Write sentences explaining what sort of job would be better for each one.**

	Кто?	Какой это человек?	Профессия	Совет
a	Лена	тихий	учительница	библиотекарша
b	Виктор	не очень энергичный	гимнаст	администратор
c	Вадим	творческий	шофёр	журналист
d	Наташа	добрый, энергичный	техник	медсестра
e	Миша	очень серьёзный	футболист	адвокат

a **<u>Лена тихий человек. Она учительница. Было бы лучше, если бы она работала библиотекаршей.</u>**

6 **Match the question with the answer.**

a Как вы ездите на работу?   **1** вечернюю

b Чем вы занимаетесь по субботам?   **2** летнюю

c Какую газету он читает?   **3** домашним хозяйством

d Какой галстук он обычно носит?   **4** ранним автобусом

e Какую юбку она обычно носит?   **5** синий

Listen and understand

ряд	*row*
кака́я глу́пость!	*how stupid!*
надева́ть/наде́ть	*to put on*
очки́	*glasses*
всё в поря́дке	*everything is in order*
повнима́тельнее	*a bit more carefully*
(внима́тельный)	*(attentive, careful)*
роль (f.)	*role*
антра́кт	*interval*
сто́ит посмотре́ть	*it is worth watching*

16.03 *Boris has found his seat at the theatre and is waiting for the play to begin.*

1 Why does the person he is sitting next to want to borrow his programme?

Де́вушка	Извини́те, пожа́луйста, како́е э́то ме́сто?
Бори́с	Со́рок пя́тое.
Де́вушка	Прости́те, но э́то моё ме́сто. Я ду́маю, что вы оши́блись ме́стом.
Бори́с	Мину́точку … мо́жет быть я и оши́бся … вот мой биле́т … восьмо́й ряд, со́рок шесто́е ме́сто … Ой, прости́те, вы пра́вы.
Де́вушка	Ничего́, ничего́. Э́то нева́жно.
Бори́с	Кака́я глу́пость! Я до́лжен был бы наде́ть очки́.
Де́вушка	Не беспоко́йтесь. Тепе́рь всё в поря́дке.
Бори́с	Но бы́ло бы лу́чше, е́сли бы я повнима́тельнее посмотре́л на биле́т.
Де́вушка	Пожа́луйста, не беспоко́йтесь. Ведь э́то нева́жно … А вы не зна́ете, кто в ро́ли Ма́ши сего́дня ве́чером? Я купи́ла бы програ́мму, е́сли бы зна́ла, где.
Бори́с	Пожа́луйста, вот моя́ посмотри́те … програ́мма …
Де́вушка	Спаси́бо, вы о́чень добры́.
Бори́с	Не́ за что.
Де́вушка	Как хорошо́! Игра́ет Жу́кова!
Бори́с	Жу́кова? Я её не зна́ю …

Де́вушка	О́чень да́же тала́нтливая актри́са, кото́рая так хорошо́ игра́ла О́лю в фи́льме «Ле́тним у́тром». Вы, должно́ быть, зна́ете э́тот фильм?
Бори́с	Нет, не зна́ю. Я не о́чень ча́сто хожу́ в кинотеа́тр.
Де́вушка	Почему́?
Бори́с	Ну, не зна́ю … немно́жко ску́чно.
Де́вушка	Вы мно́го теря́ете. Е́сли вы хоти́те, я объясню́ вам в антра́кте, каки́е фи́льмы сто́ит посмотре́ть.

2 Choose the correct option to complete the following sentences.

a Бори́с ошибся

1 ря́дом

2 теа́тром внима́тельно

3 число́м

4 ме́стом

b Бори́с до́лжен был бы

1 прочита́ть всю програ́мму

2 посмотре́ть на биле́т бо́лее внима́тельнее

3 наде́ть га́лстук

4 бы́стро посмотре́ть на биле́т

c Де́вушка ду́мает, что

1 Жу́кова о́чень хоро́шая актри́са

2 Жу́кова неталантливая актри́са

3 не сто́ит смотре́ть фильм «Ле́тним у́тром»

4 в кинотеа́тре немно́жко ску́чно

> **LANGUAGE TIP**
>
> It is worth learning the perfective past tense of the verb **ошиба́ться/ошиби́ться** *to be mistaken, to be wrong about something*: **он ошибся**, **она́ оши́блась**, **они́ оши́блись**; the instrumental case is needed to explain what you are mistaken/ wrong about.

Reading and writing

вещь (f.)	*thing*
в тече́ние (+ genitive)	*during*
го́рдость (f.)	*pride*
ежего́дно	*annually*
за́пись (f.)	*entry*
на том же ме́сте	*in the very same place*
но́ты	*(sheet) music*

па́мять (f.)	*memory, remembrance* (here: anniversary of his death)
«Пи́ковая да́ма»	*'Queen of Spades'*
попада́ть/попа́сть	*to turn up, to find oneself*
посети́тель (m.)	*visitor*
при жи́зни компози́тора	*in the composer's lifetime*
проводи́ть/провести́	*to spend (time)*
роя́ль (m.)	*grand piano*
свое́й жи́зни	*of his life*
сла́ва	*glory, fame*
сно́ва	*again*
«Спя́щая краса́вица»	*'Sleeping Beauty'*
станови́ться/стать (+ instrumental)	*to become*
стари́нный	*ancient*
умира́ть/умере́ть (past tense: **у́мер, умерла́**)	*to die*

16.04 Read and listen to the text, then answer the questions that follow in English.

Седьмо́го ма́я 1840-ого го́да роди́лся ма́льчик, кото́рый стал го́рдостью и сла́вой ру́сской музыка́льной культу́ры – Пётр Ильи́ч Чайко́вский. Вели́кий музыка́нт у́мер в октябре́ 1893-ого го́да. Ему́ бы́ло пятьдеся́т три го́да.

Дом-музе́й П.И.Чайко́вского нахо́дится в Клину́, стари́нном го́роде в 80 киломе́трах от Москвы́. В Клину́ вели́кий ру́сский компози́тор провёл после́дние де́вять лет свое́й жи́зни, в тече́ние кото́рых он написа́л, наприме́р, о́перу «Пи́ковая да́ма», бале́т «Спя́щая краса́вица», симфо́нии («Манфред», Пя́тую и Шесту́ю). Ежего́дно дом-музе́й принима́ет сто ты́сяч посети́телей. Традицио́нно днём откры́тия музе́я счита́ется 9 декабря́ 1894-ого го́да – да́та пе́рвой за́писи в кни́ге регистра́ции посети́телей. Когда́ вхо́дишь в э́тот ста́рый дом, ка́жется, что попада́ешь в про́шлое … Ка́ждая вещь – но́ты, кни́ги, портре́ты, ме́бель – на том же ме́сте, что и при жи́зни компози́тора. Роя́ль всё ещё занимает центральное место кабинета-гостиной. Два раза в год – в день рождения композитора и в день его памяти – известные пианисты снова играют на этом рояле.

(Дом-музей П.И.Чайковского в Клину)

a What happened on 7 May 1840?
b How old was Tchaikovsky when he died?
c How long did he live in Klin?
d How many people visit the museum every year?
e Why is it generally considered that the museum first opened in October 1894?
f Why do visitors feel that they are going back into the past when they enter the museum?
g When is Tchaikovsky's grand piano used nowadays?

 # Speaking

 16.05 Can you remember how to say the following in Russian? Listen to the audio and practise saying each phrase.

a Let's hope for the best.
b When will she be free?
c It would be better …
d Isn't that right?
e It would be a bit boring.

Test yourself

1 Which Russian word do you need to use to translate *which, what* in questions and exclamations?

2 Do you need adjective or noun endings for the word кото́рый *who, which*?

3 Which tense follows е́сли when what you are talking about is still possible?

4 Which tense follows е́сли when what you are talking about is no longer possible?

5 Which case would you use with ошиба́ться/ошиби́ться to say that you are wrong about something?

6 How would you say *I myself prefer …*?

7 What does the verb сто́ить usually mean? And what does it mean in the following sentence? По-мо́ему, не сто́ит покупа́ть биле́ты на э́ту пье́су.

8 Which preposition do you use if you are buying tickets *for* an event?

9 Which pronoun would you use when talking to someone you have not met before?

10 What do the phrases мо́жет быть and должно́ быть mean?

SELF CHECK

I CAN...
… express my opinion about arrangements and events.
… indicate preference in arrangements.
… express hopes and intentions about arrangements.
… make hypothetical statements.
… express statements contrary to fact.

Дава́й загля́нем в бюро́ путеше́ствий

Let's pop into the travel agent's

In this unit you will learn how to:

▶ *talk about holidays and holiday accommodation.*
▶ *talk about what is best and most comfortable.*
▶ *give more information in the negative.*

CEFR: (B2) *Can express his/her ideas and opinions with precision; can explain a problem which has arisen and make it clear that the provider of the service must make a concession.*

Óтпуск *Holiday/leave*

This is the word for *annual holiday/leave from work*, as distinct from *school holidays* (**кани́кулы**) and *holiday* in the general sense of rest, relaxation from work (**о́тдых**). Since the fall of the Soviet Union, many more Russians are going on holiday abroad, enjoying exactly the same seaside resorts and cultural hotspots as their Western European neighbours.

With their Mediterranean climate and spectacular scenery, resorts on the Black Sea Coast remain a popular holiday destination. Moscow and St Petersburg attract both Russian and foreign tourists, with a wide choice of hotels and other places to stay. Many Russians will spend not only holidays but also weekends out of town at the family **да́ча**, which these days can be anything from a modest wooden cottage to a palatial country residence. In modern Russian hotels (**гости́ницы** or **оте́ли**) the tourist can expect the same customer service arrangements as anywhere else in the world. The main reception desk deals with most queries, and most hotels also now having a concierge service. Note that, in Russia, the **пе́рвый эта́ж** (lit. *first floor*) is the *ground floor*, **второ́й эта́ж** (lit. *second floor*) is the *first floor* and so on.

Match up the following popular holiday destinations.

1 Ту́рция	**2** Кипр	**3** Ита́лия	**4** Финля́ндия
5 Испа́ния	**6** А́нглия	**7** Фра́нция	**8** Чёрное мо́ре

a Cyprus	**b** Finland	**c** Turkey	**d** Italy
e France	**f** Black Sea	**g** Spain	**h** England

Vocabulary builder

17.01 Complete the missing English expressions. Then listen to the audio and repeat the Russian until you can say all the words with confidence.

НА́ДО ЗНАТЬ! *ESSENTIALS*

ка́шлять	*to (have a) cough*
вот что беспоко́ит меня́	*that's what's worrying _____*
ка́шель (m.)	*a _____*
тебе́ ну́жно отдохну́ть (отдыха́ть/отдохну́ть)	*_____ need a holiday*
одна́ (оди́н)	*alone* (lit. _____)
реша́ть/реши́ть	*to decide*
лу́чший	*best*
слы́шать/услы́шать (2nd conjugation)	*to hear*
выле́чиваться/вы́лечиться	*to be cured, recover*
дава́й загля́нем	*let's pop into*
душ	*_____*
спра́шивать/спроси́ть	*to ask*
усло́вие	*condition*
лече́ние	*(medical) treatment*

ТУРИ́СТУ НА́ДО ЗНАТЬ *TOURIST ESSENTIALS*

мне не́ с кем пое́хать	*_____ no one to go with*
о́тпуск	*_____*
куро́рт	*resort*
мя́гкий кли́мат	*mild _____*
морско́й во́здух	*_____ air*
мо́ре	*_____*
са́мые комфорта́бельные	*the most _____*
гости́ницы	*_____*
экзоти́ческий	*_____*

бюро́ путеше́ствий	travel _____
авиабиле́т	_____
зака́зывать/заказа́ть	to book
но́мер на двои́х	a _____ room

Dialogue

 17.02 *Ira's mother has not been well, and Ira is trying to persuade her to take a holiday.*

1   Where do Ira and her mother decide to go?

И́ра	Ма́ма, как ты себя́ чу́вствуешь сего́дня? Тебе́ лу́чше?
Ма́ма	Немно́жко. И́ра, не беспоко́йся обо мне. Я немно́жко уста́ла, и всё.
И́ра	Но ты всё вре́мя ка́шляешь, вот что беспоко́ит меня́ …
Ма́ма	Тебе́ не́ о чем беспоко́иться, ведь ка́шель ско́ро пройдёт.
И́ра	Наде́юсь … но слу́шай, ма́ма, тебе́ ну́жно отдохну́ть. Ты уже́ поду́мала об о́тпуске? Куда́ ты пое́дешь?
Ма́ма	Никуда́ не пое́ду.
И́ра	Не понима́ю, а почему́?
Ма́ма	Мне не́ с кем пое́хать в о́тпуск, а е́хать одна́ не хочу́.
И́ра	Ма́мочка, э́то не пра́вда … Ведь у меня́ ско́ро бу́дет о́тпуск. Я с удово́льствием пое́ду с тобо́й в Со́чи …
Ма́ма	… Ага́, всё поня́тно. Зна́чит ты уже́ реши́ла, куда́ мы пое́дем? Ну, скажи́, како́й э́то куро́рт?
И́ра	Да, я слы́шала, что Со́чи – э́то лу́чший куро́рт, е́сли хо́чешь и отдохну́ть и вы́лечиться. Там мя́гкий кли́мат и морско́й во́здух, тёплое мо́ре и са́мые комфорта́бельные гости́ницы, экзоти́ческие рестора́ны … и
Ма́ма	Зна́чит, ты уже́ была́ в бюро́ путеше́ствий?
И́ра	Да, оди́н раз то́лько … а за́втра у́тром я бу́ду свобо́дна, е́сли …
Ма́ма	Ну, ла́дно, дава́й загля́нем в бюро́ путеше́ствий за́втра у́тром. Спро́сим об авиабиле́тах.
И́ра	Хорошо́! Зака́жем но́мер на двои́х, … с ду́шем, коне́чно … на две неде́ли в гости́нице «Дагомы́с».
Ма́ма	Э́то лу́чшая гости́ница, что ли?

224

Йра
Коне́чно! … Вот у меня́ в су́мке брошю́ра … «Дагомы́с – туристи́ческий центр на Чёрном мо́ре, отли́чные усло́вия для тури́зма, о́тдыха и лече́ния».

> **LANGUAGE TIP**
>
> In the dialogue **вот** is used with **что** to give emphasis to Ira's concerns (*that's what …*).
> You can also use **вот** with *why*: **вот почему́ он не хоте́л купи́ть биле́ты!** *that's why he didn't want to buy the tickets!*

2 True or false?
   a Ira is worried about her mother.
   b Her mother wants to go on holiday on her own.
   c Ira wants to go to Novosibirsk.
   d Ira will be free tomorrow morning.
   e Ira doesn't know anything about the hotel 'Dagomys'.

3 Answer the following questions.
   a Как ма́ма себя́ чу́вствует сего́дня?
   b Что ей ну́жно?
   c Кто мо́жет пое́хать с ма́мой в о́тпуск?
   d Како́й куро́рт Йра вы́брала (*choose*)?
   e Когда́ они пойду́т в бюро́ путеше́ствий?

Language discovery

SUPERLATIVE

1 The following sentences contain adjectives in the superlative form. Can you work out how this is formed in Russian and what these sentences mean?

Э́то са́мый краси́вый куро́рт в Ита́лии.

Э́то са́мая комфорта́бельная гости́ница на куро́рте.

Э́то са́мые интере́сные па́мятники в стране́.

The superlative in English is formed by using *most* with an adjective or by adding *-est* to an adjective: *the most expensive hotel, the dearest hotel*. In Russian the superlative is formed by using the adjective **са́мый** in front of the adjective you wish to make superlative.

This applies to all adjectives in Russian, apart from a very small number: *big/small*, *good/bad*, *old/young*, *high/low*. For these exceptions, the superlative can be formed in any of the following ways:

using **са́мый** + ordinary adjective: Э́то са́мая хоро́шая
                                              гости́ница

using **са́мый** + comparative adjective: Э́то са́мая лу́чшая
                                              гости́ница

using just the comparative adjective: Э́то лу́чшая гости́ница

All three variants mean: *This is the best hotel.*

If you want to say *This is one of the best hotels*, **из** + genitive must be used:

Э́то одна́ из лу́чших гости́ниц   *This is one of the best hotels*

> **LANGUAGE TIP**
>
> For the comparative, the endings of **бо́лее** *more* or **ме́нее** *less* never change (see Unit 14). For the superlative, the endings of **са́мый** *most* do change to agree with the noun they are describing:
>
> **Э́то бо́лее комфорта́бельная гости́ница**
> **Э́то са́мая комфорта́бельная гости́ница**

БЕСПОКО́ИТЬ(СЯ)/ПОБЕСПОКО́ИТЬ(СЯ) *TO BE/MAKE ANXIOUS*

Note how this verb is used reflexively (i.e. with the endings **-сь**, **-ся**) when it means *to worry* in the sense of *to be anxious*. When it means *to worry* in the sense of *to make (someone/something) anxious*, it must be used without the reflexive endings.

YOUR TURN (Да́вайте)

2 What do the following two sentences mean?

Йра беспоко́ится о ма́ме.   Ка́шель беспоко́ит её.

This use of the reflexive applies to a number of common verbs (e.g. *to begin*, *to finish*, *to return*).

YOUR TURN (Да́вайте)

3 What do the following two sentences mean?

Ле́кция начина́ется в семь   Он всегда́ начина́ет ле́кцию
часо́в ве́чера.   шу́ткой.

NEGATIVES

We have already met a group of negative expressions which all begin with **ни-** and which are all used with **не** + verb.

4 So, how would you translate the following sentences?

Я никуда́ не пое́ду в о́тпуск.   Я ничего́ не зна́л(а) об э́той гости́нице.

Никому́ не говори́те об э́том!

In this unit we have seen different negative expressions, for example:

Тебе́ не́ о чем беспоко́иться   *There is nothing for you to worry about*

This type of negative is always followed by an infinitive (*nothing to worry about*) and starts with **не́**.

5 Can you match the following Russian sentences with their English translation?

a	Не́где рабо́тать.	**1**	There is nothing to drink.
b	Не́куда идти́.	**2**	There is no time to watch TV.
c	Не́когда смотре́ть телеви́зор.	**3**	There is nowhere to work.
d	Не́чего пить.	**4**	There is no one to invite to supper.
e	Не́кого приглаша́ть на у́жин.	**5**	There is nowhere to go.

If you want to say, for example, *I have no time to watch the television/there is no time for me to watch the television*, simply use the dative of **я**, *for me*:

Мне не́когда смотре́ть телеви́зор.

Note that **не́что** and **(не́)кто** must be used in the correct case form. If a preposition is used with them, it splits them up:

Ива́ну не́ на что жа́ловаться   *Ivan has nothing to complain about*

Мне не́ с кем говори́ть   *I've no one to talk to*

> **LANGUAGE TIP**
>
> A negative starting with:
> ▶ **ни-** is followed by **не** and a verb in a tense
> ▶ **не́-** is followed by an infinitive.
> **Она́ никогда́ не звони́т мне:**   *She never rings me. She's got no time to talk*
> **ей не́когда говори́ть**

GENERALIZING STATEMENTS

If you want to make a general statement where you might use *you* in English (or, in a previous age, *one*), Russian can use the **ты** or **вы** form of the verb without the pronouns **ты** or **вы**:

если хо́чешь [хоти́те] отдохну́ть …

if you wish (one wishes) to have a rest/holiday …

Practice

1 Match the questions with the answers.

a	Куда́ вы пое́дете в о́тпуск?	**1**	На две неде́ли
b	Како́й э́то куро́рт?	**2**	В Оде́ссу
c	Где вы обы́чно отдыха́ете?	**3**	С ва́нной и с телефо́ном
d	На ско́лько неде́ль?	**4**	Са́мый краси́вый в Росси́и
e	Како́й но́мер вы хоти́те заказа́ть?	**5**	На бе́регу мо́ря (*at the seaside*)

выходно́й	*day off*
вы́бор	*choice*
гора́	*mountain*
мечта́	*dream*
побере́жье	*coast*

2 Look at the advertisement, then complete the statements that follow.

a This company offers a large choice of _____ and apartments.

b Holidays can be spent either by the sea or _____.

c Holidays are offered in the following countries: _____, _____, _____, United Arab Emirates (ОАЭ), _____, _____, Czech Republic (Чехия).

3 **You're feeling enthusiastic about your holiday plans! Answer the questions according to the model.**

a Кака́я э́то гости́ница? (комфорта́бельная)

b Како́й э́то куро́рт? (прия́тный)

c Ка́ко́й э́то по́езд? (бы́стрый)

d Како́й э́то кли́мат? (мя́гкий)

e Кака́я э́то програ́мма? (интере́сный)

f Како́е э́то зда́ние? (краси́вый)

Э́то самая комфорта́бельная гости́ница в стране́.

4 **Look at the list, then make up sentences explaining why none of the people are able to do the things listed (think about which forms of не́что and не́кто will be needed).**

Кто?	Заня́тие	Почему́ нельзя́?
a Ива́н	пойти́ в теа́тр за́втра	не́кто/с
b На́дя	смотре́ть телеви́зор	не́когда
c Ва́ля	писа́ть письмо́	не́что
d Бори́с	идти́ сего́дня ве́чером	не́куда
e Мари́на	рабо́тать	не́где
f И́горь	жа́ловаться	не́что/на
g Со́ня	подари́ть кни́гу	не́кто

a **Ива́ну не́ с кем пойти́ в теа́тр за́втра.**

Listen and understand

одея́ло	*blanket*
что́-нибудь	*anything*
почему́-то	*for some reason or other*
полоте́нце	*towel*
про́сьба	*request*

17.03 *Nina is having problems with her hotel room and has gone to Reception for help.*

1   What problems has Nina had?

Нина	Извините, пожалуйста …
Рецепшионист	Здравствуйте. Как вам помочь?
Нина	Я плохо спала ночью. У меня в номере холодно. Можно ещё одеяло?
Рецепшионист	Конечно … Вот, пожалуйста, возьмите.
Нина	Спасибо.
Рецепшионист	Пожалуйста. Ещё что-нибудь?
Нина	У меня в номере почему-то нет полотенца.
Рецепшионист	Ой, извините … вот вам полотенце. Всё, да?
Нина	Спасибо. Да, теперь всё в порядке … Только, знаете, телевизор не очень хорошо работает. Но это не очень важно.
Рецепшионист	Хорошо. Я сейчас пойду посмотрю.
Нина	А у меня ещё к вам просьба.
Рецепшионист	Пожалуйста.
Нина	Вы не можете заказать для меня такси?
Рецепшионист	Могу. На когда?
Нина	На послезавтра, на одиннадцать часов утра.
Рецепшионист	Куда хотите поехать?
Нина	В аэропорт.
Рецепшионист	Хорошо. Всё понятно. Я сейчас закажу.
Нина	Спасибо за помощь.
Рецепшионист	Не за что.

2   Choose the correct answer.

a Нина плохо спала, потому что
1 в номере жарко
2 номер близко от лифта
3 в номере холодно
4 в номере шумно (*noisy*)

b В номере нет
1 постели
2 телевизора
3 полотенца
4 телефона

c Нина хочет поехать в аэропорт
1 после завтрака
2 послезавтра
3 завтра
4 после обеда

Reading and writing

акти́вный	*active*
Балти́йское мо́ре	*Baltic Sea*
в окре́стностях (genitive)	*in the vicinity of*
ви́ндсерфинг	*windsurfing*
встре́ча	*meeting*
гора́	*mountain*
зака́нчивать(ся)/зако́нчить(ся)	*to finish*
Кавка́з	*Caucasus*
маршру́т	*route, itinerary*
насто́льный те́ннис	*table tennis*
незабыва́емый	*unforgettable*
не́который	*some, certain*
о́зеро	*lake*
па́русный спорт	*sailing*
похо́д	*trip, hike*
ры́бная ло́вля	*fishing*
се́верный	*northern*
теплохо́д	*ship*
тре́кинг по сиби́рской тайге́	*tracking in the Siberian taiga*
тур	*tour*
фестива́ль (m.) **иску́сств**	*arts festival*
фло́ра и фа́уна	*flora and fauna*
Эсто́ния	*Estonia*

Read the text, then answer the questions that follow in English.

Ру́сские бюро́ путеше́ствий предлага́ют все ви́ды путеше́ствий: самолётом, теплохо́дом и по́ездом, на авто́бусе и на автомоби́ле – на традицио́нные фестива́ли иску́сств, на о́тдых и лече́ние, организу́ют пое́здки для делов́ых люде́й – «би́знес-ту́ры», речны́е и морски́е круи́зы. Вот некото́рые из ту́ров и програ́мм, кото́рые предлага́ют ру́сские туропера́торы:

АВТО́БУСНЫЕ И АВТОМОБИ́ЛЬНЫЕ ТУ́РЫ И МАРШРУ́ТЫ

«Золото́е кольцо́ Росси́и» – четы́ре вариа́нта автобусных ту́ров по дре́вним ру́сским города́м: Се́ргиев Поса́д, Росто́в Вели́кий, Су́здаль, Влади́мир. Ту́ры начина́ются и зака́нчиваются в Москве́. «Большо́е Се́верное кольцо́» – путеше́ствие на автобусах из столи́цы Росси́и Москвы́ на се́веро-за́пад страны́ к Балти́йскому мо́рю в Санкт-Петербу́рг и да́лее в столи́цу и куро́ртные города́ Эсто́нии.

ТУ́РЫ «АКТИ́ВНЫЙ О́ТДЫХ»

«Тре́кинг по сиби́рской тайге́» – (5–7 дней) – в окре́стностях о́зера Байка́ла. В програ́мме 25-киломе́тровый похо́д – незабыва́емые встре́чи с фло́рой и фа́уной Сиби́ри. «Со́чи, Я́лта и Херсо́н» – спорти́вные заня́тия на куро́ртах Чёрного мо́ря – те́ннис, ви́ндсерфинг, па́русный спорт, ры́бная ло́вля, волейбо́л, баскетбо́л, насто́льный те́ннис, тури́стские похо́ды в го́ры Кавка́за и Кры́ма.

a Name the different types of transport used by Russian tour operators.

b What different types of tour do they organize?

c What is the starting point for the 'Golden Ring' tour?

d Which resorts are visited in the 'Great Northern Ring' tour?

e How long do the tracking holidays in Siberia last?

f Which different sporting activities are offered in the 'Sochi, Yalta, Kherson' tour?

LANGUAGE TIP

по + dative case is a useful preposition when talking about travel, and it can be translated in a number of ways into English:

по пути́ домо́й	*on the way home*
по Во́лге	*down the Volga*
по все́й стране́	*all over the country*

заполня́ть/запо́лнить бланк   *to fill in a form*

на второ́м этаже́   *on the first floor* (lit. *on the second floor*)

Speaking

1 17.04 You are trying to book a hotel room. Play your part, then listen to the complete conversation on the audio.

Администра́тор Вам помо́чь?

Вы   **a** *Say 'hello' and ask if there are any free rooms.*

Администра́тор Есть.

Вы   **b** *Say you want to book a room.*

Администра́тор Како́й но́мер вы хоти́те заказа́ть?

Вы   **c** *Say you want to book a single room with a shower, telephone and television.*

Администра́тор На ско́лько дней?

Вы   **d** *Say 'for five days, until* (до + genitive) *Friday'.*

Администра́тор Хорошо́. Но́мер 227 свобо́ден. Э́то на второ́м этаже́. Запо́лните, пожа́луйста, бланк.

Вы   **e** *Say 'thank you' and ask where you can get* (взять) *your key* (ключ).

Администра́тор У меня́, здесь.

2 17.05 Can you remember how to say the following in Russian? Listen to the audio and practise saying each phrase.

   a What sort of resort is it?
   b Where are you going on holiday?
   c It's the best hotel.
   d There is nothing to drink.
   e I want to book a room with a shower.

? Test yourself

1 In the following sentence, would you insert какой or который to complete the question *Which resort have you chosen?* _____ куро́рт вы вы́брали?

2 In the following sentence, would you insert нигде́ or не́где to complete the statement *I can't see Irina anywhere!* Я _____ не ви́жу Ири́ну!

3 Your hotel room doesn't have a towel. How would you ask for one?

4 If you ask someone where they are going on holiday, would you use где or куда́ for *where*?

5 You are told that your hotel room is на четвёртом этаже́. Which floor will you go to?

6 Complete the following phrase which means *in the most beautiful resort*: на _____ краси́вом куро́рте.

7 If someone says Не беспоко́йтесь! to you, what instruction are you being given?

8 Обе́д начина́ется в час *Lunch starts at one.* Why is the verb reflexive in this phrase?

9 Complete this phrase with the prepositional plural adjective endings: В сам _____ но́в _____ гости́ницах (in the newest hotels).

10 How would you say *I'd like to book a room, please*?

SELF CHECK

I CAN...

○	. . . talk about holidays and holiday accommodation.
○	. . . talk about what is best and most comfortable.
○	. . . give more information in the negative.

18 Что случи́лось?

What's happened?

In this unit you will learn how to:

▶ *ask what has happened.*
▶ *report on what has happened and what has been said.*
▶ *ask what is wrong.*
▶ *express concern and purpose.*

CEFR: (B1) *Can deal with most situations likely to arise while travelling in an area where the language is spoken; can describe experiences and events and briefly give reasons and explanations for opinions and plans; can express and respond to feelings.*

Driving in Russia

The number of cars on Russian roads has increased dramatically in the last few years, as has the choice of car available to Russian drivers. In the Soviet Union, buying a car was a very difficult business: you had to put your name on a waiting list and had a very limited choice of models. Nowadays, all the world's leading car manufacturers have outlets in Russia, including the most prestigious brands, and several produce vehicles there as well.

Traffic jams in all Russian towns and the large distances between towns mean that the car is still not always the best choice for travelling around. *Russian traffic police* (**ГАИ**) do not always have the best of reputations: they deal with accidents and with infringements of traffic regulations (for which they might impose an *on-the-spot fine*, **штраф**). A *traffic accident* is known as a **ДТП** (**доро́жно-тра́нспортное происше́ствие** – lit. *road traffic incident*) and these are, sadly, very common and often serious.

Match up these important words for a Russian car driver.

1	бензи́н	**2**	запа́сные ча́сти	**3**	запра́вочная ста́нция
4	ремо́нт	**5**	ста́нция техни́ческого обслу́живания		

a	repair	**b**	service station	**c**	spare parts
d	petrol	**e**	petrol station		

236

Vocabulary builder

18.01 Complete the missing English expressions. Then listen to the audio and repeat the Russian until you can say all the words with confidence.

НÁДО ЗНАТЬ! *ESSENTIALS*

где же	_____ on earth
что с тобóй?	what's the matter with _____ ?
ужáсно (ужáсный)	terrible, dreadful
чайкý (diminutive) хóчешь?	would you like some _____ ?
приносúть/принестú	to bring
расскажú! (расскáзывать/рассказáть)	tell (_____)
что случúлось? (случáться/случúться)	what happened? (_____)
произошлá (происходúть/произойтú)	happened (_____)
рáнен (рáненый)	hurt, injured
подбегáть/подбежáть	to run to
закричáл (кричáть/закричáть)	I/he shouted (_____)
чтóбы (+infinitive)	in order to
скóрая пóмощь	ambulance
полицейский	_____
увозúть/увезтú	to take away (by _____)
состоя́ние шóка	state of shock

НÁДО ЗНАТЬ: АВÁРИЯ *ACCIDENT ESSENTIALS*

авáрия	_____, crash
грузовúк	lorry
подъезжáть/подъéхать	to drive up to
перекрёсток	crossroads
останáвливать(ся)/остановúть(ся)	to stop
ударя́ть/удáрить	to strike, hit

Dialogue

18.02 *Anna is at Ira's flat. They are waiting for Volodya, who arrives late, looking pale and shaken.*

1 What has happened?

Йра	Ужé семь часóв! Где же Волóдя?!
Áнна	Надéюсь, что всё в порáдке.
Йра	*(Ring at the door.)* Наконéц!
Волóдя	Áнна, Йра, здрáвствуйте. Извинúте, что я пóздно пришёл.
Йра	Волóдя! Что с тобóй? Ты ужáсно выглядишь! Садúсь!
Волóдя	Спасúбо.
Áнна	Чайку хóчешь? Да? Я сейчáс принесу.
Йра	Ну, Волóдя, расскажú, что случúлось?
Волóдя	На улице произошлá авáрия. Я всё вúдел.
Йра	Бóже мой! Ты не рáнен, надéюсь?
Волóдя	Нет, нет.
Áнна	Вот тебé чай, Волóдя.
Волóдя	Спасúбо, Áнна … Вот … Я шёл по улице к стáнции метрó. Вдруг увúдел стáрую жéнщину, котóрая переходúла чéрез улицу. Онá не вúдела грузовикá, котóрый подъезжáл к перекрёстку …
Йра	Ой. Волóдя …
Волóдя	Я подбежáл к ней, закричáл, чтóбы останови́ть её, но онá не услышала меня. Грузовúк не смог останови́ться и удáрил её … Подбежáли лю́ди. Потóм скóрая пóмощь увезлá её в больнúцу …
Йра	Ужáсно!
Волóдя	Потóм, понимáете, я дóлжен был рассказáть полицéйскому обо всём, что вúдел … Он хотéл увезти́ меня в медпункт, сказáл, что я в состоя́нии шóка. Я не захотéл и сказáл, что позвоню́ в поликли́нику, éсли нáдо бýдет.

Verbs of motion have three forms of the past tense:

▶ **Он ходи́л** – *he used to go/walk; he has been going* (**ходи́ть** – habits; return journeys)
▶ **Он шёл** – *he was going* (**идти́** – one occasion, one direction)
▶ **Он пошёл** – *he has gone/set off* (**пойти́** – single action in the past).

2 True or false?

a Ira does not know where Volodya is.
b Ira says that Volodya is looking good.
c Volodya has been injured.
d A policeman asked Volodya to give a statement.
e Volodya went to the doctor's.

3 Answer the following questions.

a Как Воло́дя вы́глядит?
b Что А́нна предлага́ет ему́ вы́пить?
c Что де́лала ста́рая же́нщина, когда́ Воло́дя уви́дел её?
d Куда́ увезли́ ста́рую же́нщину?
e Воло́дя в како́м состоя́нии?

Language discovery

EMPHATIC PARTICLE ЖЕ

This is an emphatic particle – it gives an extra emphasis to a word in the sentence. In English this might be done just by the tone of voice or by adding some extra phrase such as *on earth*.

YOUR TURN (Дава́йте)

1 How would you translate the following into English?

Где же вы бы́ли?   **Когда́ же он пришёл? Кто же сказа́л э́то?**
Мы пое́дем сего́дня   **Я же вам говори́л[а]!**
же!

INDIRECT STATEMENT

This is the term used in English to describe reported statements (i.e. reports of what people have said).

 2 Reported statements in Russian work slightly differently than in English. Look at the following two examples and try to work out what this difference is, as well as translating them.

Полице́йский сказа́л, что я в состоя́нии шо́ка.

Я сказа́л, что я позвоню́ в поликли́нику.

We can see how reported statements work in English by comparing two direct speech and indirect speech sentences:

Direct speech

The policeman said, 'You are in a state of shock.'

I said, 'I will ring the clinic.'

Indirect speech

The policeman said I was in a state of shock.

I said I would ring the clinic.

As you can see, in English there is a change of tense between the direct and indirect statement (*you are → I was; I will → I would*). In Russian the tense in the indirect statement remains the same as it was in the direct statement (although, as in English, there may of course be some change of pronouns, e.g. *you are → I was*).

Direct speech

Полице́йский сказа́л: «Вы в состоя́нии шо́ка»

Я сказа́л: Я позвоню́ в поликли́нику

Indirect speech

Полице́йский сказа́л, что я в состоя́нии шо́ка

Я сказа́л, что я позвоню́ в поликли́нику

Note that in Russian the word **что** *that* always appears in indirect statements, preceded by a comma.

Here is an example of what happens when the direct statement involves the past tense – i.e. there is no change to the Russian verb, but the English verb changes from *didn't* to *hadn't*:

Direct:	**Я ничего не ви́дел**	*I didn't see anything!*
Indirect:	**Он сказа́л, что ничего́ не ви́дел.**	*He said he hadn't seen anything.*

PURPOSE

To say *in order to do something*, you need to use **что́бы**.

3 Looking at the following sentence, can you work out what happens to verbs used with что́бы and what this sentence means in English?

А́лла позвони́ла Ва́ле, что́бы узна́ть об ава́рии.

Notice that **что́бы** is always preceded by a comma (unless it is the first word in the sentence). English quite often says simply *to*, rather than *in order to*, but in Russian the only occasion when **что́бы** can be omitted is after a verb of motion:

Милиционе́р пришёл помо́чь же́нщине	*The policeman arrived to help the woman*

PREFIXED VERBS OF MOTION

We have already met a series of prefixes used with the verbs **-ходи́ть/-йти́**. The same prefixes (followed by the same prepositions) can be used with other verbs of motion and have the same meanings as with **-ходи́ть/йти́**.

4 Complete the meanings of the prefixed verbs of motion in the table.

Verb of motion	Meaning	Example of prefixed form	Meaning
-бе́гать/-бежа́ть	*to run*	**подбега́ть/подбежа́ть**	_____
-води́ть/-вести́	*to lead*	**вводи́ть/ввести́**	_____
-вози́ть/-везти́	*to transport*	**увози́ть/увезти́**	_____
-лета́ть/-лете́ть	*to fly*	**прилета́ть/прилете́ть**	_____
-носи́ть/-нести́	*to carry*	**приноси́ть/принести́**	_____
-плыва́ть/-плы́ть	*to swim, sail*	**отплыва́ть/отплы́ть**	_____

5 Note especially the prefixed forms of -езжа́ть/-е́хать. What do they mean?

подъезжа́ть/подъе́хать	(**к** + dat.)	_____
приезжа́ть/прие́хать	(**в** + acc.)	_____

переезжа́ть/перее́хать	(**че́рез** + acc.)	_____
выезжа́ть/вы́ехать	(**из** + gen.)	_____
уезжа́ть/уе́хать	(**из** + gen.)	_____
проезжа́ть/прое́хать	(**ми́мо** + gen.)	_____

> **LANGUAGE TIP**
>
> You have now met eight verbs of motion and nine prefixes, so you have the building blocks for many new verbs, e.g. to translate *to bring* in Russian, use the *arrive* prefix (**при-**) and the *carry* verbs (**-носи́ть/-нести́**): **Я принесу́ чай**.

ВСЁ, ЧТО ... *ALL THAT* ...

In order to say *everything which/that*, **что** preceded by a comma must be used:

обо всём, что случи́лось   *about everything that happened*

OBJECT OF A NEGATIVE VERB

6 In the dialogue, Volodya said Она́ не ви́дела грузовика́. Which case is used for the last word?

The genitive case may be used instead of the accusative after a negative verb. A useful everyday phrase is:

Я не обраща́л(а) внима́ния   *I wasn't paying attention*

Practice

ремо́нт	*repairs*
поворо́т	*bend, turn*
запрещён	*forbidden*
стоя́нка	*parking*

1 Match the sentences on the left with the traffic signs on the right.

a Ремо́нтные рабо́ты   **1**

b Поворот направо запрещён **2**

c Кемпинг **3**

d Пункт медицинской помощи **4**

e Место стоянки **5**

f Перекрёсток **6**

2 **Read the extract from the policeman's notebook and then write sentences based on the information given, reporting what the witness said.**

Полицейский	**Свидетель** (*witness*)
a Куда вы шли?	К станции метро
b Во сколько это было?	Это было часа в четыре
c Что вы видели?	Грузовик и старую женщину
d Что вы сделали?	Я подбежал к ней
e Как вы себя чувствуете сейчас?	Не очень хорошо
f Вы хотите поехать в медпункт?	Нет, не хочу

a **Свидетель сказал, что он шёл к станции метро.**

> **LANGUAGE TIP**
>
> In the previous exercise, an approximate time is given (*at about four o'clock*) by putting
> the unit of time first – **часá в четы́ре**. You can use this sort of inversion with other units
> of time, e.g.: **Мы жи́ли в Итáлии гóда три** *We lived in Italy for about three years.*

Великобритáния	*Great Britain*
крáжа	*theft*
фотоаппарáт	*camera*
фунт	*pound*

3 Read the police report, then answer the questions.

МВД

Управление внутренних дел
гор. Москва
20 отделение милиции
от 29 марта 2014г

Начальник 20 отделения милиции г. Москвы
/ Ка__ин В.Н.

СПРАВКА

ВЫ Дана гр. Великобритании Грин Амелии, прож.
в гостинице Можайская – 410 о том, что 28
марта 2014 года она обратилась в 20 отделение
милиции г. Москвы с заявлением по поводу
кражи из её номера следующих вещей

1 Фотоаппарат «Миранда»

2 30 фунтов стерлингов

3 5,000 рублей

---

a Where was Amelia Green staying?

b What items were stolen?

c Where were they stolen from?

d When did the theft occur?

4 **Complete the following description of Tamara's journey, using the prefixed forms of -езжать/-ехать.**

На про́шлой неде́ле Тама́ра _____ (*arrived*) в Псков на по́езде. Она́ _____ (*cross*) че́рез го́род на такси́. Они́ _____ (*drove out of*) из це́нтра го́рода и _____ (*drove past*) ми́мо ста́рых заво́дов. Наконе́ц такси́ _____ (*drove up to*) к гости́нице.

5 **Match the questions with the answers.**

a	Почему́ вы звони́те ей?	**1**	Пло́хо
b	Где произошла́ ава́рия?	**2**	Что́бы узна́ть, как дела́
c	Как вы себя́ чу́вствуете?	**3**	Полице́йскому
d	Что вы хоти́те купи́ть в апте́ке?	**4**	Недалеко́ от ста́нции метро́
e	Кому́ вы рассказа́ли обо всём э́том?	**5**	Табле́тки

6 **Read the passage about what happened to Petya yesterday, then answer the questions.**

Вчера́ по доро́ге на рабо́ту Пе́тя зашёл в универса́м. Поэ́тому (*therefore*) он по́здно пришёл на рабо́ту, часо́в в де́сять. Он пообе́дал в два часа́ в буфе́те и верну́лся на рабо́ту часа́ в три.

В четы́ре часа́ Ле́на позвони́ла ему́ и сказа́ла, что у неё два биле́та в кино́, ита́к (*and so*) вчера́ ве́чером они́ ходи́ли в кинотеа́тр.

По́сле фи́льма они́ поу́жинали в рестора́не и Пе́тя о́чень по́здно верну́лся (*to return*) домо́й … В результа́те он сего́дня ещё раз по́здно пришёл на рабо́ту … полоди́ннадцатого.

a Во ско́лько Пе́тя пришёл на рабо́ту вчера́?
b Во ско́лько он пообе́дал вчера́?
c Что он де́лал вчера́ ве́чером?
d Во ско́лько он пришёл на рабо́ту сего́дня?

Listen and understand

забыва́ть/забы́ть	*to forget* (here: *leave*)
зо́нтик	*umbrella*
опи́сывать/описа́ть	*to describe*
кошелёк	*purse*
косме́тика	*make-up*
вам везёт	*you are lucky/in luck*

18.03 *Marina is ringing the lost property office* (**бюро́ нахо́док**).

1 What two items is Marina trying to find?

Мари́на	Алло́? Бюро́ нахо́док?
Де́вушка	Да, слу́шаю.
Мари́на	Я забы́ла в кинотеа́тре «Ко́смос» зо́нтик и су́мку.
Де́вушка	Когда́?
Мари́на	Вчера́ ве́чером.
Де́вушка	Опиши́те, пожа́луйста, зо́нтик.
Мари́на	Но́вый, кра́сный.
Де́вушка	А су́мка како́го цве́та?
Мари́на	Чёрная.
Де́вушка	Что бы́ло в су́мке?
Мари́на	Кошелёк, па́спорт, косме́тика, чёрная ру́чка.
Де́вушка	Как ва́ша фами́лия?
Мари́на	Белоу́сова.
Де́вушка	Подожди́те. Я пойду́ посмотрю́…
Мари́на	Спаси́бо вам большо́е.
Де́вушка	… Вам везёт. Ва́ши ве́щи у нас. Приезжа́йте!
Мари́на	Я так ра́да! Когда́ лу́чше прие́хать?
Де́вушка	Сейча́с же, е́сли мо́жно. Ведь бюро́ закрыва́ется в 5 часо́в.
Мари́на	Спаси́бо большо́е. До свида́ния.
Де́вушка	Пожа́луйста. До свида́ния.

> **LANGUAGE TIP**
>
> **Ведь бюро́ закрыва́ется**: Like **же**, **ведь** is an emphatic particle, and is used to express a gentle warning, or to emphasize something the speaker finds surprising or very obvious. In English **ведь** might be expressed as, e.g., *you realize/know, after all, indeed* (or sometimes just by the tone of voice).

2 Complete the following sentences which summarize Marina's conversation in Russian.

a Мари́на забы́ла зо́нтик и су́мку в _____.

b Она́ звони́т в _____.

c Бюро́ закрыва́ется в _____.

d У неё _____ су́мка.

Reading and writing

война́	*war*
войска́ (n. pl.)	*troops, forces*
двoре́ц	*palace*
деревя́нный	*wooden*
гла́вный	*main*
Евро́па	*Europe*
импера́тор	*emperor*
кораблестрои́тель (m.)	*shipbuilder*
кре́пость (f.)	*fortress*
ли́чный	*personal*
Ме́дный вса́дник	*Bronze Horseman*
наводне́ние	*flood*
называ́ть/назва́ть	*to call, name*
окно́	*window*
осно́ван	*founded*
побежда́ть/победи́ть	*to conquer, vanquish*
полково́дец	*general*
сраже́ние	*battle*
среди́ (+ genitive)	*among*
удиви́тельный	*amazing, surprising*
фонта́н	*fountain*
шве́дский коро́ль	*Swedish king*
экспона́т	*exhibit*

Read the text, then answer the questions that follow in English.

Пётр I – удиви́тельный челове́к: ру́сский импера́тор, полково́дец, диплома́т и кораблестрои́тель, роди́лся в 1672 году́. Его́ де́тские го́ды прошли́ в Москве́.

В 1709 году́ под Полта́вой произошло́ гла́вное сраже́ние Се́верной войны́ (1700–1721), в кото́ром ру́сская а́рмия под кома́ндованием Петра́ I победи́ла войск шве́дского короля́ Ка́рла XII. Санкт-Петербу́рг был осно́ван Петро́м I в 1703 году́ как но́вая столи́ца Росси́и, как «окно́ в Евро́пу». Дере́вя́нный до́мик Петра́, па́мятник пе́рвых лет Санкт- Петербу́рга, мо́жно ви́деть и сего́дня. Мо́жно посети́ть и ле́тний дворе́ц Петра́, Эрмита́ж (среди́ экспона́тов кото́рого – ли́чные ве́щи Петра́), Петропа́вловскую кре́пость, го́род фонта́нов – Петродворе́ц.

Пётр I у́мер в 1725 году́. Са́мый изве́стный па́мятник Петру́ «Ме́дный вса́дник»; так называ́л Пу́шкин э́тот па́мятник, кото́рый счита́ется эмбле́мой го́рода. Пу́шкин, кото́рый после́дние го́ды про́жил иу́мер в Санкт-Петербу́рге, написа́л поэ́му «Ме́дный вса́дник». Это поэ́ма о наводне́нии, кото́рое случи́лось в Санкт-Петербу́рге в ноябре́ 1824 го́да. До сих пор э́то наводне́ние счита́ется са́мым ху́дшим наводне́нием в исто́рии го́рода.

a What different roles did Peter the Great fulfil?
b Where did he spend his childhood?
c What happened at the Battle of Poltava?
d Why did Peter the Great build Petersburg?
e Why would people interested in Peter the Great want to visit the Hermitage?
f What happened in 1824?

Speaking

 1 18.04 You are having a chat with Ivan. Play your part, then listen to the complete conversation on the audio.

Вы	**a** *Tell Ivan he looks dreadful.*
Ива́н	Да, я пло́хо себя́ чу́вствую.
Вы	**b** *Ask what's the matter with him.*
Ива́н	Я то́лько что ви́дел ава́рию.
Вы	**c** *Ask what happened.*
Ива́н	Грузови́к уда́рил ста́рую же́нщину.
Вы	**d** *Say 'that's terrible'. Tell him to sit down.*
Ива́н	Спаси́бо.
Вы	**e** *Ask him if he'd like some tea.*
Ива́н	Да, о́чень хочу́. Вы о́чень добры́.
Вы	**f** *Say 'don't mention it (you're welcome)'.*

То́лько что *only just* is easy to use – simply put it before a verb: **мы то́лько что получи́ли письмо́** *we've only just received the letter.* **Как то́лько** *as soon as* often involves the future tense: **я позвоню́, как то́лько прие́ду** *I'll ring as soon as I arrive.*

2 **18.05 Can you remember how to say the following in Russian? Listen to the audio and practise saying each phrase.**

  a What has happened?
  b What's the matter with you?
  c Where on earth have you been?
  d How are you feeling now?
  e You are very kind.

? Test yourself

1 What form of the verb *pay* would you use after чтобы if you wanted to say *in order to pay*?

2 If you wanted to ask someone what was wrong with them, would you say Что с вáми? or Что случúлось?

3 *He said he would ring me!* What tense would you have to use in Russian for *he would ring*?

4 If you wanted to explain that you were walking along the street when you bumped into a friend, which form of the past tense would you choose: мы ходúли, мы шли or мы пошлú?

5 How would you explain that you've *just* bought the tickets?

6 Мы _____ éхали чéрез мост. Which prefix would you add to make this mean *We drove across the bridge*?

7 *Where on earth are you going?* Кудá _____ ты идёшь? Add the missing word.

8 *It would be better if …* Былó _____ лýчше, éсли _____ он пришёл в 8 часóв. Add the two missing words.

9 Я забы́ла в таксú очкú! What have you done with your glasses?

10 You plan to arrive at about ten o'clock. How will you say *at about ten o'clock*?

SELF CHECK

	I CAN...
○	… ask what has happened.
○	… report on what has happened and what has been said.
○	… ask what is wrong.
○	… express concern and purpose.

19 Спаси́бо за откры́тку

Thank you for the card

In this unit you will learn how to:
▶ *write formally and informally in Russian.*
▶ *report what people have asked.*
▶ *express feelings and opinions.*

CEFR: (B1) *Can write very brief reports to a standard, conventionalized format, which pass on routine factual information and state reasons for actions.*

Written communication

Russian addresses used to start with the country and end with the name of the addressee. It is now the norm, however, to write an address as follows:

Я́блокову, В.Н.	(surname in dative, initials of first name and patronymic)
у́лица Одое́вского, д. 42, кв. 73	(street, house no., flat no.)
Пермь 36	(town and district number)
Росси́я	(country)

An e-mail address is either **электро́нный а́дрес** or **имейл**. The word **входя́щие** *inbox* comes from the prefixed verb of motion for *to enter*, and the word for the @ sign is **соба́чка** (lit. *little dog*).

As you already know, it is very important to choose to use either **вы** or **ты** when addressing someone in Russian. This is also true for written communications, and the distinction is reflected in styles of writing; either conventional letters or, more likely, e-mails.

Do you think the following Russian written salutations are formal or informal?

Уважа́емый господи́н дире́ктор!

Уважа́емый господи́н!

Уважа́емая Мари́я Никола́евна!

Глубокоуважа́емый профе́ссор Бы́ков!

Vocabulary builder

19.01 Complete the missing English expressions. Then listen to the audio and repeat the Russian until you can say all the words with confidence.

НА́ДО ЗНАТЬ! *ESSENTIALS*

я наде́юсь, что	_____ hope _____
дово́льно	*quite*
напряжённый	*pressurized, tense, strained*
бо́же мой!	*good gracious!* (lit. _____ *God*)
волнова́ться/взволнова́ться	*to be agitated, upset, worried*
догово́р	*agreement, contract*
компа́ния	_____
перебива́ть/переби́ть (перебью́, перебьёшь)	*to interrupt*
рабо́тать над (+ instrumental)	*to _____ on*
перево́д	*translation*
у́мный	*clever*
спосо́бный	*able, efficient*
что за безобра́зие!	*it's disgraceful!*
отка́зываться/отказа́ться от (+ genitive)	*to refuse*
в ка́честве (+ genitive)	*as, in the capacity _____*
перево́дчица (m. перево́дчик)	_____
то есть (т.е.)	*that is (_____)*
всем приве́т	*_____ to everyone*
чуде́сно (чуде́сный)	*wonderful*
где́-то	*some _____*
как мо́жно скоре́е	*as soon/quickly as _____*

Dialogue

 19.02 Ira has just received an e-mail from her sister, Nina, and is telling her mother about it.

1 What is Nina's news?

Ира	Мама, я сегодня получила имейл от Нины.
Мама	Я надеюсь, что у неё всё в порядке. Она долго не писала.
Ира	Не беспокойся, мама. Вот что она пишет: «Милая Ирочка! Спасибо за имейл. Прости, что так долго не писала. Последние три недели были довольно напряжёнными …»
Мама	Боже мой! Я надеюсь, что она не заболела!
Ира	Не волнуйся, мамочка … «… потому, что на работе мы готовили договор с французской компанией …»
Мама	Я же говорила ей, что было бы лучше работать учительницей …
Ира	Мама, прошу тебя, не перебивай меня! «… и, конечно, мне надо было работать над переводами разных документов. Но теперь мы кончили всю эту работу и директор сказал, что он очень доволен моей работой …»
Мама	Ну, конечно, ведь Ниночка такая умная, способная девушка!
Ира	Мама! «и вчера он спросил меня, хочу ли я поехать с ним в Париж …»
Мама	Что за безобразие! Она, конечно, отказалась от такого приглашения?
Ира	Мамочка, прошу тебя, слушай! «в качестве переводчицы. Будет очень весело и интересно, потому что Мария Николаевна, жена директора, тоже едет (ты помнишь, она работает в Эрмитаже здесь в Санкт-Петербурге). Она уже была в Париже и покажет нам самые интересные места. Мы поедем через десять дней, то есть пятнадцатого числа. Всем привет! Пиши! Целую, Нина.»
Мама	Чудесно! Где мои очки? Я их видела где-то. Я хочу сама читать имил. Потом напиши ответ как можно скорее, скажи Ниночке, что в Париже надо купить и духи, и …

2 True or false?

a Ira's mother has received an e-mail from Nina.

b Nina has been working on the contract for three weeks.

c Ira's mother keeps interrupting her.

d Ira's boss will be going to Paris with his wife.

e Ira's mother wants to phone Nina.

3 Answer the following questions.

a Когда́ И́ра получи́ла имейл?

b Кем рабо́тает Ни́на?

c Где она́ рабо́тает?

d Куда́ она́ пое́дет че́рез де́сять дней?

e Что она́ должна́ бу́дет купи́ть в Пари́же для ма́мы?

Language discovery

WRITTEN GREETINGS

Salutations and sign-offs vary depending on whether the letter/e-mail, etc. you are writing is formal or informal. Here are the formal salutations you met at the start of the unit, along with their English equivalents.

Уважа́емый господи́н дире́ктор!	*Dear Director* (lit. *Respected Director*)
Уважа́емый господи́н	*Dear Sir*
Уважа́емая Мари́я Никола́евна!	*Dear Maria Nikolaevna* (For someone you don't know well enough to call just by their first name – equivalent to the English *Dear Mrs Jones*)
Глубокоуважа́емый профе́ссор Бы́ков!	*Dear Professor Bykov* (lit. *Deeply respected Professor Bykov*)

And here are some informal salutations:

Дорого́й Бори́с	*Dear Boris*
Дорога́я Та́ня	*Dear Tanya*
Ми́лый Пе́тя	*Dear Petya* (used for your nearest and dearest)

1 **Now match the following Russian written sign-offs with their English equivalents. Then decide which are formal and which are informal.**

a	С уваже́нием	**1**	All the best
b	И́скренне Ваш (Ва́ша)	**2**	All the very best
c	С глубо́ким уваже́нием	**3**	Love from (lit. I kiss)
d	Целу́ю	**4**	See you soon
e	Всего́ хоро́шего/до́брого	**5**	Yours (most) sincerely (lit. with deep respect)
f	Всего́ вам са́мого наилу́чшего	**6**	Yours faithfully/yours sincerely (lit. with respect)
g	До ско́рого свида́ния	**7**	Yours sincerely
h	Твой Пе́тя	**8**	Yours, Galya
i	Ва́ша Га́ля	**9**	Yours, Petya

INSTRUMENTAL CASE

In the phrase **после́дние три неде́ди бы́ли дово́льно напряжёнными** the adjective **напряжённый** is in the instrumental case. This is because words that follow the verb *to be* in the past or future are often in the instrumental case, especially if they are describing a temporary state.

YOUR TURN (Дава́йте)

2 **Can you translate the following sentence, identify the word(s) in the instrumental and suggest why this case has been used?**

Де́сять лет наза́д (*ago*) **он был студе́нтом, а тепе́рь он перево́дчик.**

INDIRECT QUESTIONS

In English we introduce an indirect question by using either *if* or *whether*.

Direct question: *He asked 'Do you want to go to Paris?'*

Indirect question: *He asked if/whether I wanted to go to Paris.*

We have seen that Russian indirect statements retain the tense of the original statement and this also applies to indirect questions. In Russian there is only one way to introduce an indirect question – with the particle **ли** (never use **е́сли** in an indirect question).

Word order is important in indirect questions:

he asked (*they wondered*, etc.) → comma → verb → **ли** → subject

3 How would you translate the following sentences?

Он спросúл меня, хочý ли я поéхать в Парúж.

Мáма хотéла знать, отказáлась ли Нина.

Нина не знáла, поéдут ли онú.

> **LANGUAGE TIP**
>
> In English we can use the word *if* for conditions and for indirect questions. If you can replace *if* with *whether*, you know you're dealing with an indirect question. Never try to use **éсли** in an indirect question in Russian – use **ли** instead.

КАК МÓЖНО ... *AS ... AS POSSIBLE*

The formula **как мóжно** + comparative adverb can be used in a number of useful expressions.

4 How would you translate the following expressions?

как мóжно бóльше   как мóжно лýчше   как мóжно тúше

NUMBERS IN TIME PHRASES

In time phrases such as **до девятú часóв** *before nine o'clock*, the number **дéвять** *nine* is in the genitive case (**до** + genitive = *until, as far as, before*).

All numbers use case endings, in the same way as nouns and adjectives. It is particularly useful to know these when you are dealing with time phrases:

Nominative	**два/две**	**три**	**четы́ре**
Accusative	**два/две**	**три**	**четы́ре**
Genitive	**двух**	**трёх**	**четы́рёх**
Dative	**двум**	**трём**	**четы́рём**
Instrumental	**двумя**	**тремя**	**четырьмя́**
Prepositional	**двух**	**трёх**	**четырёх**

Numbers such as **де́вять** which end in a soft sign have the same endings as a feminine soft sign noun (e.g. **дверь**).

YOUR TURN (Дава́йте)

5 How would you translate the following two sentences?

Он рабо́тал с восьми́ до оди́ннадцати.

Приезжа́йте, пожа́луйста, к трём часа́м.

6 Having translated the previous two sentences, can you complete the following?

с	+	_____ case	means	_____
до	+	_____ case	means	_____
к	+	_____ case	means	_____

ГДЕ́-ТО

This means *somewhere*. The particle **-то** can be used in a similar way with other question words (*when? how? who? what?*).

7 Can you work out what the following words and sentence mean?

когда́-то   кто́-то   что́-то

Кто́-то позвони́л тебе́ часо́в в во́семь.

When you want to say not *somewhere*, but *anywhere*, a different particle is used: **-нибудь.**

YOUR TURN (Дава́йте)

8 How would you translate the following words?

когда́-нибудь   кто́-нибудь   что́-нибудь   куда́-нибудь

LANGUAGE TIP

In English there is not always a clear-cut difference between *somewhere* and *anywhere*. In Russian, use **-нибудь** rather than **-то** when in English you could use *any-* instead of *some-*.

SURNAMES

Russian surnames hold a few surprises. For example, masculine surnames ending in **-ов**, **-ев** or **-ин** decline exactly like a regular masculine noun ending in a consonant, except for the instrumental which ends in **-ым**. Feminine surnames which end in **-ова**, **-ева** or **-ина** decline like a regular feminine noun ending in an **-а**, except for the genitive, dative and instrumental which all end in **-ой**. Surnames which end in **-ский** decline exactly like adjectives. So, in addresses, **И.П. Петро́вич**, **В.М. Петро́ва** and **Н.Б. Петро́вский** would appear as:

Петро́вичу, И.П.   **Петро́вой, В.М.**   **Петро́вскому, Н.Б.**

Practice

1 Look at the details of the following people and then write out the address of each one as you would on a parcel.

   a Бори́с Никола́евич Шмелёв живёт в Санкт-Петербу́рге (109262); а́дрес: у́лица Заце́па, дом 20, кварти́ра 57

   b Мари́я Алекса́ндровна Пло́тникова живёт в Воро́неже (394001); а́дрес: Ряби́новая у́лица, дом 21, кварти́ра 76

   c Фёдор Ива́нович Соколо́вский живёт в Москве́ (117552); а́дрес: Ми́нская у́лица, дом 62, кварти́ра 15

опубликова́ние, публика́ция	*publication*
присужда́ться	*to be awarded*
писа́тель (m.)	*writer*
достопримеча́тельности (f., pl.)	*sights*
совреме́нный	*contemporary, modern*

2 Look at the following advertisement for a competition and answer the questions.

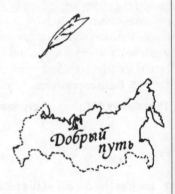
a How often is the prize offered?
b What is it awarded for?
c Who can take part in the competition?
d What can competitors write about?

3 **What would Natasha say to Petya if she did not know the answers to his questions?**

Пётя	Наташа
a Мама уже получила мой имейл?	<u>Я не знаю, получила ли она имейл</u>
b Нина сказала, что она поедет в Париж?	
c Борис приедет сегодня?	
d Вадим любит смотреть телевизор?	
e Валя прочитала всю книгу?	
f Директор подписал (*sign*) договор?	

женат   *married* (of a man)

замужем   *married* (of a woman)

4 **Read the following information about Lyuda.**

Люда живёт в Новосибирске. У неё один брат Саша, который живёт с мамой в Москве. Саша не женат. Люда замужем. Мужа зовут Николай. Люда старается писать маме имейл раз в неделю, но иногда она так занята́, что у неё про́сто нет вре́мени. Тогда́ она́ звони́т ма́ме по телефо́ну, хотя́ иногда́ э́то то́же тру́дно. Она́ предпочита́ет писа́ть име́йл, е́сли есть вре́мя.

Now answer these questions.

about Lyuda:	and about yourself:
a Где Лю́да живёт?	Где вы живёте?
b У неё есть сестра́?	У вас есть бра́тья и сёстры?
c Как зову́т её му́жа?	Вы жена́ты/за́мужем?
d Она́ ча́сто пи́шет ма́ме?	Вы предпочита́ете писа́ть име́йл и́ли говори́ть по телефо́ну?
e Почему́ иногда́ она́ не мо́жет писа́ть?	

психо́лог	psychologist
вы включены́	you are included
уча́стник	participant
сообща́ть/сообщи́ть	to communicate, announce
подтвержда́ть/подтверди́ть	to confirm
рейс	flight

5 Read the e-mail and answer the questions.

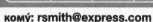

кому́: rsmith@express.com
от: sekretar@kongresspsikh.ru
заголо́вок: XII конгре́сс психо́логов
20 апре́ля 2015 го́да

Уважа́емый профе́ссор Смит!

Организацио́нный комите́т XII конгре́сса психо́логов информи́рует, что вы включены́ в число́ уча́стников Конгре́сса.

В конце́ ию́ня – нача́ле ию́ля мы сообщи́м вам, где мо́жно получи́ть авиабиле́т.

Про́сим подтверди́ть ва́ше уча́стие в Конгре́ссе, сообщи́в да́ту, но́мер ре́йса не поздне́е 1 а́вгуста 2015г.

С уваже́нием,

Секрета́рь

И.С. Хмеле́вский

a Кем рабо́тает профе́ссор Смит?

b Когда́ он узна́ет, где мо́жно получи́ть авиабиле́т?

c Когда́ он до́лжен подтверди́ть, что прие́дет на Конгре́сс?

Listen and understand

режиссёр	*director/producer*
в чём и́менно состои́т рабо́та?	*what exactly does the job involve?*
тво́рческий	*creative*
снима́ть/снять фильм	*to shoot a film*
теорети́чески	*in theory*
на пра́ктике	*in practice*
телесту́дия	*television studio*

19.03 *A journalist is interviewing Marina Vladimirovna, a television producer.*

1 What was Marina Vladimirovna's profession before she became a television producer?

Журнали́ст	Мари́на Влади́мировна, кем вы рабо́таете?
Мари́на	Я режиссёр.
Журнали́ст	В чём и́менно состои́т ва́ша рабо́та?
Мари́на	Я режиссёр документа́льных фи́льмов.
Журнали́ст	Каки́х, наприме́р?
Мари́на	Ну, … фи́льмов по литерату́ре, по исто́рии …
Журнали́ст	Ско́лько лет вы рабо́таете режиссёром?
Мари́на	Лет де́сять. До э́того я рабо́тала перево́дчицей.
Журнали́ст	И каку́ю рабо́ту вы предпочита́ете?
Мари́на	Коне́чно, интере́сно бы́ло рабо́тать перево́дчицей, но я бо́льше люблю рабо́тать режиссёром.
Журнали́ст	Почему́?
Мари́на	Ну, … рабо́та така́я интере́сная, тво́рческая.
Журнали́ст	Мари́на Влади́мировна, над чем вы сейча́с рабо́таете?
Мари́на	Сейчас мы снима́ем фильм о жи́зни в Санкт-Петербу́рге в нача́ле э́того ве́ка.
Журнали́ст	Ско́лько часо́в в день вы рабо́таете?
Мари́на	Тру́дно сказа́ть, но теорети́чески я рабо́таю с девяти́ до шести́.

Журналист	А на практике?
Марина	На практике я ещё в телестудии в десять, даже в одиннадцать часов вечера.

> **LANGUAGE TIP**
>
> Note the use of the instrumental case in this dialogue when talking about people's jobs: **Кем вы работаете?** lit. *as whom do you work?*; **Я работала переводчицей** *I worked as a translator.*

2 Choose the correct option to complete the following sentences.

a Марина режиссёр
1 романтических фильмов
2 музыкальных передач
3 спортивных программ
4 документальных фильмов

b Десять лет назад она работала
1 режиссёром
2 переводчицей
3 учительницей
4 врачом

c Сейчас она снимает фильм
1 о Москве
2 о Санкт-Петербурге
3 о журналистах
4 о писателях

d Теоретически она работает
1 с восьми утра до девяти вечера
2 с девяти утра до десяти
3 с девяти утра до шести вечера
4 с десяти утра до шести вечера

Reading and writing

возможность (f.)	*opportunity*
впереди	*ahead, in front*
дача	*holiday home; house in the country*
коллега	*colleague*
новости (f., pl.)	*news*
позади	*behind*
поэтому	*therefore*
путешествовать	*to travel*
родственник	*relative, relation*

сообщение	message
составля́ть/соста́вить	to make up, put together, compose
уче́бный год	academic year

 19.04 Read and listen to this message, then answer the questions that follow in English.

7 сентября́ 2014г.

Дорого́й Джон!

Мне бы́ло о́чень прия́тно получи́ть ва́ше сообще́ние и узна́ть, что о́тпуск ваш прошёл хорошо́.

Я то́же дово́льна свои́м о́тдыхом. Отпуск преподава́телей ву́зов и шко́льных учителе́й составля́ет в на́шей стране́ 48 рабо́чих дней (то есть 8 неде́ль), так что у меня́ была́ возмо́жность занима́ться дома́шними дела́ми и путеше́ствовать – после́днее мне о́чень нра́вится. К концу́ уче́бного го́да (то есть к концу́ ию́ня) я почу́вствовала, что о́чень уста́ла. Поэ́тому в нача́ле ию́ля, как то́лько я вы́шла в о́тпуск, я уе́хала за́город к ро́дственникам (на ле́тнюю кварти́ру, и́ли, как мы говори́м, на «да́чу»). Там я пла́вала, гуля́ла (температу́ра днём до 35 гра́дусов) и помога́ла мои́м ро́дственникам в саду́, где ле́том всегда́ мно́го рабо́ты. Пото́м я уе́хала на куро́рт на Черномо́рское побере́жье – чуде́сно! – мя́гкий кли́мат, тёплое мо́ре и хоро́шие усло́вия для о́тдыха.

Сейча́с мой о́тпуск уже́ позади́; впереди́ мно́го рабо́ты – в э́том году́ мы перехо́дим на но́вые уче́бные пла́ны. И до́ма есть рабо́та – пора́ сде́лать ремо́нт в кварти́ре.

Вот пока́ и все мои́ но́вости. Переда́йте, пожа́луйста, приве́т ва́шим колле́гам, с кото́рыми я познако́милась, когда́я была́ в ва́шей стране́ в про́шлом году́. Пиши́те! Мне бу́дет интере́сно узна́ть о ва́шем ле́тнем путеше́ствии (где, в каки́х места́х бы́ли, что ви́дели интере́сного). Жду ва́шего отве́та!

Ва́ша Гали́на.

a What was Galina pleased to learn from John's message?
b How much holiday do teachers get every year in Russia?
c What does Galina like to do most of all in her holidays?
d How did she feel towards the end of June?
e Where did she go as soon as her holiday began?
f What was the temperature at the beginning of July?
g What was her opinion of the Black Sea resort?

> **LANGUAGE TIP**
>
> Galina's letter includes lots of useful time phrases, such as:
>
> | | |
> |---|---|
> | **в нача́ле ию́ля** | *at the beginning of June* |
> | **в э́том году́** | *this year* |
> | **днём** | *during the day* |
> | **к концу́ ию́ня** | *towards the end of June* |
> | **как то́лько** | *as soon as* |
> | **ле́том** | *in the summer* |

Speaking

19.05 Can you remember how to say the following in Russian? Listen to the audio and practise saying each phrase.

a Dear Boris …
b Yours sincerely …
c As soon as possible.
d I hope everything is all right.
e Good gracious!

? Test yourself

1 In which of the following ways would you begin an e-mail to a new business contact in Russia: Уважаемая Мария Ивановна / Дорогая Мария?

2 If you are addressing a letter in Russian, which case do you need to use for the person's surname?

3 What does the following question mean: Можно послать по имейлу?

4 Which particle will you always find in an indirect question?

5 How would you say *as quickly as possible* in Russian?

6 When translating the phrase *Have you bought anything?* would you use что-то or что-нибудь?

7 Which case is being used for the numbers in the following sentence and why? Я работаю с девяти до пяти часов.

8 How would you say *I work as a businessman* in Russian? Which case do you need to use for *businessman*?

9 Why is the animate accusative used for the word husband in the following sentence? Мужа зовут Николай (lit. *husband they call Nikolai*).

10 In which of the following ways would you sign off an e-mail to a new business contact in Russia: целую/с уважением?

SELF CHECK

I CAN...

- ◯ ... write formally and informally in Russian.
- ◯ ... report what people have asked.
- ◯ ... express feelings and opinions.

20 Приезжа́йте к нам опя́ть!

Come and see us again!

In this unit you will learn how to:
▶ *talk about yourself in more detail.*
▶ *use numbers with adjectives and nouns.*
▶ *use other ways of expressing appreciation and thanks.*

CEFR: (B2) *Can pass on detailed information reliably.*

Сувени́ры *Souvenirs*

Any trip to Russia will be full of opportunities to buy traditional souvenirs. The most instantly recognizable and most popular are the matryoshka dolls. These are wooden, with successively smaller identical dolls fitted one inside the other. They can be traditionally painted as if in peasant dress or have a more modern theme to appeal to international tourists: famous figures from Russian history, popular culture, etc. Other popular souvenirs are the *fur hat* (**мехова́я ша́пка**) and the *samovar* (**самова́р**) – a sort of decorative urn for boiling water to make tea.

You might also consider buying a balalaika. This is a stringed musical instrument (usually 2–4 strings) with a triangular body – the Russian version of a guitar. It is commonly used in a **фолькло́рный анса́мбль** to accompany national folk songs and dances. Balalaikas come in different sizes, and there are balalaika orchestras (with instruments ranging in size from that of a violin to a double bass).

Match the following Russian souvenirs to their English equivalents.

1	ка́рта	**2**	икра́	**3**	во́дка
4	кни́га	**5**	конфе́ты	**6**	шкату́лка
a	vodka	**b**	map	**c**	caviar
d	jewellery box	**e**	book	**f**	sweets

Vocabulary builder

20.01 Complete the missing English expressions. Then listen to the audio and repeat the Russian until you can say all the words with confidence.

НА́ДО ЗНАТЬ! *ESSENTIALS*

ты принёс с собо́й	_____ *have brought with you*
чей э́то бока́л?	*whose champagne glass is this?*
за свои́х ру́сских друзе́й	*to my _____ friends*
пребыва́ние	*stay*
для тех, кто	*for those _____*
интере́снее всего́	*most _____ of all*
благода́рный	*grateful*
все свои́ сувени́ры	*all your _____*
плато́к	*shawl*
матрёшка	_____
племя́нница (*m.* племя́нник)	*niece (_____)*
для себя́	*_____ yourself*
пока́ ничего́	*nothing yet*
я так и ду́мала	*I _____ as much*
приезжа́йте к нам опя́ть	*come and see _____ again*

Dialogue

20.02 *Anna is spending her last evening in Moscow at Ira's flat. Sasha and Volodya are there too.*

1 Which souvenirs has Anna bought?

Йра	А вот и Са́ша. Ты принёс с собо́й буты́лку шампа́нского, да?
Са́ша	Да, вот она́. *(Pours out champagne.)* Воло́дя сейча́с придёт. Он сказа́л, что принесёт свой фотоаппара́т … А вот и он.
Йра	Приве́т … Ну, чей э́то бока́л? Мой, да? … Хорошо́, я предлага́ю тост за А́нну!
Все	За А́нну!
А́нна	Спаси́бо. Я то́же хочу́ предложи́ть тост … за свои́х ру́сских друзе́й!

Йра	Спаси́бо, А́нна ... Ну, скажи́, как тебе́ понра́вилось твоё пребыва́ние в Москве́?
А́нна	О́чень. Всё удиви́тельно интере́сно.
Воло́дя	Да́же на ле́кциях о жи́вописи?
Йра	Что ты, Воло́дя! Ведь таки́е ле́кции о́чень интере́сны для тех, кто лю́бит иску́сство.
А́нна	Да ... но для меня́ интере́снее всего́ бы́ло познако́миться с И́рой и с её друзья́ми.
Йра	Спаси́бо, А́нна!
А́нна	Я действи́тельно о́чень благода́рна вам всем за всё – за биле́ты в теа́тр, и за пое́здку за́город ... Спаси́бо.
Йра	Ещё шампа́нского!
Са́ша	Во ско́лько самолёт вылета́ет за́втра, А́нна?
А́нна	Полдеся́того.
Воло́дя	Ты уже́ купи́ла все свои́ сувени́ры?
А́нна	Да, я купи́ла два краси́вых платка́ (э́то ма́ме и тёте), футбо́лку для бра́та, матрёшку для племя́нницы, пять–шесть интере́сных книг для друзе́й ...
Йра	Мно́го! А что ты купи́ла для себя́?
А́нна	*(Sighs.)* Пока́ ничего́. Вре́мени не́ было.
Йра	Я так и ду́мала! ... Ну вот. А́нна, э́то пода́рок от нас всех ... ру́сская балала́йка.
А́нна	Спаси́бо. Вы о́чень добры́.
Йра	Пожа́луйста ... приезжа́йте к нам опя́ть! Мы бу́дем о́чень ра́ды.

> **LANGUAGE TIP**
>
> To say *I am grateful for*, use the short form of the adjective **благода́рный за** + accusative: **я благода́рен** (m.) / **я благода́рна** (f.) / **мы благода́рны за всё** *I/we are grateful for everything*.

2 True or false?

a Volodya has brought a bottle of champagne.

b Ira proposes a toast to Sasha.

c Anna thanks all her Russian friends.

d Anna's plane is scheduled to leave at 09:30.

e Anna has bought a balalaika for her brother.

3 Answer the following questions.

   a Какóй тост предлагáет Áнна?

   b Как Áнне понрáвилось пребывáние в Москвé?

   c За чтó онá благодари́т Йру, Сашу и Волóдю?

   d Что Áнна купи́ла мáме?

   e Какóй подáрок Áнна получáет от Йры, Волóди и Сáши?

Language discovery

TALKING ABOUT THINGS THAT BELONG TO YOU – СВОЙ

1 What does the word свой mean in each of the following sentences?

Я купи́ла свой биле́т	**Ты забы́л свой ключ**
Он несёт свой пáспорт	**Мы встречаемся со свои́ми друзьями**
Вы ви́дите свой чемодáн?	**Они пи́ли своё шампáнское**

As we can see in the examples, the way that we translate **свой** into English changes according to who is doing the action in the sentence. We are already used to using **мой**, etc. to mean *my*, **твой** to mean *your*, **наш** to mean *our* and **ваш** to mean *your*. **Свой** can be an alternative to all of these.

The key idea to remember is that when you can add the word *own* to *my*, *your*, etc. in English, then in Russian you can use **свой**. This is particularly common in conversational Russian.

The only times when **свой** changes the meaning significantly are when translating *his*, *her* or *their*.

YOUR TURN (Давáйте)

2 Remember that the key idea of свой is *own*, so what is the difference between the following two sentences?

Бори́с читáет свою́ кни́гу.   **Бори́с читáет егó кни́гу.**

Remember that because **свой** depends on the person doing the action in a sentence, **свой** can never describe this person – in other words, **свой** is not usually found in the nominative case. So, if you want to describe the person doing the action in a sentence, you must use **мой**, **твой**, **егó**, **наш**, **ваш**, **их**:

| Моя сестра преподаёт итальянский язык | *My sister teaches Italian* |
| Он сказал, что его сестра уже купила балалайку | *He said that his sister had already bought a balalaika* |

TALKING ABOUT YOURSELF – СЕБЯ

3 What do the following sentences mean?

Я купила себе футболку	Ты говоришь о себе?
Он несёт паспорт с собой	Мы закрыли за собой дверь
Вы видите себя на фотографии?	Они купили билеты для себя

As we can see from the examples, **себя** means *myself, yourself, himself, herself, ourselves, yourselves, themselves*, according to who is doing the action of the sentence. It is used in all cases except the nominative:

Accusative	**себя**
Genitive	**себя**
Dative	**себе**
Instrumental	**собой**
Prepositional	**себе**

ASKING WHO OWNS THINGS – ЧЕЙ

4 What do the following sentences mean?

| чей: Чей это бокал? | чья: Чья это матрёшка? |
| чьё: Чьё это письмо? | чьи: Чьи это сувениры? |

As we can see from the examples, Russian has a separate word for *whose* when you are asking a question. It has masculine, feminine, neuter and plural forms.

NUMBERS

Numbers in Russian are a bit complicated and need to be followed by specific cases.

5 Look at the following examples and try to work out the rules before you continue:

один русский друг	одна русская матрёшка
одно интересное письмо	два английских футболиста
две русских матрёшки	три американских фильма
четыре ирландских туриста	пять интересных магазинов

де́сять хоро́ших книг	два́дцать дешёвых биле́тов
два́дцать оди́н но́вый журна́л	два́дцать два вку́сных блина́
два́дцать пять испа́нских фана́тов	два миллио́на шестьсо́т ты́сяч четы́реста пятьдеся́т оди́н тури́ст

In Russian, the number *one* has a masculine, feminine and neuter form. The number *one* (and its compounds, such as 21 or 101) does not affect the endings of the nouns and adjectives that follow it.

However, all other Russian numbers do affect the endings of the nouns and adjectives that follow them.

▶ After *two*, *three* and *four*, and their compounds (32, 44, etc.) you use the genitive plural of the adjective and the genitive singular of the noun. Note that the number *two* has a feminine form (**две**).

▶ After all other numbers you use the genitive plural of both adjectives and nouns.

> **LANGUAGE TIP**
>
> It is possible with feminine nouns following the numbers *two*, *three* and *four* (and their compounds) to use either the nominative or the genitive plural of the adjective, but you must always use the genitive singular of the feminine noun: **три ру́сские (ру́сских) балала́йки** *three Russian balalaikas*.

USEFUL EXPRESSIONS WITH THE WORD TOT

The basic meaning of **тот** is *that*. However, you are most likely to meet it in a few set expressions:

▶ The construction **тот**, **кто** means *the person who*, *he who*.

YOUR TURN (Дава́йте)

6 How would you therefore translate the following sentence?

Ты говори́шь о том, кто купи́л балала́йку?

▶ **Те**, **кто** means *those who*, but note that the verb following this expression is usually in the singular.

YOUR TURN (Дава́йте)

7 How would you therefore translate the following sentence?

для тех, кто лю́бит иску́сство

▶ **Тот же** means *the same* and **тот же са́мый** *the very same* – both **тот** and **са́мый** must agree with the noun they describe.

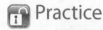

8 How would you therefore translate the following sentence?

Он чи́тал ту же (са́мую) газе́ту ка́ждый день.

Practice

1 Match the questions with the answers.

a	Во ско́лько самолёт вылета́ет?	**1**	Свою́ балала́йку
b	Что ты принёс с собо́й?	**2**	О́чень. Всё так интере́сно!
c	Чья э́то кни́га?	**3**	За пое́здку за́город
d	Как вам нра́вится э́тот го́род?	**4**	К трём часа́м
e	За что вы благодари́те их?	**5**	Моя́

бижуте́рия	*jewellery*
вы́лет	*departure*
о́бувь	*footwear*
проду́кты	*food*
това́ры	*goods*

2 Look at the advertisement and answer the questions.

a Apart from footwear and jewellery, what can be bought at the shop?
b Where exactly is the shop situated?
c Which season's collection is on show?

3 **You have just returned from a holiday in Moscow and decide to write and thank your Russian friend. Read the extracts from your diary and address book, and thank your friend for each point mentioned. Address the card appropriately.**

Суббо́та:	2 биле́та в теа́тр на бале́т «Снегу́рочка»
Воскресе́нье:	Пое́здка за́город (собира́ли грибы́ два часа́!)
Понеде́льник:	Экску́рсия в дом-музе́й П.И. Чайко́вского
Вто́рник:	Обе́д в рестора́не «Колобо́к»

Губа́нов, А.П. (Анато́лий)

Первома́йская ул., д. 45, кв. 29

105554 Москва́

LANGUAGE TIP

▶ On a specific day of the week: **В** + accusative case

В понеде́льник мы бу́дем в Ло́ндоне   *On Monday we shall be in London*
▶ Habits/general: **ПО** + dative plural

По понеде́льникам обы́чно я рабо́таю до́ма   *On Mondays I usually work at home*

сти́рка	*washing*
химчи́стка	*dry cleaning*
отъе́зд	*departure*
наименова́ние	*name/naming*
по́дпись (f.)	*signature*
ежедне́вно	*daily*
оставля́ть/оста́вить	*to leave*

4 **Look at the form and answer the questions.**

БЛАНК-ЗАКАЗ НА СТИРКУ/ХИМЧИСТКУ

Номер комнаты: _____

Фамилия: _____

Дата отъезда: _____

Наименование вещей: _____

Подпись: _____ Дата: _____

Примечание: 1.   Приём заказа ежедневно до 11:00 утра.

                        2.   Заполните бланк и оставьте на столе.

a What information must you provide if you want washing/dry cleaning done?

b How often are orders taken for this service?

c What must you do with the form when you have completed it?

на пéнсии	*retired* (lit. *on a pension*)
семья́	*family*
внук	*grandson*
расска́зывать/рассказа́ть	*to tell, relate*
скри́пка	*violin*
учи́ться	*to study*
увлека́ться/увлéчься (+ instr.)	*to be enthusiastic about*

5 **Read the following information about Ли́дия Па́вловна Ка́рпова, then answer the questions that follow.**

Ли́дия Па́вловна живёт в Иркутске, в Сиби́ри. Иркутск нахо́дится на восто́ке страны. Она́ на пéнсии и живёт одна́ потому́, что её муж у́мер дéсять лет наза́д. У неё в семьé сын, его жена и два вну́ка. К сча́стью, её сын, Ко́ля, живёт недалеко́ от неё, и он ча́сто помога́ет ей: наприме́р, éсли она́ больна́, он дéлает поку́пки. У Ли́дии два вну́ка, Пётр и Андрéй. Вот что Ли́дия расска́зывает о свои́х вну́ках: «Пéтя студéнт, хо́чет стать врачо́м. Он о́чень интересу́ется му́зыкой, прекра́сно игра́ет на скри́пке – серьёзный тако́й ма́льчик. Андрю́ша всё ещё у́чится в шко́ле. Он увлека́ется футбо́лом и на́до сказа́ть, что он не очень лю́бит занима́ться кни́гами! Они́ ча́сто захо́дят ко мне, помога́ют мне.»

О Ли́дии	О себе́
a Где нахо́дится Ирку́тск?	Где нахо́дится ваш го́род?/ва́ша дере́вня?
b Почему́ Ли́дия живёт одна́?	Кто есть в ва́шей семье́?
c Кто есть в её семье́?	Как их зову́т?
d Как зову́т её вну́ков?	Что они́ де́лают в свобо́дное вре́мя?
e Что они́ де́лают в свобо́дное вре́мя?	Расскажи́те, чем вы интересу́етесь, что вы де́лаете в свобо́дное вре́мя.

Listen and understand

колле́га	colleague
нетерпе́ние	impatience
ждать с нетерпе́нием	to look forward to
прие́зд	arrival
лабора́нт	laboratory assistant
скуча́ть	to miss (**по** + dative of nouns, **по** + prepositional of pronouns)
от и́мени всего́ коллекти́ва	on behalf of all the staff

20.03 *Alla is leaving for a new job and has come to say goodbye to her boss.*

1 What has Alla's boss done on her behalf to help her in her new job?

Дире́ктор	Ита́к, вы за́втра уезжа́ете, да?
А́лла	Да. Самолёт вылета́ет в шесть часо́в у́тра.
Дире́ктор	Наде́юсь, что вы не волну́етесь!
А́лла	Насчёт ре́йса, нет … но, коне́чно, я немно́жко беспоко́юсь о свое́й но́вой рабо́те.

Директор	Не надо. Я уверен, что вам понравится эта новая работа. И я знаю, что ваши будущие коллеги с большим нетерпением ждут вашего приезда.
Алла	Почему вы так думаете?
Директор	Я только что говорил по телефону с директором фабрики «Медведково» и объяснил ему, какой вы способный лаборант.
Алла	Спасибо вам, Николай Петрович.
Директор	Не за что … Я хочу поблагодарить вас, Алла Константиновна, за всю вашу работу здесь у нас. Если я не ошибаюсь, вы уже десять лет работаете в нашей лаборатории, да?
Алла	Правильно.
Директор	Я знаю, что ваши коллеги будут скучать по вас! Примите, пожалуйста, эту ручку от имени всего коллектива.
Алла	Золотая ручка! Спасибо большое!
Директор	Мы желаем вам всего самого наилучшего – успеха, здоровья и счастья.
Алла	Спасибо Николай Петрович, я очень благодарна вам за всё.
Директор	Если вы будете в Екатеринбурге, приезжайте к нам, Алла Константиновна. Мы будем очень рады.

2 True or false?

a Алла уезжает послезавтра.

b Она беспокоится о новой работе.

c Она работает переводчицей.

d Она десять лет работает в этой фирме.

e Она получает золотые часы от коллег.

Reading and writing

вспоминать/вспомнить	to recall, remember, reminisce
добро	good
закон	law
«Идиот»	'The Idiot'
коробка	box

красота́	*beauty*
нанима́ть/наня́ть	*to rent, hire*
папиро́са	*cigarette*
переу́лок	*lane, alleyway*
переустро́йство	*reorganization*
«Преступле́ние и наказа́ние»	*'Crime and Punishment'*
создава́ть/созда́ть	*to create*
состоя́ть	*to consist of*
спустя́	*later, after*
цель (f.)	*goal, aim*

20.04 Read and listen to the text, then answer the questions that follow in English.

Е́сли вы бу́дете в Санкт-Петербу́рге, посети́те музе́й-кварти́ру вели́кого ру́сского писа́теля Фёдора Достое́вского (1821–1881). А́дрес музе́я: Кузне́чный переу́лок, дом 5. Здесь Достое́вский прожи́л с семьёй – жено́й А́нной Григо́рьевной и двумя́ детьми́, Фе́дей и Лю́бой – после́дние го́ды свое́й жи́зни. «Кварти́ру на́няли: на углу́ Я́мской и Кузне́чного переу́лка …» сообщи́л Фёдор Миха́йлович бра́ту Никола́ю в октябре́ 1878 го́да. А́нна Григо́рьевна вспомина́ла «Кварти́ра на́ша состоя́ла из шести́ ко́мнат и находи́лась на второ́м этаже́».

Век спустя́ со́здали в до́ме на Кузне́чном литерату́рно- мемориа́льный музе́й. Из о́кон гости́ной, где Достоевский читал де́тям «Капита́нскую до́чку» Пу́шкина, «Тара́са Бу́льбу» Го́голя, «Бородино́» Ле́рмонтова (но никогда́ не чита́л им своего́), тепе́рь открыва́ется тот же вид, что и мно́го лет наза́д. Тот же са́мый поря́док в кабине́те, где роди́лся рома́н «Бра́тья Карама́зовы» – «Газе́ты, коро́бки с папиро́сами, пи́сьма, кни́ги … всё должно́ бы́ло лежа́ть на своём ме́сте …» вспомина́ла дочь Достое́вского, Любо́вь Фёдоровна.

Достое́вский ду́мал о переустро́йстве ми́ра по зако́нам приро́ды и пра́вды, добра́ и красоты́; он писа́л об э́том в «Идио́те», в «Преступле́нии и наказа́нии». Достое́вского называ́ли и называ́ют психо́логом. «Непра́вда, – говори́л Достое́вский, – я реали́ст. Моя́ цель – найти́ в челове́ке челове́ка.»

a Where is the Dostoevsky Museum situated?
b How many children did Dostoevsky have?
c How did his wife describe the flat?
d What did Dostoevsky do in the sitting room?
e What did he like to have around him in his study?
f In what way did he want to change the world?

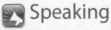 # Speaking

 1 20.05 Play your part in the conversation, then listen to the complete conversation on the audio.

Воло́дя	Чем вы интересу́етесь?
Вы	**a** *Say you're interested in Russian music.*
Воло́дя	Вы лю́бите спорт?
Вы	**b** *Say 'yes', you sometimes play tennis in the summer.*
Воло́дя	Что вы обы́чно де́лаете по суббо́там?
Вы	**c** *Say you do the shopping, work in the garden and sometimes go to the cinema.*
Воло́дя	Когда́ вы уезжа́ете?
Вы	**d** *Say 'tomorrow'. Your plane leaves at 10 a.m.*

 2 20.06 Can you remember how to say the following in Russian? Listen to the audio and practise saying each phrase.

a Whose is this camera?
b I propose a toast to you
c More champagne!
d Come and see us again!
e What time does the plane leave?

Test yourself

1 What does the following sentence mean? Онá дéсять лет рабóтает в лаборатóрии. Which tense is the verb in and why?

2 Can you remember the two different ways of asking *at what time* in Russian?

3 How would you say the following number phrases: 1 день *one day*, 21 недéля *21 weeks*, 41 окнó *41 windows*? (Окнó can also mean *window* in the sense of a space in your schedule.)

4 What are you being asked when a Russian says: Вам/тебé понрáвилась Москвá? Can you explain why Москвá is in the nominative case and вам/тебé is in the dative case?

5 Give your reasons for matching up the following Russian and English expressions:

a вéчер	**1** the day before yesterday
b вчерá	**2** evening
c позавчерá	**3** the day after tomorrow
d послезáвтра	**4** yesterday

6 How would you translate the underlined words in the following sentences, and why are they spelled differently? <u>Чей</u> это паспорт? <u>Чья</u> это книга? <u>Чьи</u> это дéньги?

7 What is the difference in meaning between мы игрáли в тéннис в понедéльник and мы игрáли в тéннис по понедéльникам?

8 How do you say *the same* in Russian? Why is this a bit more complicated than in English?

9 Which tense is used in the first half of this sentence and why? Éсли вы бýдете в Москвé, приезжáйте к нам!

10 Борис выпил егó шампáнское. Why might Boris be in trouble?

SELF CHECK

	I CAN...
○	...talk about myself in more detail.
○	...use numbers with adjectives and nouns.
○	...use other ways of expressing appreciation and thanks.

Appendix: Grammar

Spelling rules

1   Never write **ы**, **ю**, **я** after **г**, **к**, **х**, **ж**, **ч**, **щ**, **ш**; instead write **и**, **у**, **а** (except for some nouns of foreign origin, e.g. **парашю́т**, **жюри́**).

2   Never write unstressed **о** after **ж**, **ч**, **ш**, **щ**, **ц**; instead write **е**.

Nouns

NB: The animate accusative is formed in exactly the same way as the genitive case. It affects masculine singular animate objects and all plural animate objects.

MASCULINE NOUNS – DECLENSION

Singular

Nom.	журна́л	трамва́й	автомоби́ль
Acc.	журна́л	трамва́й	автомоби́ль
Gen.	журна́ла	трамва́я	автомоби́ля
Dat.	журна́лу	трамва́ю	автомоби́лю
Instr.	журна́лом	трамва́ем	автомоби́лем
Prep.	о журна́ле	о трамва́е	об автомоби́ле

Some masculine nouns take **-у́** or **-ю́** in the prepositional singular:

аэропо́рт	*airport*	в аэропорту́
бе́рег	*shore, bank*	на берегу́
год	*year*	в году́
Дон	*River Don*	на Дону́
край	*edge*	на краю́
Крым	*Crimea*	в Крыму́
лёд	*ice*	на льду́
лес	*forest*	в лесу́
мост	*bridge*	на мосту́
порт	*port*	в порту́
рот	*mouth*	во рту
сад	*garden*	в саду́

снег	snow	в снегу́
у́гол	corner	в углу́

Some masculine nouns ending in **-а**, **-я** (e.g. **де́душка** *grandfather*, **дя́дя** *uncle*) decline like feminine nouns.

Plural

Nom.	журна́лы	трамва́и	автомоби́ли
Acc.	журна́лы	трамва́и	автомоби́ли
Gen.	журна́лов	трамва́ев	автомоби́лей
Dat.	журна́лам	трамва́ям	автомоби́лям
Instr.	журна́лами	трамва́ями	автомоби́лями
Prep.	о журна́лах	о трамва́ях	об автомоби́лях

Some masculine nouns have the nominative plural ending **-а́** or **-я́**:

а́дрес	address	адреса́
бе́рег	shore, bank	берега́
ве́чер	evening, party	вечера́
глаз	eye	глаза́
го́лос	voice	голоса́
го́род	town	города́
дом	house	дома́
до́ктор	doctor	доктора́
лес	forest	леса́
мех	fur	меха́
но́мер	number, room	номера́
о́стров	island	острова́
па́спорт	passport	паспорта́
по́езд	train	поезда́
учи́тель	teacher	учителя́
цвет	colour	цвета́

Note the declension of **друг** *friend* and **сын** *son*:

Nom.	друзья́	сыновья́
Acc.	друзе́й	сынове́й
Gen.	друзе́й	сынове́й
Dat.	друзья́м	сыновья́м
Instr.	друзья́ми	сыновья́ми
Prep.	о друзья́х	о сыновья́х

Nouns ending in **-анин** or **-янин** in the plural: **англича́нин** *Englishman*:

Nom.	**англича́не**
Acc.	**англича́н**
Gen.	**англича́н**
Dat.	**англича́нам**
Instr.	**англича́нами**
Prep.	**об англича́нах**

Irregular plurals: **де́ти** *children*, **лю́ди** *people*:

Nom.	**де́ти**	**лю́ди**
Acc.	**детей**	**людей**
Gen.	**детей**	**людей**
Dat.	**де́тям**	**лю́дям**
Instr.	**детьми́**	**людьми́**
Prep.	**о де́тях**	**о лю́дях**

Nouns ending in **ж**, **ч**, **ш** and **щ** have the genitive plural ending **-ей**.

FEMININE NOUNS – DECLENSION

Singular

Nom.	**ко́мната**	**неде́ля**	**ста́нция**	**дверь**
Acc.	**ко́мнату**	**неде́лю**	**ста́нцию**	**дверь**
Gen.	**ко́мнаты**	**неде́ли**	**ста́нции**	**две́ри**
Dat.	**ко́мнате**	**неде́ле**	**ста́нции**	**две́ри**
Instr.	**ко́мнатой**	**неде́лей**	**ста́нцией**	**две́рью**
Prep.	**о ко́мнате**	**о неде́ле**	**о ста́нции**	**о две́ри**

Plural

Nom.	**ко́мнаты**	**неде́ли**	**ста́нции**	**две́ри**
Acc.	**ко́мнаты**	**неде́ли**	**ста́нции**	**две́ри**
Gen.	**ко́мнат**	**неде́ль**	**ста́нций**	**дверей**
Dat.	**ко́мнатам**	**неде́лям**	**ста́нциям**	**деверя́м**
Instr.	**ко́мнатами**	**неде́лями**	**ста́нциями**	**деверя́ми**
Prep.	**о ко́мнатах**	**о неде́лях**	**о ста́нциях**	**о деверя́х**

Note the irregular feminine nouns **дочь** *daughter* and **мать** *mother*:

	Singular	Plural	Singular	Plural
Nom.	**дочь**	**до́чери**	**мать**	**ма́тери**
Acc.	**дочь**	**дочере́й**	**мать**	**матере́й**
Gen.	**до́чери**	**дочере́й**	**ма́тери**	**матере́й**
Dat.	**до́чери**	**дочеря́м**	**ма́тери**	**матеря́м**
Instr.	**до́черью**	**дочерьми́**	**ма́терью**	**матеря́ми**
Prep.	**о до́чери**	**о дочеря́х**	**о ма́тери**	**о матеря́х**

NEUTER NOUNS – DECLENSION

Singular

Nom.	**ме́сто**	**мо́ре**	**зда́ние**
Acc.	**ме́сто**	**мо́ре**	**зда́ние**
Gen.	**ме́ста**	**мо́ря**	**зда́ния**
Dat.	**ме́сту**	**мо́рю**	**зда́нию**
Instr.	**ме́стом**	**мо́рем**	**зда́нием**
Prep.	**о ме́сте**	**о мо́ре**	**зда́нии**

Plural

Nom.	**места́**	**моря́**	**зда́ния**
Acc.	**места́**	**моря́**	**зда́ния**
Gen.	**мест**	**море́й**	**зда́ний**
Dat.	**места́м**	**моря́м**	**зда́ниям**
Instr.	**места́ми**	**моря́ми**	**зда́ниями**
Prep.	**о места́х**	**о моря́х**	**о зда́ниях**

Note the declension of neuter nouns ending in **-мя**:

	Singular	Plural
Nom.	**вре́мя**	**времена́**
Acc.	**вре́мя**	**времена́**
Gen.	**вре́мени**	**времён**
Dat.	**вре́мени**	**времена́м**
Instr.	**вре́менем**	**времена́ми**
Prep.	**о вре́мени**	**о времена́х**

STRESS PATTERNS IN NOUNS

In many Russian nouns the stress remains constant throughout the declension of the noun, but in some nouns the pattern changes. The most effective approach is to learn the most common examples of where stress changes in a noun's declension:

▶ We have already seen, for example, that some masculine nouns take stressed endings in the plural (e.g. **дом**, **го́род** etc.).

▶ Some common feminine nouns which are stressed on the ending throughout the singular are stressed on the stem throughout the plural, e.g.:

гроза́	*thunderstorm*
игра́	*game*
сестра́	*sister* (pl. **сёстры**)
страна́	*country*

▶ Some common feminine nouns are stressed on the ending except in the accusative singular and nominative and accusative plural, e.g.:

вода́	*water*
голова́	*head*
нога́	*leg, foot*
рука́	*arm, hand*
сторона́	*side, direction*

▶ Some common feminine nouns are stressed on the stem except in the plural oblique (gen., dat., instr., prep.) cases, e.g.:

вещь	*thing*
дверь	*door*
ло́шадь	*horse*
но́вость	*news*
часть	*part*
че́тверть	*quarter*

▶ Some common neuter nouns are stressed on the endings throughout the singular and on the stem throughout the plural, e.g.:

вино́	*wine*
кольцо́	*ring*

окно́	window
письмо́	letter
число́	number, date

▶ Some common neuter nouns are stressed on the stem through the singular and on the endings throughout the plural, e.g.:

де́ло	matter, affair
ме́сто	place
мо́ре	sea
по́ле	field
пра́во	right
се́рдце	heart
сло́во	word

Adjectives – declension

UNSTRESSED

	Masc.	Fem.	Neut.	Pl.
Nom. (*new*)	но́вый	но́вая	но́вое	но́вые
Acc.	но́вый	но́вую	но́вое	но́вые
Gen.	но́вого	но́вой	но́вого	но́вых
Dat.	но́вому	но́вой	но́вому	но́вым
Instr.	но́вым	но́вой	но́вым	но́выми
Prep.	о но́вом	о но́вой	о но́вом	о но́вых

STRESSED

	Masc.	Fem.	Neut.	Pl.
Nom. (*young*)	молодо́й	молода́я	молодо́е	молоды́е
Acc.	молодо́й	молоду́ю	молодо́е	молоды́е
Gen.	молодо́го	молодо́й	молодо́го	молоды́х
Dat.	молодо́му	молодо́й	молодо́му	молоды́м
Instr.	молоды́м	молодо́й	молоды́м	молоды́ми
Prep.	о молодо́м	о молодо́й	о молодо́м	о молоды́х

SOFT

Nom. *(early)*	**ра́нний**	**ра́нняя**	**ра́ннее**	**ра́нние**
Acc.	**ра́нний**	**ра́ннюю**	**ра́ннее**	**ра́нние**
Gen.	**ра́ннего**	**ра́нней**	**ра́ннего**	**ра́нних**
Dat.	**ра́ннему**	**ра́нней**	**ра́ннему**	**ра́нним**
Instr.	**ра́нним**	**ра́нней**	**ра́нним**	**ра́нними**
Prep.	**о ра́ннем**	**о ра́нней**	**о ра́ннем**	**о ра́нних**

Note the following carefully:

1 тре́тий *third*

Nom.	**тре́тий**	**тре́тья**	**тре́тье**	**тре́тьи**
Acc.	**тре́тий**	**тре́тью**	**тре́тье**	**тре́тьи**
Gen.	**тре́тьего**	**тре́тьей**	**тре́тьего**	**тре́тьих**
Dat.	**тре́тьему**	**тре́тьей**	**тре́тьему**	**тре́тьим**
Instr.	**тре́тьим**	**тре́тьей**	**тре́тьим**	**тре́тьими**
Prep.	**о тре́тьем**	**о тре́тьей**	**о тре́тьем**	**о тре́тьих**

2 мой (твой, свой) and **наш (ваш)**

Nom.	**мой/наш**	**моя́/на́ша**	**моё/на́ше**	**мои́/на́ши**
Acc.	**мой/наш**	**мою́/на́шу**	**моё/на́ше**	**мои́/на́ши**
Gen.	**моего́/ на́шего**	**мое́й/на́шей**	**моего́/ на́шего**	**мои́х/ на́ших**
Dat.	**моему́/ на́шему**	**мое́й/на́шей**	**моему́/ на́шему**	**мои́м/ на́шим**
Instr.	**мои́м/ на́шим**	**мое́й/на́шей**	**мои́м/ на́шим**	**мои́ми/ на́шими**
Prep.	**о моём/ на́шем**	**о мое́й/ на́шей**	**о моём/ на́шем**	**о мои́х/ на́ших**

3 Irregular short comparative adjectives

бли́зкий	*near*		**бли́же**
бога́тый	*rich*		**бога́че**
большо́й	*big*		**бо́льше**
высо́кий	*high, tall*		**вы́ше**
глубо́кий	*deep*		**глу́бже**
гро́мкий	*loud*		**гро́мче**

далёкий	*distant*	да́льше
дешёвый	*cheap*	деше́вле
дорого́й	*dear, expensive*	доро́же
жа́ркий	*hot*	жа́рче
коро́ткий	*short*	коро́че
кре́пкий	*strong*	кре́пче
лёгкий	*light, easy*	ле́гче
ма́ленький	*little*	ме́ньше
молодо́й	*young*	моло́же
ни́зкий	*low*	ни́же
плохо́й	*bad*	ху́же
по́здний	*late*	по́зже
ра́нний	*early*	ра́ньше
ти́хий	*quiet*	ти́ше
у́зкий	*narrow*	у́же
хоро́ший	*good*	лу́чше
ча́стый	*frequent*	ча́ще
чи́стый	*clean*	чи́ще
широ́кий	*wide*	ши́ре

4 Suffix **-айший** or **-ейший**

This is sometimes added to adjectives to form the superlative. This form of the superlative is most frequently met in written Russian, thus you might read about Pushkin, for example:

Пу́шкин – велича́йший   *Pushkin is the greatest Russian poet*
ру́сский поэ́т   (from the adjective **вели́кий** *great*)

Pronouns – declension

PERSONAL PRONOUNS

Nom.	я	ты	он/оно́	она́	мы	вы	они́
Acc.	меня́	тебя́	его́	её	нас	вас	их
Gen.	меня́	тебя́	его́	её	нас	вас	их
Dat.	мне	тебе́	ему́	ей	нам	вам	им
Instr.	мной	тобо́й	им	ей	на́ми	ва́ми	и́ми
Prep.	обо мне	о тебе́	о нём	о ней	о нас	о вас	о них

NB: Always add **н** to the beginning of **его́/ему́/им/её/ей/их/и́ми** if they are preceded by a preposition.

REFLEXIVE PRONOUNS

Acc.	**себя́**
Gen.	**себя́**
Dat.	**себе́**
Instr.	**собо́й**
Prep.	**о себе́**

INTERROGATIVE PRONOUNS

Nom.	**кто**	**что**
Acc.	**кого́**	**что**
Gen.	**кого́**	**чего́**
Dat.	**кому́**	**чему́**
Instr.	**кем**	**чем**
Prep.	**о ком**	**о чём**

DEMONSTRATIVE PRONOUNS

	Masc.	Fem.	Neut.	Pl.
Nom.	**э́тот/тот**	**э́та/та**	**э́то/то**	**э́ти/те**
Acc.	**э́тот/тот**	**э́ту/ту**	**э́то/то**	**э́ти/те**
Gen.	**э́того/того́**	**э́той/той**	**э́того/того́**	**э́тих/тех**
Dat.	**э́тому/тому́**	**э́той/той**	**э́тому/тому́**	**э́тим/тем**
Instr.	**э́тим/тем**	**э́той/той**	**э́тим/тем**	**э́тими/те́ми**
Prep.	**об э́том/о том**	**об э́той/о той**	**об э́том/о том**	**об э́тих/о тех**

DETERMINATIVE PRONOUNS

	Masc.	Fem.	Neut.	Pl.
Nom.	**весь**	**вся**	**всё**	**все**
Acc.	**весь**	**всю**	**всё**	**все**
Gen.	**всего́**	**всей**	**всего́**	**всех**
Dat.	**всему́**	**всей**	**всему́**	**всем**
Instr.	**всем**	**всей**	**всем**	**все́ми**

Prep.	обо всём	о всей	обо всём	о всех
Nom.	сам	сама́	само́	са́ми
Acc.	сам	саму́	само́	са́ми
Gen.	самого́	само́й	самого́	сами́х
Dat.	самому́	само́й	самому́	сами́м
Instr.	сами́м	само́й	сами́м	сами́ми
Prep.	о само́м	о само́й	о само́м	о сами́х

Prepositions

Preposition	Case	Meaning
без	+ genitive	*without*
в	+ accusative	*into, to*
в	+ prepositional	*in, at*
вме́сто	+ genitive	*instead of*
для	+ genitive	*for*
до	+ genitive	*until, as far as, before*
за	+ accusative	*for, on behalf of*
за	+ instrumental	*behind, beyond*
из	+ genitive	*from*
к	+ dative	*towards, to the house of*
кро́ме	+ genitive	*except, apart from*
ме́жду	+ instrumental	*between*
ми́мо	+ genitive	*past*
на	+ accusative	*onto, to; (intended) for*
на	+ prepositional	*on, at*
над	+ instrumental	*over*
о/об	+ prepositional	*about*
о́коло	+ genitive	*near, approximately*
от	+ genitive	*from*
пе́ред	+ instrumental	*in front of; before*
по	+ dative	*along, according to*
под	+ instrumental	*under*
по́сле	+ genitive	*after*

при	+ prepositional	*at the time of, in the reign of, in the presence of*
про́тив	+ genitive	*against, opposite*
ра́ди	+ genitive	*for the sake of*
с	+ genitive	*from, since*
с	+ instrumental	*with*
среди́	+ genitive	*among, in the middle of*
у	+ genitive	*by, at the house of*
че́рез	+ accusative	*across, through*

Note the following nouns, which cannot be used with **в** + prepositional to mean *in* or *at*, and must be used with **на** + prepositional to mean *in* or *at*:

вокза́л	*station*	**се́вер**	*north*
восто́к	*east*	**спекта́кль**	*performance*
вы́ставка	*exhibition*	**стадио́н**	*stadium*
заво́д	*factory*	**ста́нция**	*station*
за́пад	*west*	**у́лица**	*street*
конце́рт	*concert*	**Ура́л**	*Urals*
куро́рт	*seaside resort*	**уро́к**	*lesson*
ле́кция	*lecture*	**фа́брика**	*factory*
пло́щадь	*square*	**факульте́т**	*faculty*
по́чта	*post office*	**экза́мен**	*exam*
рабо́та	*work*	**юг**	*south*
ры́нок (fleeting **о**)	*market*		

Numbers

All numbers decline, and we have seen in the units how to use numbers in the nominative case and in expressions of time.

FURTHER NOTES ON NUMBERS

1 40 (**со́рок**), 90 (**девяно́сто**) and 100 (**сто**) have only two forms: **со́рок, девяно́сто, сто** (nom., acc.) and **сорока́, девяно́ста, ста** (all other cases). With 50 (**пятьдеся́т**), 60 (**шестьдеся́т**), 70 (**се́мьдесят**) and 80 (**во́семьдесят**), both halves of the number decline:

Nom./Acc.	**пятьдеся́т**
Gen.	**пяти́десяти**
Dat.	**пяти́десяти**
Instr.	**пятью́десятью**
Prep.	**о пяти́десяти**

Both halves of the hundreds of numbers decline too:

Nom./Acc.	**две́сти**	**пятьсо́т**
Gen.	**двухсо́т**	**пятисо́т**
Dat.	**двумста́м**	**пятиста́м**
Instr.	**двумяста́ми**	**пятьюста́ми**
Prep.	**о двухста́х**	**о пятиста́х**

2 Use of numbers with:
▶ animate accusative nouns:

2, 3, 4 have an animate form:

Он ви́дит двух ма́льчиков. *He sees two boys.*

5 and above (including compounds of 2, 3, 4) behave as they would in the nominative:

Она́ зна́ет три́дцать три *She knows 33 students.*
студе́нта.

▶ numbers in all other cases except nominative/accusative:

The number and the noun must be in the same case, and the noun will take plural endings (except after *one*):

Он идёт в теа́тр с одно́й *He is going to the theatre with*
де́вушкой. *one girl.*

Он идёт в теа́тр с тремя́ *… with three girls.*
де́вушками.

Он идёт в теа́тр с *… with 25 girls.*
двадцатью́ пятью́ де́вушками.

▶ numbers with distance (**в** + prepositional of the number and of the measurement):

Заво́д нахо́дится в трёх *The factory is three kilometres*
киломе́трах от го́рода. *from town.*

Verbs

REGULAR VERBS

First conjugation	Second conjugation
я рабо́таю	**я говорю́**
ты рабо́таешь	**ты говори́шь**
он рабо́тает	**он говори́т**
мы рабо́таем	**мы говори́м**
вы рабо́таете	**вы говори́те**
они́ рабо́тают	**они́ говоря́т**

IRREGULARITIES

1   In second conjugation verbs the first person singular of the present and future perfective has a consonantal change if the stem of the verb ends in:

б → бл	**люби́ть**	*to like, love*	**я люблю́, ты лю́бишь**
в → вл	**гото́вить**	*to prepare*	**я гото́влю, ты гото́вишь**
д → ж	**ви́деть**	*to see*	**я ви́жу, ты ви́дишь**
з → ж	**вози́ть**	*to transport*	**я вожу́, ты во́зишь**
п → пл	**спать**	*to sleep*	**я сплю, ты спишь**
с → ш	**носи́ть**	*to carry*	**я ношу́, ты но́сишь**
т → ч	**лете́ть**	*to fly*	**я лечу́, ты лети́шь**
ст → щ	**посети́ть**	*to visit*	**я посещу́, ты посети́шь**

2   Verbs in **-овать** and **-евать** in the present and future perfective tense lose the **-ов/-ев** of the infinitive, e.g. **сове́товать** *to advise*:

-ую	**сове́тую**
-уешь	**сове́туешь**
-ует	**сове́тует**
-уем	**сове́туем**
-уете	**сове́туете**
-уют	**сове́туют**

3   Verbs in **-авать** (except **пла́вать** *to swim*) lose the syllable **-ав** throughout the present tense, e.g. **дава́ть** *to give*:

даю́	даём
даёшь	даёте
даёт	даю́т

4 Some common irregular verbs:

брать *to take* (imperfective)	**беру́, берёшь, берёт, берём, берёте, беру́т**
взять *to take* (perfective)	**возьму́, возьмёшь, возьмёт, возьмём, возьмёте, возьму́т**
есть *to eat*	**ем, ешь, ест, еди́м, еди́те, едя́т**
ждать *to wait*	**жду, ждёшь, ждёт, ждём, ждёте, ждут**
жить *to live*	**живу́, живёшь, живёт, живём, живёте, живу́т**
éхать *to travel*	**éду, éдешь, éдет, éдем, éдете, éдут**
идти́ *to walk*	**иду́, идёшь, идёт, идём, идёте, иду́т**
класть *to put*	**кладу́, кладёшь, кладёт, кладём, кладёте, кладу́т**
мочь *to be able*	**могу́, мо́жешь, мо́жет, мо́жем, мо́жете, мо́гут**
писа́ть *to write*	**пишу́, пи́шешь, пи́шет, пи́шем, пи́шете, пи́шут**
хоте́ть *to want*	**хочу́, хо́чешь, хо́чет, хоти́м, хоти́те, хотя́т**

5 Imperative (see Unit 3). Note that if the first person singular of the verb has an unstressed ending preceded by a single consonant, the imperative ends in **-ь** (**ты**), **-ьте** (**вы**):

отве́тить *to answer* (perfective)   **я отве́чу → отве́ть! отве́тьте!**

Note that imperatives formed from the imperfective infinitive are generally more polite/friendly, while those formed from the perfective infinitive are more of a brusque order:

Сади́тесь, пожа́луйста!	*Please (do) sit down!*
Ся́дьте!	*Sit down!*

Key to the exercises

Note that t = true and f = false.

THE CYRILLIC ALPHABET

Practice

1 a London **b** Washington **c** Madrid **d** Dublin **e** Amsterdam **f** Aberdeen **g** Toronto **h** Birmingham **i** Wellington **j** Melbourne **2 a** Steph Carlton, 208 **b** Cheryl Clark, 202 **c** Olivia Johanssen, 209 **d** Chad Harrison, 207 **e** Simon Mackenzie, 205 **f** Miguel Sanchez, 206 **g** David Cogan, 201 **h** Nick Taylor, 210 **i** Maria Perez, 203 **j** Lily McDonald, 204

UNIT 1

Russian names
Алексе́й

Vocabulary builder
passport, visa, baggage/luggage, American, tourist

Dialogue
1 Are you a tourist? Are you English? What is your surname? **2 a** f **b** f **c** t **3 a** Yes **b** Prince

Language discovery
1 There is no Russian word for *a/an* **2** There is no Russian word for *are* **3** The word order doesn't change **4** Most of them end in -a **5** я, он, она́, вы **6** The word *your* changes from ваш to ва́ша

Practice
1 a Russian **b** Vorobyova **c** consultant **2 b** Мари́я англича́нка. Она́ студе́нтка **c** Макси́м ру́сский. Он инжене́р **d** За́ра ирла́ндка. Она́ актри́са **e** Си́лвио италья́нец. Он студе́нт **3** St Petersburg **4 a** 4 **b** 3 **c** 1 **d** 2

Listen and understand
1 Tsvetov **2** his ticket **3** seat 5B

Reading and writing

1 a t **b** f **c** f, only three are mentioned: Bolshoi Theatre, Moscow University and the Kremlin **2 a** Вот моя деклара́ция **b** Вот мой телефо́н **c** Вот мой бага́ж **d** Вот мой журна́л **e** Вот моя ви́за

Speaking

1 a Моя фами́лия – Принц **b** Да, я англича́нин **c** Да, я – студе́нт
2 a Ваш па́спорт, пожа́луйста! **b** Как ва́ша фами́лия? **c** До свида́ния
d Здра́вствуйте! **e** Спаси́бо

Test yourself

1 It will end in either -a or -я **2** There is no word for *the* in Russian **3** Writing: just put a question mark at the end; Speaking: raise your voice at the end **4** Because the words for *my* and *your* must agree with the noun they are describing – so, if a noun is feminine (like ви́за) then you must use the feminine form of *my* and *your* **5** It's a Russian middle name based on the father's first name and used in formal situations **6** пожа́луйста **7** где? **8** До свида́ния **9** Answers will vary **10** Вы

UNIT 2

Major Russian cities

Арха́нгельск = Arkhangel'sk, Владивосто́к = Vladivostók, Екатеринбу́рг = Yekaterinburg, Москва́ = Moscow, Новосиби́рск = Novosibirsk, Омск = Omsk, Сама́ра = Samara, Санкт-Петербу́рг = St Petersburg

Vocabulary builder

live, London, school, centre, interesting

Dialogue

1 That her name is Ira, she is Anna's guide, she lives in Moscow, she works in the centre, she works in a tour agency, she speaks English, she speaks Spanish, she speaks German **2 a** f **b** f **c** t **3 a** well **b** in Bristol **c** English teacher in a school **4** по-ру́сски **5** me = меня́, they call = зову́т, direct translation: me they call …

Language discovery

1 call/be named, speak/talk, study, live, work **2** рабо́таю, рабо́таете **3** -ешь, -ет, -ем, -ют **4** -шь, -т, -м, -те **5** In -ать verbs, the vowel sound is the same in the *I* and *they* endings, whereas in -ить verbs, the vowel sound is different **6** -ю, -ишь, -ит, -им, -ите, -ят **7 a** я **b** Ира **c** Анна **8** It's Москве́ instead of Москва́ **9** Ло́ндоне, ви́зе, письме́ **10** Уэ́льсе, Испа́нии, Шотла́ндии, Ирла́ндии

Practice

1 a рабо́таем **b** изуча́ет **c** живёте **d** зна́ют **e** говорю́ **2 a** Class **b** salad **c** chocolate cake **d** coffee **e** 292-00-50 **3 a** Ви́ктор рабо́тает в университе́те **b** Са́ша рабо́тает в Екатеринбу́рге **c** Ты рабо́таешь в шко́ле **d** Гали́на рабо́тает в А́нглии **e** Вы рабо́таете в о́фисе **f** Я рабо́таю в гости́нице **g** Бори́с рабо́тает в Москве́ **4 a** Анна живёт в Бри́столе. Она говори́т по-англи́йски **b** Я живу́ в Би́рмингеме. Я говорю́ по-англи́йски **c** Ни́кола живёт в Пари́же. Он говори́т по-францу́зски **d** Мари́я и Рафа́л живу́т в Испа́нии. Они́ говоря́т по-испа́нски **e** Вы живёте в Москве́. Вы говори́те по-ру́сски **f** Ты живёшь в Берли́не. Ты говори́шь по-неме́цки

Listen and understand

1 because he sometimes works in Russia (as a journalist) **2 a** f **b** t **c** t **d** f **e** f

Reading and writing

a a large cultural and administrative centre **b** it's about 5 million **c** in the centre in a flat **d** it's very beautiful – e.g. Winter Palace, Hermitage **e** university

Speaking

a Как вас зову́т? **b** Меня́ зову́т А́нна **c** О́чень прия́тно **d** Я рабо́таю в Москве́ **e** Я живу́ в Ло́ндоне

Test yourself

1 я рабо́таю, я говорю́, вы рабо́таете, вы говори́те **2** жить, я живу́, он живёт **3** Меня́ зову́т … and your name! **4** В университе́те, в шко́ле, в письме́ **5** Вы говори́те по-ру́сски? **6** here, there, very, yes, no **7** When you meet someone for the first time **8** When you're saying *excuse me, please.* NB: This phrase can also be used when you're apologizing **9** Я живу́ в … и я рабо́таю в …; e.g.: Я живу́ в Ли́дсе и я рабо́таю в о́фисе в Брэдфорде I live in Leeds and work in an office in Bradford **10** Мой па́спорт; моя́ ви́за; ва́ша гости́ница

UNIT 3

Russian addresses

Borodinskaya Street, block 145, building 2, flat number 67

Vocabulary builder

I don't know, plan, I have got, to see, restaurant, the left, to understand, address

Dialogue

1 none, they do not know where the hotel is **2 a** f **b** f **c** t **3 a** restaurant **b** house 120, block 3, flat 5 **c** from the chemist's, go straight on, then left

Language discovery

1 nominative used for subject of the sentence, prepositional used for saying *in/on somewhere* **2** The word for *restaurant* stays the same, but аптéку is used instead of аптéка 3 **a** университéт **b** Москвý **c** план **4** в + acc. means *to* **5** you go (by foot), идёт, идём, идёте, they go (by foot) **6** вúжу, вúдит, вúдим, вúдите, they see **7** The я form is я вúжу **8** he, she, we, you, they

Practice

1 a кудá **b** в Óмске **c** в университéте **d** в аптéку **e** в ресторáне **2 a** Москвý **b** Маша **c** Óльгу **3 a** concert by the group Na-Na **b** You should go to the central stadium at 7 p.m. on 17 July **4 b** Вúктор живёт в Кúеве **c** Я живý в Áнглии **d** Ты живёшь в Одéссе **e** Слáва и Кúра живýт в Итáлии **5 a** Как вас зовýт? **b** Где вы живёте? **c** Где вы рабóтаете? **d** Кудá вы идёте? **e** У вас есть план? **6 a** У меня (есть) пáспорт **b** У тебя́ (есть) пáспорт? **c** У них (есть) вúза **d** У нас (есть) вúза

Listen and understand

1 the Cosmos cinema **2** metro station, hotel Cosmos, space museum **3 a** 3 **b** 2 **c** 1 **d** 1

Reading and writing

a Mashatin **b** works in chemist's shop (in the suburbs) **c** three years **d** in a flat on the outskirts of Moscow **e** not big; kitchen, bathroom, bedroom and sitting room **f** supermarket, chemist's, cinema, school, metro station

Speaking

1 a Как пройти́ в апте́ку? **b** Э́то далеко́? **c** Спаси́бо большо́е **2 a** Спаси́бо большо́е **b** У вас есть план? **c** Скажи́те, пожалуйста **d** Как пройти́ в театр? **e** Э́то далеко́?

Test yourself

1 куда́?, где? **2** как дела́? how are things?, как вас зову́т what are you called?, как пройти́ в … how do I get to …? **3** Add the word не in front of the verb: e.g. я не зна́ю I don't know **4** извини́те, пожа́луйста; скажи́те, пожа́луйста; спаси́бо большо́е **5** напра́во, нале́во, пря́мо, далеко́ **6** The subject is the person or thing performing an action, and the object is the person or thing that has an action done to it: e.g. I (subject) see (verb) the restaurant (object): Я ви́жу рестора́н **7** accusative **8** апте́ку, рестора́н (no change), метро́ (no change) **9** в теа́тр means *to the theatre* (accusative case), but в теа́тре means *in the theatre* (prepositional case) **10** У вас есть соба́ка? Да, у меня́ есть соба́ка

UNIT 4
The museum
Do not take photographs in the Zoological Museum!

Vocabulary builder

take photographs, in the museum you cannot take photographs, buy tickets, you want, to want, to like, buy, tickets, ticket office/cash desk, it is not possible/you may not

Dialogue

1 What is the building on the left? **2 a** t **b** t **c** f **3 a** В ка́ссе **b** Ка́рту и деревя́нный стул **c** Фотографи́ровать

Language discovery

1 The Russian equivalent of the English *s* (to show a plural) is either -ы or -и **2** -ы, газе́ты, -и, cars, -ь,-и, две́ри, -и, трамва́и, trams, -я, -и, ста́нции, (metro) stations, па́рки, parks, -a, -и, де́вушки **3** Which film do you want to see? What a beautiful church! **4** In the shop you can buy postcards; In Russia, you must visit the Kremlin in Moscow! **5** лю́бит, лю́бим, лю́бите, лю́бят **6** я гото́влю, ты гото́вишь, он/она́ гото́вит, мы гото́вим, вы гото́вите, они́ гото́вят

Practice

1 a 3 **b** 1 **c** 4 **d** 2 **2 a** Don't smoke in the lift **b** Don't smoke in bed **c** Chocolate **3 b** це́рковь? **c** -о́й, музе́й? **d** -о́е, зда́ние? **e** Кака́я это кни́га? **f** Како́й это дом? **4** Пря́мо, напра́во, пря́мо, напра́во, пря́мо, напра́во **5 a** Меня́ зову́т … **b** Я живу́ в … **c** Я рабо́таю в … **d** Я живу́ в … **e** У меня́ (e.g.) ма́ленькая кварти́ра

Listen and understand

1 Is the wi-fi free in the hotel? **2 a** f **b** t **c** f **d** f **e** t **f** f

Reading and writing

a Golden ring **b** old, beautiful, historic, cultural, Russian **c** churches, cathedrals, museums, monuments **d** tractors, computers, beautiful crystal **e** because it has museums, monuments, ancient architecture **f** beautiful gardens and kitchen gardens with cucumbers and tomatoes

Speaking

1 a Извини́те, пожа́луйста **b** Как пройти́ в це́рковь? **c** Спаси́бо. Где музе́й? **d** Где мо́жно купи́ть биле́ты? **e** Спаси́бо. До свида́ния **2 a** Где мо́жно купи́ть откры́тки? **b** На́до купи́ть биле́т **c** Како́й э́то музе́й? **d** Здесь нельзя́ кури́ть! **e** Ла́дно

Test yourself

1 Мо́жно (usually followed by an infinitive – the to do part of the verb) **2** Although it is second conjugation, so works like говори́ть in the present tense, the я form has an additional л: люблю́ **3** -ы and -и **4** -ое **5** Either that you may not or it is not possible to do something **6** како́й, кака́я, како́е, каки́е **7** Лю́ди **8** Do you want? Would you like? **9** на́до **10** After г, к, х, ж, ч, ш, щ

UNIT 5
Shopping
1 d **2** c **3** e **4** a **5** b

Vocabulary builder

theatre/opera, ticket, to the left, not far, tickets, tickets, roubles, roubles

Dialogue

1 to go to the theatre; yes, as she buys two tickets at a kiosk to see a Chekhov play **2 a** f **b** f **c** t **3 a** Биле́ты в цирк **b** На у́лице, сле́ва от апте́ки, недалеко́ от ста́нции метро́ **c** шестьсо́т рубле́й

Language discovery

1 ticket, a lot of, theatre, two **2** автомобиля, -я, of (a/the) hotel, недéли, of (a/the) station, -ь, -а, мóре, здáния

Practice

1 four: Áнны, билéта, Чéхова, сестры́ **2 a** У вас есть пáспорт? **b** Где нахóдится киóск? **c** Скóлько стóит план гóрода? **d** Где он рабóтает? **e** Вы лю́бите Чéхова? **3** b **4 b** У Вади́ма есть автомоби́ль и телефóн, но у негó нет собáки **c** У Ни́ны есть собáка и автомоби́ль, но у неё нет телефóна **d** У Алексéя есть автомоби́ль и телефóн, но у негó нет собáки **5 a** Ви́ктора – object of sentence, animate accusative **b** пьéса – subject of sentence, nominative of a feminine noun **c** óперу – object of sentence, accusative of a feminine noun **d** пьéсу – на + accusative means for **e** Влади́мир – subject of sentence, nominative case

Listen and understand

1 two bottles of mineral water, three bread rolls, three portions of soup, one bun (no chocolate, as they don't have any); 700 roubles **2 a** 3 **b** 2 **c** 2 **d** 1

Reading and writing

a Ukraine **b** 'The mother of Russian cities' **c** approximately 3 million **d** It's very beautiful – there are parks, forests, gardens, campsites, hotels, monuments **e** planes, televisions, motorcycles

Speaking

a У вас есть билéты? **b** Скóлько стóит билéт? **c** Скóлько с меня́? **d** Недалекó от теáтра **e** Слéва от шкóлеы

Test yourself

1 Скóлько стóит? Скóлько с меня́? **2** The Russian unit of currency is the rouble (рубль), and it is divided into 100 kopeks (сто копéек) **3** It has alternative forms depending on the gender of the noun, so: оди́н билéт one ticket, однá буты́лка one bottle, однó мéсто one place, seat **4** They are followed by nouns in the genitive singular: два музéя two museums, три гости́ницы three hotels, четы́ре здáния four buildings **5** To explain what belongs to whom: Nina's ticket = the ticket of Nina = би́лет Ни́ны **6** без, для, до, из, от, пóсле, с, у **7** They are all phrases containing quantities: a lot of luggage, half a kilo of sugar, a bottle of wine, there isn't any milk **8** далекó/недалекó от **9** If you have a masculine animate noun which is the object of a sentence, remember that the masculine animate accusative endings are just the same as the genitive: Она́ лю́бит Никола́я She loves Nikolai **10** If you want to buy a ticket for a particular event, then remember you'll need to use на + accusative: биле́т на о́перу на за́втра a ticket for the opera tomorrow

UNIT 6
Sport and fitness in Russia
1 g **2** e **3** a **4** c **5** d **6** h **7** b **8** f

Vocabulary builder
hockey, three, very much, fruit, you, you, portrait, interesting

Dialogue
1 Ira enjoys it, Volodya is bored and Anna is ready to leave after three hours at the museum **2 a** t **b** t **c** f **d** f **e** f **3 a** Нет, не о́чень **b** О́чень краси́вые карти́ны **c** Потому́, что она́ худо́жник **d** Чай

Language discovery
1 to play football **2** to play the guitar **3** We have been playing for two hours **4** accusative **5** учи́телю, -ю, to/for (a/the) dog, Оле, to/for Maria, -ь, -у, мо́ре, зда́нию **6** tickets, me, to Viktor's (house), telephone, work, smoke, I, to rest

Practice
1 a зна́ете **b** Да, вот он **c** рабо́тает **d** Да, мо́жно **e** багажа́ **f** Бори́су **2 a** молока́ **b** Бори́су **c** нам **d** гости́ницы **e** мне **3 b** Воло́дя предпочита́ет игра́ть на гита́ре **c** Вади́м предпочита́ет игра́ть на кларне́те **d** Лё на предпочита́ет игра́ть в хокке́й **e** Све́та предпочита́ет игра́ть в ша́хматы

Listen and understand
1 She studies mathematics, enjoys the course, watches TV, reads a lot, really likes to swim but swims only occasionally – the pool is a long way away; she plays volleyball and basketball in the university sports centre **2 a** 2 **b** 4 **c** 4

Reading and writing
a beautiful, typically Russian **b** in the centre of Moscow, near metro station Tretyakovskaya **c** Sergei Mikhailovich Tretyakov, a rich Muscovite merchant **d** 19th-century painters, who depict life and problems of 19th-century Russia

Speaking

1 a В го́роде есть музе́и? **b** Э́ти музе́и недалеко́ от гости́ницы? **c** Что есть в музе́е? **d** Ско́лько сто́ит биле́т в музе́й? **e** Спаси́бо большо́е и до свида́ния **2 a** Что вы предпочита́ете?/Что ты предпочита́ешь? **b** Бо́льше всего́ я люблю́ футбо́л **c** Я предпочита́ю игра́ть на гита́ре **d** Ты лю́бишь / Вы лю́бите э́ту карти́ну? / Тебе́ нра́вится эта карти́на?/Вам нра́вится эта карти́на? **e** Вы лю́бите спорт? / Ты лю́бишь спорт? / Тебе́ / Вам нра́вится спорт?

Test yourself

1 Accusative, because *Boris* would be the subject and *opera* and *ballet* the objects: Бори́с предпочита́ет о́перу и́ли бале́т? **2** Prepositional, because you would be explaining where at: Я рабо́таю в о́фисе **3** Genitive, because you will be using the preposition от: мой дом нахо́дится далеко́ от вокза́ла **4** Genitive, because you will be saying *the book of Olga*: кни́га О́льги **5** Accusative, because you are asking where to: Вы идёте в гости́ницу? **6** Dative, because the word на́до is used to express need: Сего́дня Влади́миру на́до рабо́тать. Today it is necessary for Vladimir to work **7** Genitive **8** Accusative, e.g.: Спаси́бо за вино́ Thank you for the wine **9** Accusative (to play at): Я люблю́ игра́ть в те́ннис **10** Dative, because you will need to use the preposition к: Ты идёшь к А́нне сего́дня ве́чером?

UNIT 7
At the post office

авиа. means *airmail* and наземн. means *surface mail*

Vocabulary builder

25, e-mail, need

Dialogue

1 envelopes, stamps and postcards **2** apart from, except **3 a** f **b** t **c** f **4 a** Краси́вые **b** Пять **c** А́нна хо́чет посла́ть име́йл домо́й

Language discovery

1 автомоби́лей, museums, неде́ли, stations, -и, -я, зда́ний **2** -ый, -ая, -ое **3** 500, 11, 100

Practice

1 b пять театра́льных биле́тов **c** оди́н килогра́мм помидо́ров **d** два́дцать ру́сских сувени́ров **e** три буты́лки во́дки **f** два́дцать шесть краси́вых ма́рок **2 b** Па́трик хо́чет купи́ть шесть ма́рок в Аме́рику. Зна́чит ему́ на́до купи́ть шесть ма́рок по се́мьдесят пять рубле́й **c** Ты хо́чешь купи́ть три ма́рки в И́ндию. Зна́чит тебе́ на́до купи́ть три ма́рки по два́дцать рубле́й **d** Мы хоти́м купи́ть семь ма́рок в Испа́нию. Зна́чит нам на́до купи́ть семь ма́рок по три́дцать пять рубле́й **e** Са́ша хо́чет купить две марки в Петербу́рг. Зна́чит ему́ на́до купи́ть две ма́рки по два́дцать рубле́й **f** Я хочу́ купи́ть де́сять ма́рок в Кана́ду. Зна́чит мне на́до купи́ть де́сять ма́рок по сто рубле́й **3 a** 3 **b** 1 **c** 2 **d** 5 **e** 4 **4 a** Как **b** Ско́лько **c** Куда́ **d** где **e** Как **f** Каки́е

Listen and understand

1 to the post office – Olya to buy envelopes and Natasha to send a parcel to her brother for his birthday (a jumper) **2 a** 3 **b** 3 **c** 2

Reading and writing

a 'The father of Russian cities' **b** 9th **c** Moscow to St Petersburg **d** there are many beautiful old churches and interesting monuments **e** religious picture of saint(s) **f** restoring frescoes of the 14th century **g** many years

Speaking

1 a Извини́те, пожа́луйста **b** Ско́лько сто́ит посла́ть откры́тку в А́нглию? **c** Да́йте, пожа́луйста, пять ма́рок по пятна́дцать рубле́й **d** Да, спаси́бо, э́то всё **2 a** Что тебе́/вам ну́жно? **b** У меня́ до́ма **c** Тебе́/вам что́-нибудь ну́жно? **d** Я хочу́ посла́ть име́йл **e** Э́то всё?

Test yourself

1 На по́чте: remember that по́чта is one of the words you must use with на, never with в (see Unit 5) **2** If someone tells you the price per item, you will hear the word по and then the price: Э́ти откры́тки по 20 рубле́й These postcards are 20 roubles each **3** До́ма means *at home* and в до́ме means *in the house* **4** Я иду́ домо́й **5** почему́? and потому́ что; they both start with п, so try to remember which is which by noticing that because is a longer word than why and similarly потому́ что is longer than почему́ **6** Because one is followed by the nominative singular (оди́н биле́т), two is followed by the genitive singular (два биле́та), five is followed by the genitive plural (пять биле́тов) **7** For nouns in the plural, all animate nouns (masculine and feminine) and their adjectives must be put into the animate accusative if they are the object of the sentence. The plural animate accusative case is exactly the same as the genitive plural: Я зна́ю но́вых ма́льчиков и де́вушек I know the new boys and girls **8** Just two:

-ых or -их for all genders **9** конвертов, марок, посылок, писем, имейлов
10 The second spelling rule: never put an unstressed o after ж, ц, ч, ш or щ

UNIT 8
Restaurant
beef Stroganoff, soup, hamburger, pizza, chicken Kiev, Russian pancakes, (open) sandwich, Russian salad

Vocabulary builder
my, lot, not, not, how much, please, you, you; please, menu, with, not very, rice, portion, lemon, tea

Dialogue
1 two portions of cucumbers with soured cream, two portions of homemade burgers with rice, ice-cream and tea with lemon **2 a** t **b** f **c** f **d** t **e** t **3 a** в ресторане **b** огурцы со сметаной и грибы **c** Нет, они не очень голодны́ **d** моро́женое **e** чай с лимо́ном

Language discovery
1 I, my, you, your, he/she, him/her, we, our, you, your, they, them **2** The infinitive of a reflexive verb will end in -ся, the я and вы forms will end in -сь (because the verb ends in a vowel) and all the other forms (ты, он, она́, мы, они́) will end in -ся **3** я сижу́, вы сади́тесь; all other forms end in -ся **4** занята́, за́нято, за́няты, откры́т, откры́то, откры́ты, вку́сно, вку́сны, дово́льно, дово́льны, свобо́дно, свобо́дны, согла́сно, согла́сны **5** учи́телем, Алексе́ем, крова́тью, тётей, -ей, -ем, зда́нием **6** я́годами, -ами

Practice
1 b Са́ша предпочита́ет суп с помидо́рами и́ли с гриба́ми? Он предпочита́ет суп с гриба́ми **c** Са́ша предпочита́ет котле́ты с ри́сом и́ли с карто́шкой? Са́ша предпочита́ет котле́ты с ри́сом **d** Са́ша предпочита́ет ры́бу с гарни́ром и́ли с жа́реной карто́шкой? Са́ша предпочита́ет ры́бу с жа́реной карто́шкой **e** Са́ша предпочита́ет бифште́кс с ри́сом и́ли с гарни́ром? Са́ша предпочита́ет бифште́кс с гарни́ром **2 a** 3 **b** 1 **c** 5 **d** 2 **e** 6 **f** 4 **3 a** закры́т **b** свобо́дно **c** рад **d** за́няты **e** дово́льны (or ра́ды), вку́сны **f** согла́сна **4 a** сала́т с помидо́рами **b** суп с гриба́ми **c** омле́т с сы́ром **d** фру́кты **e** сок и чай

Listen and understand

1 He buys a ham sandwich instead of a cheese sandwich for Vadim **2 a** 1 **b** 4 **c** 3 **d** 4

Reading and writing

a cold, hot, fish, meat, vegetable **b** cabbage **c** with sour cream and with garlic **d** fish **e** flour, butter, egg, salt

Speaking

1 a (Да́йте) мне, пожа́луйста, сала́т с помидо́рами **b** Спаси́бо, нет. Я не о́чень го́лоден/голодна́ **c** Ско́лько сто́ит бефстро́ганов? **d** (Да́ йте) мне, пожа́луйста, бефстро́ганов **e** (Да́йте) мне, пожа́луйста, моро́женое **f** (Да́ йте) мне, пожа́луйста, сок и чай с лимо́ном **2 a** Это место свобо́дно? **b** Да́йте, пожа́луйста, счёт **c** Мо́жно заказа́ть? **d** Что вы хоти́те пить? **e** Извините за оши́бку

Test yourself

1 Извини́те за пробле́му (see Unit 3 for the accusative case) **2** Кто что хо́чет? **3** At the end of the meal, because счёт means bill **4** At the beginning of the meal, because заку́ски are starters **5** Чай с лимоном – instrumental case **6** (Я хочу́ заказа́ть) бифште́кс с гриба́ми **7** She will prefer о́вощи vegetables, because мя́со is meat **8** You would use the word како́й which, what sort of, what a: Каки́е у вас бутербро́ды? (See Unit 4 to revise како́й) **9** Рестора́н закры́т or just За́крыто **10** It would have to be a long adjective. You can only use short form adjectives in simple statements where the word order is X is Y. So, if you're saying *the restaurant is new*, you could say рестора́н нов, but if you want to say *I prefer the new restaurant*, you'll need to use the long form: Я предпочита́ю но́вый рестора́н

UNIT 9

The train

1 c **2** d **3** a **4** b

Vocabulary builder

group, 20, 40, seven, we, ticket, St Petersburg, ticket, platform, good

Dialogue

1 carriage 6, compartment 4, berth 24 **2 a** f **b** t **c** f **d** f **e** t **3 a** В по́лночь **b** В семь часо́в **c** Она́ говори́т, что это краси́вый го́род **d** Потому́, что тепло́ и прия́тно **e** У неё обра́тный биле́т

Language discovery

1 masculine, feminine, neuter, plural **2** Is that all/everything? Yes, thank you, that's all/everything **3** train, bus, plane **4** ты, you will be, -ет, he/she will be, мы, we will be, -ете, you will be, они, they will be **5** два, три, четы́ре, пять, шесть, семь, во́семь, де́вять, де́сять, оди́ннадцать, двена́дцать, 1st, 2nd, 3rd, 4th, 5th, 6th, 7th, 8th, 9th, 10th, 11th, 12th; they have the same endings as adjectives **6** Because you need the nominative singular after one, genitive singular after two, three and four, and the genitive plural after five and above **7** four, five, ten, four, 20, 25, four, five, 20, quarter, ten, five, five o'clock **8** midday and midnight **9** The preposition в is used, except in the case of minutes to the hour and half past the hour **10** через + time expression means *in x minutes' time*; in 40 minutes **11** I, three **12** го́род, goes, го́род, is going, авто́бусом, work, Анна, St Petersburg **13** Bon appétit/Enjoy your meal!, All the best!

Practice

1 a Шесть часо́в **b** Два часа́ **c** Полшесто́го **d** Без двадцати́ де́вять **e** Де́сять мину́т оди́ннадцатого **f** Че́тверть девя́того **2 b** В шесть часо́в ве́чера **c** В полови́не девя́того/полдевя́того у́тра **d** в полови́не двена́дцатого/полдвена́дцатого ве́чера **3 a** Business, tourism **b** Sleepers **c** Europe and Asia **d** Have a pleasant journey!

Listen and understand

1 how she gets to work **2 a** 3 **b** 3 **c** 2 **d** 2

Reading and writing

a A large red letter 'M' **b** Because it is well organized, quick, convenient, trains run quickly and frequently **c** Between 90 seconds and 10 minutes (average time 2.5 minutes)

Speaking

1 a Ско́лько сто́ит биле́т в Я́лту? **b** Да́ йте пожа́луйста, два биле́та в Я́лту **c** Вот пятьсо́т рубле́й **d** Извини́те, у меня́ нет ме́лочи **e** Во ско́лько идёт/отхо́дит по́езд? **f** От како́й платфо́рмы отхо́дит по́езд? **2 a** Ско́лько сейча́с вре́мени? Кото́рый час? **b** Во сколько отходит поезд? **c** От како́й платфо́рмы отхо́дит по́езд? **d** По́езд отхо́дит че́рез десять мину́т **e** Ско́лько дней ты там бу́дешь вы там бу́дете?

Test yourself

1 Genitive: всего хорошего, because the verb желать must be followed by the genitive case, and even though you don't actually say *I wish* (я желаю), the rule still applies **2** The stem is буд- and the first and second persons are я буду, ты будешь. If you know these three things, then it's easy to remember the rest of the future of the verb *to be* **3** Остановка means *stop* and пересадка means *change*. Did you notice the genitive plural of these words in the Dialogue section? Через шесть остановок after six stops and без пересадок without changes. (To revise the way the genitive plural is formed, see Unit 7.) **4** Accusative, because when you ask for a ticket to a place, you are dealing with direction, not position (i.e. you're not already in Moscow, but you want to get there) **5** You would need to add the word утра (lit. of the morning) – i.e. the genitive case of утро morning **6** Сначала means *at first, first* and потом means *then, next* **7** You would be asking: What time is it? **8** We need to form the present tense from the first infinitive, because we are dealing with an action that happens often (and not once) **9** Tomorrow evening; remember that lots of time phrases involve the use of the instrumental case (see the Language discovery section) **10** Потому что – because (почему? means *why?* – see Unit 7)

UNIT 10

Russian meals

1 c **2** d **3** e **4** a **5** b **6** i **7** f **8** g **9** j **10** h

Vocabulary builder

, nine, lunch, lunch, supper, work, administrative

Dialogue

1 On Mondays he works in the studio, where he does administrative work: answering letters and consulting colleagues. On Wednesdays, he works at home writing film scripts **2** a t **b** f **c** f **d** t **e** t **3** a сценаристом **b** работает дома, пишет сценарии **c** на машине **d** рано утром **e** сидит дома, слушает радио, смотрит телевизор, читает интересную книгу

Language discovery

1 -ет, -ем, -ете; -ет, -ем, -ете **2** -у, -ю, -е, -и, -у, -ю **3** Spelling rule 1: you cannot write ы after г, к, х, ж, ч, ш, щ (you have to write –и instead); Spelling rule 2: you cannot write an unstressed о after ж, ч, ш, щ or ц **4** 21, 2, six **5** change -ая to -ую

Practice

1 b чёрную ю́бку **c** деревя́нный стул **d** интере́сную кни́гу **e** ру́сский журна́л **f** но́вую ка́рту **2 a** Italian **b** Russian, Maths, English **3** живёт, рабо́тает, говори́т, хо́дит, мо́жет, лю́бит, игра́ет, пи́шет, пла́вает, гуля́ет **4 a** Я живу́ в (Ло́ндон)е **b** Я живу́ в (до́ме/кварти́ре) **c** Я рабо́таю (инжене́р)ом, (бизнесме́нк)ой **d** Мне (41 год/43 го́да/46 лет) **e** Обы́чно по утра́м я встаю́ в (6) часо́в **f** Я е́зжу на рабо́ту (авто́бус)ом/(маши́н)ой **g** Я начина́ю рабо́тать в (9) часо́в **h** Я обе́даю в (час) **i** Обы́чно по вечера́м я (изуча́ю ру́сский язы́к) **j** По суббо́там и по воскресе́ньям, я обы́чно (отдыха́ю до́ма)

Listen and understand

1 six **2 a** 3 **b** 4 **c** 2 **d** 4

Reading and writing

a radio and television programmes, cinema, theatre, reading, sport, tourism **b** a multitude of different ones **c** they have sections entitled 'crosswords, humour, chess' **d** everywhere – home, park, school **e** Russia, Germany, Canada, Mexico, France, USA

Speaking

1 a Я встаю́ в семь часо́в (утра́) **b** На трамва́е **c** Я начина́ю рабо́тать в де́вять часо́в (утра́) **d** Часо́в де́вять **2 a** Я встаю́ в во́семь часо́в **b** Я обы́чно обе́даю в час **c** Я всегда́ е́зжу на метро́ **d** Ско́лько ему́ лет? **e** Во ско́лько вы начина́ете рабо́тать?

Test yourself

1 Say the word for hour(s) first and leave the number till later: часа́ в три at about three o'clock **2** год is the word to use when the last number is one, го́да when the last number is two, three or four, лет for everything else **3** He watches television three hours per day – в here means *per* **4** Genitive case, because if you want to explain that someone is not at home, you need to use the genitive case for the person who is absent **5** Ско́лько вам (тебе́) лет? **6** в пя́тницу means *on Friday* but по пя́тницам means *on Fridays* **7** Because you need to use the accusative in the second phrase and these are the feminine adjective and noun endings **8** the infinitive **9** This verb is slightly irregular because it loses the middle syllable in the present tense: я встаю́ **10** я пишу́, я могу́

UNIT 11
Weather
(it is) hot, (it is) cold, (it is) warm, (it is) cool/chilly

Vocabulary builder
day, female, female, radio, you, where, platform; weather, weather, cold, weather, forecast, warm, hot, cool/chilly; тепло sounds a little like the English word *tepid*, and the first syllable of холодно sounds similar to *cold*

Dialogue
1 Ira has an English guest, Anna, and is not sure about the weather because today is cold and wet, but Sasha suggests listening to the weather forecast on the radio and, if it is good, he will ring at eight o'clock the following day **2 a** t **b** f **c** f **d** t **3 a** Потому, что там будут грибы **b** На автобусе **c** В метро **d** В семь часов

Language discovery
1 идёт, it walks **2** shining, blowing **3** adverbs; because you must use an adjective (not an adverb) and make it agree with погода **4** because there is no verb to be in the present tense in Russian **5** -ет; -ем; -те

Practice
1 a будет играть **b** напишу **c** буду делать **d** позвоню **e** будут обедать **2 a** Холодно, идёт снег **b** Тепло/жарко, светит солнце **c** Идёт дождь **d** Ветер дует **3 b** Серёжа живёт в Архангельске, очень далеко от Москвы. Сегодня идёт снег, очень холодно **c** Елена живёт в Киеве, далеко от Москвы. Сегодня туман, тепло **d** Юрий живёт в Ташкенте, очень далеко от Москвы. Сегодня светит солнце, душно **e** Галя живёт в Екатеринбурге, далеко от Москвы. Сегодня дует ветер, пасмурно **4 a** News **b** Documentary film 'Suzdal' **c** Tennis at 18:30 on Tuesday and hockey at 19:15 on Thursday **d** 'Hello, music', 'Musical kiosk' and 'Musical telephone' **e** Monday, 20:15, Spanish, and Tuesday, 19:30, Italian

Listen and understand
1 Misha **2 a** 3 **b** 2 **c** 4 **d** 3

Reading and writing
a no rain at the beginning of the week, then showers and thunderstorms **b** water temperature will be 16–18° **c** St Petersburg **d** Central Asia **e** in forests of Central Asia **f** Northern Urals **g** St Petersburg

Speaking

1 a Спаси́бо, я не могу́, потому́ что сего́дня ве́чером мне на́до бу́дет рабо́тать **b** Извини́те, за́втра я пое́ду/пойду́ к О́льге **c** Спаси́бо, а сего́дня о́чень хо́лодно. Е́сли в четве́рг бу́дет хо́лодно, я бу́ду смотре́ть телеви́зор до́ма **d** Ла́дно, я позвоню́ вам в сре́ду часо́в в во́семь **e** Не зна́ю, э́то зави́сит от пого́ды **2 a** Каки́е у вас пла́ны на за́втра? **b** Кака́я сего́дня пого́да? **c** За́втра бу́дет жа́рко **d** Я позвоню́ вам сего́дня ве́чером **e** Где встре́тимся?

Test yourself

1 Definitely your fur hat, because моро́з means *frost* and so три́дцать гра́дусов моро́за means *–30°* **2** Кака́я сего́дня пого́да? See Unit 4 if you're not sure about како́й (meaning *which, what sort of, what a*) **3** Каки́е у вас/тебя́ пла́ ны на вто́рник? **4** Э́то зави́сит от А́нны – i.e. the genitive case after от **5** The imperfective future always describes actions in the future that are incomplete, repeated or continuing **6** The perfective future always describes actions in the future that are single and complete **7** Я бу́ду чита́ть рома́н «Война́ и мир» за́втра́ suggests that you will be reading a part of *War and Peace*, but not finishing it, whereas Я прочита́ю рома́н «Война́ и мир» за́втра means that you will finish reading *War and Peace* **8** Use за́втра instead of сего́дня and insert the word бу́дет: За́втра мо́жно бу́дет смотре́ть телеви́зор **9** The dative case is needed for the person you will ring and в + accusative when you ring a place **10** Use за́втра instead of сего́дня, insert the word бу́дет before the weather word and use бу́дет again to form the imperfective future: За́втра бу́дет хо́лодно и я бу́ду сиде́ть до́ма

UNIT 12
Telephone

1 пятьсо́т пятьдеся́т пять, двена́дцать, два́дцать четы́ре **2** три́ста во́семьдесят де́вять, шестьдеся́т шесть, се́мьдесят во́семь **3** восемьсо́т двена́дцать, три́дцать три, со́рок пять **4** четы́реста девяно́сто пять, ноль шесть, шестьдеся́т два **5** четы́реста девяно́сто де́вять, девяно́сто, ноль три **6** девятьсо́т шестьдеся́т три, два́дцать два, пятьдеся́т шесть

Vocabulary builder

I, tomorrow, we, was, we; number, not, I, you

Dialogue

1 Outside the Bolshoi Theatre at 6:30 p.m. to go to the opera **2 a** t **b** t **c** f **d** f **3 a** Нет, она хочет позвонить Ире **b** Анне/Ей очень понравилась поездка **c** Послезавтра **d** У входа в Большой театр

Language discovery

1 (We) thank you for your letter; Thank you for the new book; It is necessary to pay for our theatre tickets **2** The imperfective past tense is used for actions which are repeated, continuing or incomplete. The perfective past tense is used for single, completed actions **3** -е, -е, -и

Practice

1 a 4 **b** 1 **c** 5 **d** 3 **e** 2 **2 a** играл **b** написала **c** делала **d** смотрели, позвонил **e** прочитала, пообедала **3** marketing/management **4 b** Вчера я позвонил(а) Ире. Мы говорили о поездке в Сергиев Посад **c** Вчера я позвонил(а) Максиму. Мы говорили о французском фильме **d** Вчера я позвонил(а) Алле. Мы говорили о новом учебнике **e** Вчера я позвонил(а) Володе. Мы говорили о плохой погоде

Listen and understand

1 Because he knows that there is an important meeting, but he has forgotten the time **2 a** 2 **b** 3 **c** 3

Reading and writing

1 a live without their mobile phones **b** life without mobile phones **c** their personal and social life **d** about three hours **e** mobile shopping and social networking **2 a** В 7 часов **b** На кухне **c** Она работала в библиотеке 2 часа **d** В буфете **e** Она приготовила ужин, позвонила маме, и смотрела телевизор **3** Вчера Вадим был очень занят. Он встал полшестого и позавтракал на кухне. Утром он работал на заводе пять часов, потом он пообедал в ресторане. После обеда он работал на заводе три часа. Вечером он играл в футбол, смотрел телевизор и читал газету **4** Model answers: **a** Я встал(а) (полшестого). **b** Я позавтракал(а) (на кухне.) **c** Утром я (работал(а) на заводе пять часов,). **d** Я пообедал(а) в ресторане.) **e** Вечером я (играл(а) в футбол, смотрел(а) телевизор и читал(а) газету)

Speaking

a Кто это говорит? **b** Виктор дома? **c** Всё было очень интересно **d** Ещё раз спасибо! **e** Всего доброго

Test yourself

1 It means *all the best*, so it is a good phrase to use at the end of a telephone conversation with a friend; it is in the genitive case because the verb жела́ть *to wish* is understood (see Unit 9) **2** until tomorrow, until Monday, goodbye (lit. *until meeting*) **3** Accusative; спаси́бо за вку́сный у́жин **4** The imperfective will deal with process and the perfective with result **5** It is irregular: шёл, шла, шло, шли **6** -ли, because it always has to be plural, even if you are talking to one person **7** но́вый дом, но́вый дом, но́вого до́ма, но́вому до́му, но́вым до́мом, но́вом до́ме **8** но́вая маши́на, но́вую маши́ну, но́вой маши́ны, но́вой маши́не, но́вой маши́не, но́вой маши́не **9** но́вое письмо́, но́вое письмо́, но́вого письма́, но́вому письму, но́вым письмом, но́вом письме **10** три́ста семна́дцать – два́дцать во́семь – со́рок пять

UNIT 13
The doctor
1 c **2** a **3** b **4** d **5** f **6** h **7** e **8** g

Vocabulary builder
you, I advise, very, you, want, to order, I, you; you, you, are you, I, sore, I, doctor's, doctor, soon

Dialogue
1 stay in bed, call a doctor, don't go on the trip, rest, drink tea with lemon **2 a** t **b** f **c** f **d** f **3 a** нева́жно **b** Го́рло и голова́ **c** Нет, А́нне о́чень хо́чется пить **d** Се́ргиев Поса́д

Language discovery
1 мне, вам, ему́; they are all about 'feeling' **2** good, hot, she **3** boring, lecture, interesting, Russian **4** In the present tense the -ова and -ева change to -у

Practice
1 b О́ле хо́лодно **c** Макси́му пло́хо **d** Ви́ктору ску́чно **2 a** У меня́ боли́т голова́ **b** У меня́ боли́т го́рло **c** У меня́ боля́т ру́ки **d** У меня́ боли́т живо́т **e** У меня́ боли́т спина́ **3 b** Врач рекоменду́ет мне лежа́ть в посте́ли **c** Врач рекоменду́ет мне не пить во́дку **d** Врач рекоменду́ет мне пить чай с лимо́ном **4 a** 3 **b** 2 **c** 3 **d** 2

Listen and understand
1 Because his stomach hurts and he has lost his appetite **2 a** f **b** f **c** t
d t **e** f **f** t

Reading and writing
1 a health **b** children **c** diabetes **d** not all are free **e** looking for fruit and
vegetables **f** eat **2 b** У Тáни/ногá болúт/онá должнá/ей нельзя́ **c** У
вас/болúт спинá/вы должны́/вам нельзя́ **d** У Áллы/болúт гóрло/онá
должнá/ей нельзя́ **e** У негó/болúт глаз/он дóлжен/емý нельзя́

Speaking
1 a Здрáвствуйте, дóктор. У меня́ болúт гóрло **b** Я дýмаю/мне кáжется,
что у меня́ высóкая температýра **c** Что мне дéлать? **d** Когдá мне
принимáть таблéтки? **2 a** Что с тобóй? **b** Мне плóхо **c** Тебé лýчше?
d Не беспокóйся **e** Тебé хóчется пить?

Test yourself
1 Мне хóлодно **2** Нé за что **3** У меня́ болúт головá **4** Я заболел(а)
гриппом **5** Я жáлуюсь на спину **6** It is in the plural to agree with tablets
7 нельзя́ (see Unit 6) **8** Мне чай с лимóном, пожáлуйста **9** Don't worry!
10 Мне лýчше

UNIT 14
Department store
1 b **2** d **3** e **4** c **5** a

Vocabulary builder
me, bright, colour, I usually, us

Dialogue
1 a jumper and a fur hat **2 a** f **b** t **c** t **d** t **e** f **3 a** Недалекó от станции
метрó Академúческая **b** Потомý что я́рко-крáсный свúтер мал **c** Потомý
что чёрный свúтер ей óчень идёт **d** Я́ркие, весёлые цветá **e** Чёрный

Language discovery
1 The most important thing to remember about negative expressions
(nothing, no one, nowhere, etc.) is that when they are used with a verb, не
must always be added before the verb **2** anything, anyone **3** genitive

4 Do you prefer the bright red dress or the pale pink? **5** too big (for me), this dress is too long (for me), are too short (for me), is too small (for me), these trousers are too narrow (for me), is too wide (for me) **6** -ёт, -ём, -ёте, -ут; -ёт, -ём, -ёте, -ут **7** b and e **8** This shirt is more fashionable

Practice

1 a ничего́ не **b** никого́ не **c** нигде́ не **d** никогда́ не **e** никуда́ не **2 a** two **b** two – men's and children's **c** Kievskaya **d** three **3 a** 3 **b** 1 **c** 5 **d** 4 **e** 2 **4** accusative case; **b** чёрную ю́бку/краси́вее/кра́сная ю́бка **c** зелёный сви́тер/дешё́вле/чё́рный сви́тер **d** кра́сное пла́тье/я́рче/се́рое пла́тье **e** но́вый га́лстук/веселе́е/ста́рый га́лстук **5 a** Чита́ть рома́ны **b** Романти́ческие **c** Биогра́фию **d** В кни́жном магази́не

Listen and understand

1 a dark blue t-shirt for 500 roubles and a size 58 fur hat for 1,500 roubles **2 a** 4 **b** 3 **c** 3 **d** 1

Reading and writing

a father and son **b** Moscow Textiles Institute **c** Russia, Japan, Australia, India **d** classic (English) suit **e** music and painting **f** teacher and constant example

Speaking

1 a Извини́те, пожа́луйста, у вас есть меховы́е ша́пки? **b** Покажи́те, пожа́луйста, э́ту ша́пку … вон там, нале́во **c** Мо́жно её приме́рить? **d** Я ду́маю/мне ка́жется, что она́ мне велика́ **e** Пожа́луйста, да **f** Да, вы пра́вы. Я возьму́ э́ту ша́пку **2 a** Я никогда́ не смотрю́ телеви́зор **b** Да, мо́жет быть вы пра́вы **c** Вы хоти́те приме́рить э́ту мехову́ю ша́пку? **d** Зелёный сви́тер тебе́ о́чень идёт **e** Э́та ю́бка намно́го лу́чше

Test yourself

1 Мо́жно её приме́рить? **2** Се́рый свитер. Russian has different words for *brown* and *grey*, depending on what is being described: седо́й for grey hair (otherwise use се́рый); ка́рий for brown eyes (otherwise кори́чневый) **3** не **4** бо́лее **5** The dative case -тебе́ **6** чем **7** To take the green shirt **8** Я возьму́ её (notice её – the accusative of она and referring to the shirt **9** Я уве́рен(а), что ты прав(а) **10** Я никогда́ ничего́ не понима́ю (lit. *I never nothing don't understand*)

UNIT 15
A holiday
1 d **2** e **3** b **4** a **5** c

Vocabulary builder
original(ly), sock, secret, how old are you?, to be born, mathematics, mathematics, me, date, compliment; holiday, birthday, you, toast to, holiday (festive occasion), champagne, bottle

Dialogue
1 38, 35, 8 March **2 a** t **b** f **c** f **d** t **e** t **3 a** Потому́ что он лю́бит спорт **b** За Воло́дю **c** три́дцать во́семь лет **d** В Екатери́нбурге, на Ура́ле **e** э́то междунаро́дный же́нский день

Language discovery
1 -ых, -ах **2** -их, -ях **3** -ых, -их, -ах, -их, -их, -ах, -их, -ях, -ых, -ах **4** янва́рь, февра́ль, март, апре́ль, май, ию́нь, ию́ль, а́вгуст, сентя́брь, октя́брь, ноя́брь, дека́брь **5** They are ordinal numbers; the months are in the genitive case; on a date in Russian is in the genitive case **6** He opens the door and goes into the library **7** The imperfective forms are all based on ходи́ть and the perfective forms are all based on идти́ **8** The waiter approached our table. I hope that he will arrive on time! He quickly crosses the street. The doctor entered the room. The tourists are going out of the museum now. All the children will get off the bus. Volodya has already left. She always goes past the school. I usually pop into the supermarket **9 a** 6 **b** 7 **c** 4 **d** 5 **e** 3 **f** 2 **g** 1

Practice
1 a 5 **b** 4 **c** 7 **d** 6 **e** 2 **f** 1 **g** 3 **2 a** New Year **b** Birthday **3** Оле́г Петро́вич Быко́в ру́сский, роди́лся в Я́лте 12-ого апре́ля 1972-ого го́да. Оле́г живёт в Краснода́ре, где он рабо́тает учи́телем **4 a** больши́х рестора́нах **b** кни́га о спортсме́нах **c** иностра́нным тури́стам **d** ру́сских музе́ях **e** све́жего молока́ **f** но́вых кварти́рах **5** прихо́дит, выхо́дит, подхо́дит, схо́дит, перехо́дит, вхо́дит, прохо́дит, вхо́дит

Listen and understand
1 Valentina will invite the guests and make the party snacks, and Oleg will buy a present and the champagne **2 a** седьмо́го а́вгуста **b** Оле́г **c** ду́хи и́ли джи́нсы **d** он ста́рый друг

Reading and writing

a tree **b** a kind old man with a white beard, white fur coat and a big sack of presents **c** his granddaughter, the Snow Maiden **d** to the old year (that has just finished) **e** happiness, health, success

Speaking

1 a Моя фами́лия Бра́ун **b** Я англича́нин/англича́нка **c** Я роди́лся/ родила́сь двена́дцатого апре́ля ты́сяча девятьсо́т шестьдеся́т восьмо́го го́да **d** Я роди́лся/ родила́сь в Ли́дсе, на се́вере А́нглии **e** Я рабо́таю журнали́стом/ журнали́сткой **2 a** С днём рожде́ния! **b** С Но́вым го́дом! **c** Ско́лько тебе́ лет? **d** Я роди́лся/родила́сь в ты́сяча девятьсо́т шестьдеся́т восьмо́м го́ду **e** Поздравля́ю!

Test yourself

1 C is missing, as you are saying (I congratulate you) with … **2** masculine **3** Како́го числа́? Note that this is in the genitive case **4** седьмо́м and году́ **5** из **6** в **7** на этой неде́ле **8** Кем вы рабо́таете? (lit. *as whom do you work?*) **9** Я предлага́ю тост за Ви́ктора (note that Ви́ктора is in the animate accusative – see Unit 5) **10** в лу́чших рестора́нах (prepositional plural)

UNIT 16
Moscow's theatres

1 concert hall, Tchaikovsky **2** theatre, Gogol **3** dramatic theatre, Stanislavsky **4** theatre, Pushkin

Vocabulary builder

lecture, serious, thing, light, amusing, true, to try, better, better, best; Igor, theatre, Puss, comedy

Dialogue

1 Either to the Gogol Theatre to watch the Zoshchenko comedy 'Respected Comrade' or the musical theatre to see Tchaikovsky's ballet 'Snow Maiden' **2 a** f **b** t **c** f **d** t **e** t **f** t **3 a** В четве́рг **b** Опера «Оте́лло» **c** В Центра́льном теа́тре ку́кол **d** Он ду́мает, что бы́ло бы ску́чно **e** Когда́ он доста́нет биле́ты

Language discovery

1 Алекса́ндр: 17, 18, 19, 20, 21; Бори́с: 1, 2; Влади́мир: 3, 4, 5, 6; Еле́на: 10, 11, 12; Ири́на: 7, 8, 9; Ната́лья: 13, 14; Ольга: 15, 16 **2** It means *who*, *whom*, *that* or *which* **3** Кото́рый must agree with the noun it refers to in number (singular or plural) and gender (masculine, feminine or neuter), but its case is determined by what follows; Olga, who works at the museum, is five years older than me. Olga, whom you already know, works at the museum. Olga, whom you met at the lecture, has invited us to the theatre. The museum, which is in the centre, opens at ten o'clock. **4** -его; -ей, -ей, -ей; -ее, -его, -ему, -им, -ем; -их **5** Use the past tense with бы to form the conditional in Russian; It would be (would have been) better to invite her to the theatre. She would prefer (would have preferred) something lighter. She would choose (would have chosen) a comedy herself. It would be (would have been) a bit boring.

Practice

1 a кото́рый **b** кото́рой **c** кото́ром **d** кото́рого **e** кото́рыми **f** кото́рую **2 a** November **b** 19th **c** Dostoevsky **d** 19:00 **3** Sample answers **b** Е́сли бы у меня́ бы́ло мно́го де́нег, я купи́ла бы но́вую маши́ну **c** Е́сли бы я пло́хо себя́ чу́вствовал(а), я пошёл (пошла́) бы в поликли́нику **d** Е́сли бы я потеря́л(а) соба́ку, я позвони́л(а) бы в полице́йский уча́сток **4 a** – Что вы лю́бите бо́льше, спорт, му́зыку и́ли живопи́сь? – Бо́льше всего́ я люблю́ му́зыку **b** – Что вы лю́бите бо́льше, теа́тр, кино́ и́ли цирк? – Бо́льше всего́ я люблю́ кино́ **c** – Что вы лю́бите бо́льше, о́перу, бале́т и́ли футбо́л? – Бо́льше всего́ я люблю́ о́перу **5 b** Ви́ктор не о́чень энерги́чный челове́к. Он гимна́ст. Бы́ло бы лу́чше, е́сли бы он рабо́тал администра́тором **c** Вади́м тво́рческий челове́к. Он шофёр. Бы́ло бы лу́чше, е́сли бы он рабо́тал журнали́стом **d** Ната́ша до́брый, энерги́чный челове́к. Она́ техник. Бы́ло бы лу́чше, е́сли бы она́ рабо́тала медсестро́й **e** Ми́ша о́чень серьёзный челове́к. Он футболи́ст. Бы́ло бы лу́чше, е́сли бы он рабо́тал адвока́том **6 a** 4 **b** 3 **c** 1 **d** 5 **e** 2

Listen and understand

1 She wants to know who is playing the role of Masha and doesn't know where to buy a programme of her own **2 a** 4 **b** 2 **c** 1

Reading and writing

a P.I. Tchaikovsky born **b** 53 **c** nine years **d** 100,000 **e** first entry in visitors' book dates from then **f** everything is just as it was in his lifetime **g** on Tchaikovsky's birthday and the anniversary of his death

Speaking

a Бу́дем наде́яться на лу́чшее **b** Когда́ она будет свобо́дна? **c** Бы́ло бы лу́чше … **d** Не пра́вда ли? **e** Бы́ло бы немно́жко ску́чно

Test yourself

1 какой **2** adjective **3** the future **4** the conditional **5** the instrumental case **6** я сам/сама́ предпочита́ю … **7** to cost; to be worth **8** на + accusative case **9** вы **10** perhaps, maybe; it must be

UNIT 17
Holiday/leave
1 c **2** a **3** d **4** b **5** g **6** h **7** e **8** f

Vocabulary builder

me, cough, you, one, shower; I have, holiday/leave, climate, sea, sea, comfortable, hotels, exotic, agency/bureau, air/plane ticket, double

Dialogue

1 Sochi, Hotel 'Dagomys', Black Sea, tourist centre **2** a **t** b **f** c **f** d **t** e **f** 3 **a** Немно́жко лу́чше **b** Ей ну́жно отдохну́ть **c** И́ра **d** Со́чи – лу́чший куро́рт, е́сли хо́чешь и отдохну́ть, и вы́лечиться **e** За́втра у́тром

Language discovery

1 In front of each adjective, add са́мый with the same ending as the adjective: This is the most beautiful resort in Italy. This is the most comfortable hotel in the resort. These are the most interesting monuments in the country **2** Ira is worried about her mother. The cough is worrying her **3** The lecture begins at 7 p.m. He always starts the lecture with a joke **4** I'm not going on holiday anywhere. I didn't know anything about this hotel. Don't tell anyone about this! **5** a 3 **b** 5 **c** 2 **d** 1 **e** 4

Practice

1 a 2 **b** 4 **c** 5 **d** 1 **e** 3 **2** a hotels **b** in the mountains **c** Egypt, Thailand, Turkey, Israel, Scandinavia **3** b Э́то са́мый прия́тный куро́рт в стране́ **c** Э́то са́мый бы́стрый по́езд в стране́ **d** Э́то са́мый мя́гкий кли́мат в стране́ **e** Э́то са́мая интере́сная програ́мма в стране́ **f** Э́то са́мое краси́вое зда́ние в стране́ **4** b На́де не́когда смотре́ть телеви́зор **c** Ва́ле не́чем писа́ть письмо́ **d** Бори́су не́куда идти́ сего́дня ве́чером **e** Мари́не не́где рабо́тать **f** И́горю не́ на что жа́ловаться **g** Со́не не́кому подари́ть кни́гу

Listen and understand

1 She didn't sleep well, it is cold in her room, she needs an extra blanket, she needs a towel, the TV doesn't work (she wants to order a taxi to the airport) **2** a 3 **b** 3 **c** 2

Reading and writing

a plane/ship/train/bus/car **b** to arts festivals/rest and treatment/business trips/river and sea cruises **c** Moscow **d** Estonian **e** 5–7 days **f** tennis/windsurfing/sailing/fishing/volleyball/basketball/table tennis/mountain hikes

Speaking

1 a Здра́вствуйте. Есть свобо́дные номера́? **b** Я хочу́ заказа́ть но́мер **c** Но́мер на одного́ с ду́шем, с телефо́ном и с телеви́зором, пожа́луйста **d** На пять дней, до пя́тницы **e** Спаси́бо. Где мо́жно взять ключ? **2 a** Како́й э́то куро́рт? **b** Куда́ вы (по)е́дете в о́тпуск? **c** Это лу́чшая гости́ница **d** Не́чего пить **e** Я хочу́ заказа́ть но́мер с ду́шем

Test yourself

1 Како́й, because it is a word used for asking questions; кото́рый is a word which makes a link in a sentence, giving further information **2** Нигде́, because you are using it with a verb in the present tense **3** Да́йте, пожа́луйста, полоте́ нце (у меня́ в но́мере нет полоте́нца) **4** You would use куда́ , because your question is about direction, not position **5** The third floor. Literally, на четвёртом этаже́ means *on the fourth floor*, but remember that in Russian the first floor (пе́рвый эта́ж) is the ground floor **6** На са́мом краси́вом куро́рте **7** Don't worry! (from the verb беспоко́иться/по-) **8** Because lunch is starting itself **9** В са́мых но́вых гости́ницах **10** Я хоте́л/хоте́ла бы заказа́ть но́мер, пожа́луйста

UNIT 18
Driving in Russia

1 d **2** c **3** e **4** a **5** b

Vocabulary builder

where, you, tea, to tell, to happen, to happen, to shout, policeman, transport; accident

Dialogue

1 There has been an accident. An old woman has been knocked down by a lorry, and Volodya has had to give a statement to the police **2 a** t **b** f **c** f **d** t **e** f **3 a** Ужа́сно **b** Чай (чайку́) **c** Она́ переходи́ла че́рез у́лицу **d** В больни́цу **e** Он в состоя́нии шо́ка

Language discovery

1 Where (on earth) have you been? When (on earth) did he arrive? Who (on earth) said that? We'll go today (this very day)! I told you so! **2** In Russian, the tense of the reported statement is always the tense in which the original statement was made: The policeman said that I was in a state of shock. I said that I would ring the clinic **3** The verb following чтобы must be in the infinitive: Alla rang Valya to find out about the accident **4** to run up to, to lead in, to take away (by transport), to arrive by plane/to fly in, to bring, to swim/sail away **5** (by transport) to approach, to arrive, to cross, to exit, to leave, to pass by **6** genitive

Practice

1 a 4 **b** 1 **c** 6 **d** 5 **e** 2 **f** 3 **2 b** Свидéтель сказáл, что э́то бы́ло часá в четы́ре **c** Свидéтель сказáл, что он ви́дел грузови́к и стáрую жéнщину **d** Свидéтель сказáл, что он подбежáл к ней **e** Свидéтель сказáл, что он не óчень хорошó себя́ чу́вствует **f** Свидéтель сказáл, что он не хóчет поéхать в медпу́нкт **3 a** Hotel Mozhaiskaya **b** camera, £30 sterling and 5,000 roubles **c** her room **d** 28 March 2014 **4** приéхала, переéхала, вы́ехали, проéхали, подъéхало **5 a** 2 **b** 4 **c** 1 **d** 5 **e** 3 **6 a** Часóв в дéсять **b** В два часá **c** Он ходи́л в кинотеáтр с Лёной **d** Полоди́ннадцатого

Listen and understand

1 new red umbrella, black bag containing her purse, passport, make-up and black pen **2 a** кинотеáтре **b** бюрó нахóдок **c** 5 часóв **d** чёрная

Reading and writing

a Emperor, general, diplomat and shipbuilder **b** Moscow **c** Peter conquered the troops of the Swedish king **d** As the new capital of Russia and a 'window on Europe' **e** Exhibits include his personal things **f** Worst flood in Petersburg's history

Speaking

1 a Вы ужáсно вы́глядите! **b** Что с вáми? **c** Что случи́лось? **d** Э́то ужáсно. Сади́тесь **e** Хоти́те чай/чáйку? **f** Нéзачто/Пожáлуйста **2 a** Что случи́лось? **b** Что с вáми? **c** Где же вы бы́ли? **d** Как вы себя́ чу́вствуете сейчáс? **e** Вы óчень добры́

Test yourself

1 You would use the infinitive: чтóбы заплати́ть **2** Что с вáми? (Что случи́лось? means What has happened?) **3** The future, because what the person said at the time was I will ring you **4** Мы шли по у́лице, because the sentence is describing the action in progress on a specific occasion and in a specific direction **5** Я то́лько что купи́л(а)биле́ты **6** пере (Мы перее́хали че́рез мост) **7** же **8** The missing word for both blanks is бы **9** You've left (forgotten) them in the taxi (забыва́ть/забы́ть) **10** Часо́в в де́сять

UNIT 19
Written communication
They are all formal

Vocabulary builder
I, that, my, company, work, of, translator/interpreter, i.e., greetings, where, possible

Dialogue
1 She has been very busy at work, has just finished a contract with a French company and will be going on a business trip to Paris **2 a** f b t **c** t **d** t **e** f **3 a** Сего́дня **b** Перево́дчицей **c** В Санкт-Петербу́рге **d** В Пари́ж **e** Духи́

Language discovery
1 a b 6 7 **c** 5 **d** 3 **e** 1 f 2 **g** 4 **h** 9 **i** 8; formal: a–c; informal: d–i **2** Ten years ago he was a student, but now he is a translator; student, because it follows the past tense of the verb *to be*, indicating a temporary state **3** He asked me if/whether I wanted to go to Paris; Mother wanted to know if/whether Nina had refused. Nina didn't know if they would go **4** as much as possible; as well as possible; as quietly as possible **5** He worked from eight until eleven; Please be here by three **6** genitive, from; genitive, until; dative, by **7** sometime (with some specific time in mind); someone (with some specific person in mind); something (with some specific thing in mind); Someone rang you at about eight **8** anytime, anyone, anything, anywhere

Practice
1 a Шмелёву, Б.Н. У́лица Заце́па, д.20, кв.57, Санкт-Петербу́рг 109262 Росси́я **b** Пло́тниковой, М.А. Воро́неж 394001 Ряби́новая у́лица, д.21, кв.76 Росси́я **c** Соколо́вскому, Ф.И. Ми́нская у́лица, д.62, кв.15, Москва́ 117552 Росси́я **2 a** every year **b** best publication about tourism in Russia **c** foreign writers **d** tourist journey, sights, nature, historical and cultural monuments of Russia, meetings with Russian people, tours, excursions, national cuisine and modern life of Russia **3 b** Я не зна́ю, сказа́ла ли Ни́на,

что она́ пое́дет в Пари́ж **c** Я не зна́ю, прие́дет ли Бори́с сего́дня **d** Я не зна́ю, лю́бит ли Вади́м смотре́ть телеви́зор **e** Я не зна́ю, прочита́ла ли Ва́ля всю кни́гу **f** Я не зна́ю, подписа́л ли дире́ктор догово́р **4 a** В Новосиби́рске **b** Нет, у неё нет сестры́. У неё брат **c** Её му́жа зову́т Никола́й **d** Она́ стара́ется писа́ть раз в неде́лю **e** Потому́ что она́ так занята́ **5 a** Он рабо́тает психо́логом **b** В конце́ ию́ня – нача́ле ию́ля **c** Не поздне́е 1 а́вгуста/до 1 а́вгуста

Listen and understand
1 She worked as a translator/interpreter **2 a** 4 **b** 2 **c** 2 **d** 3

Reading and writing
a that his holiday went well **b** 48 working days/8 weeks **c** travel **d** very tired **e** to her relations' dacha/summer flat/holiday home **f** During the day it was up to 35 degrees **g** Wonderful! – mild climate, warm sea, good conditions for a holiday

Speaking
a Дорого́й Бори́с **b** С уваже́нием **c** Как мо́жно скоре́е **d** Я наде́юсь, что всё в порядке **e** Бо́же мой!

Test yourself
1 Уважа́емая Мари́я Ива́новна **2** the dative of the person's surname **3** Can (I) send it by e-mail? **4** ли **5** как можно скоре́е **6** что-нубудь **7** genitive, as both of these prepositions are followed by the genitive case **8** я работаю бизнесменом, instrumental case **9** You need to use the accusative of the person whose name is given (and му́жа is animate accusative) **10** с уважением

UNIT 20
Souvenirs
1 b **2** c **3** a **4** e **5** f **6** d

Vocabulary builder
you, Russian, who, interesting, souvenirs, matryoshka doll, nephew, for, thought, us

Dialogue
1 two beautiful shawls, a t-shirt, a Russian doll, five or six books **2 a** f **b** f **c** t **d** t **e** f **3 a** Тост за свои́х ру́сских друзе́й **b** О́чень, всё удиви́тельно

интере́сно **c** За всё. За биле́ты в теа́тр, за пое́здку за́ город **d** Краси́вый платóк **e** Она́ получа́ет ру́сскую балала́йку

Language discovery

1 own: I bought my (own) ticket, You forgot your (own) key, He carries his (own) passport, We meet up with our (own) friends, Do you see your (own) suitcase? They drank their (own) champagne **2** Boris is reading his (own) book; Boris is reading his book (i.e. a book belonging to someone else) **3** I bought myself a t-shirt; Are you talking about yourself? He carries his passport with him(self); We closed the door behind us; Can you see yourself in the photograph? They bought tickets for themselves **4** Whose is this (champagne) glass? Whose is this matryoshka doll? Whose is this letter? Whose are these souvenirs? **5** (see main text) **6** Are you talking about the person who bought a balalaika? **7** for those who love art **8** He read the (very) same paper every day.

Practice

1 a 4 **b** 1 **c** 5 **d** 2 **e** 3 **2 a** clothes, souvenirs, children's goods, food **b** Sheremetyevo airport departure lounge **c** winter **3** sample answer: Дорого́й Анато́лий! Спаси́бо вам большо́е за биле́ты в теа́тр: мне о́чень понра́вился бале́т «Снегу́рочка». Спаси́бо за пое́здку за́город. Спаси́бо то́же за экску́рсию в дом музе́й Чайко́вского и обе́д в рестора́не «Колобо́к». Всё бы́ло о́чень интере́сно. Всего́ хоро́шего; address: Губано́ву, А.П./Первома́йская ул., д.45, кв.29/105554 Москва́/Росси́я **4 a** room number, surname, date of departure, name of things, signature, date **b** every day before 11 a.m. **c** Leave it on the table **5 a** В Сиби́ри, на восто́ке страны́ **b** Потому́ что её муж у́мер де́сять лет наза́д **c** Сын, его́ жена́ и два вну́ка **d** Пётр (Пе́тя) и Андре́й (Андрю́ша) **e** Пе́тя игра́ет на скри́пке, а Андрю́ша игра́ет в футбо́л

Listen and understand

1 He has rung her new boss to say how good she is at her job **2 a** f **b** t **c** f **d** t **e** f

Reading and writing

a in St Petersburg on Kuznechnyi Lane **b** two: Fedya and Lyuba (son and daughter) **c** as having 6 rooms and situated on the second (i.e. first) floor **d** read to his children **e** newspapers, boxes of cigarettes, letters, books **f** to reorganize it according to the laws of nature, truth, good and beauty

Speaking

1 a Я интересу́юсь ру́сской му́зыкой **b** Да, иногда́ я игра́ю в те́ннис ле́том **c** Я де́лаю поку́пки, рабо́таю в саду́, иногда́ хожу́ в кинотеа́тр **d** За́втра. Самолёт вылета́ет в 10 часо́в у́тра **2 a** Чей э́то фотоаппара́т? **b** Я предлага́ю тост за вас **c** Ещё шампа́нского! **d** Приезжа́йте к нам опя́ть! **e** Во ско́лько вылета́ет самолёт?

Test yourself

1 It means: she has been working in the laboratory for 10 years. You use the present tense to express how long someone has been doing something **2** В кото́ром часу́? Во ско́лько? **3** оди́н день, два́дцать одна́ неде́ля, со́рок одно́ окно́ **4** You are being asked if you liked Moscow (lit. *to you pleased Moscow?*) To ask someone how they like something, use the verb нра́виться/понра́виться *to be pleasing*. Remember that the construction is a) dative of person b) verb in the right tense, and agreeing with what is pleasing **5 a** 2 **b** 4 **c** 1 **d** 3; Послезавтра means *the day after tomorrow* because literally it means *after tomorrow*; Вчера means *yesterday* so позавчера means *the day before yesterday*; Вечер means *evening* **6** Whose – used with a masculine, a feminine and a plural noun; **7** We played tennis on Monday; we played tennis on Mondays **8** You use тот же, but you need to make sure that тот agrees with the word it is describing. If you add са́мый to mean the very same, then са́мый must also agree **9** The future tense: when if refers to a future event, Russian uses the future tense (even though the present tense would be used in English). So, е́сли вы бу́дете в Москве́, приезжа́йте к нам! literally means If you will be in Moscow, come to us **10** This sentence means *Boris drank his* (i.e. somebody else's) *champagne!*

Russian–English vocabulary

а	*and, but*
ава́рия	*accident*
а́вгуст	*August*
авто́бус	*bus, coach*
автомоби́ль (m.)	*car*
адвока́т	*solicitor*
англи́йский	*English*
англича́нин (pl. англича́не)	*Englishman*
англича́нка	*Englishwoman*
А́нглия	*England*
антра́кт	*interval*
апре́ль (m.)	*April*
апте́ка	*chemist's shop*
бага́ж	*luggage*
бассе́йн	*swimming pool*
бе́гать/бежа́ть (бегу́, бежи́шь, бегу́т)/ побежа́ть	*to run*
бе́дный	*poor*
без (+ gen.)	*without*
бе́лый	*white*
бензи́н	*petrol*
бе́рег (pl. берега́)	*bank, shore*
беспла́тный	*free, at no charge*
беспоко́иться/побеспоко́иться	*to worry, be anxious*
биле́т	*ticket*
благодари́ть/поблагодари́ть (за + асс.)	*to thank (for)*
благода́рный	*grateful*
бланк	*form*
ближа́йший	*closest*
бли́зкий	*near*
блины́	*pancakes*
бога́тый	*rich*
боль (f.)	*pain*
больни́ца	*hospital*
больно́й	*ill*

бо́льше всего́	most of all
большо́й	big
борода́	beard
брат (pl. бра́тья)	brother
брать (беру́, берёшь)/взять (возьму́, возьмёшь)	to take
брю́ки (f.)	trousers
бу́дущий (adj.)	future
буты́лка	bottle
бы́стрый	quick
бюро́ (indeclinable)	office
бюро́ нахо́док	lost property office
в (+ acc.)	to, into
в (+ prep.)	in, at
ва́жный	important
ва́нная	bathroom
ваш	your
вдруг	suddenly
ведь	you realize/know, after all, indeed
везде́	everywhere
век	century
вели́кий	great
велосипе́д	bicycle
вертолёт	helicopter
весёлый	cheerful
весна́	spring
весь, вся, всё, все	all
ве́тер (fleeting e)	wind
ве́чер (pl. вечера́)	evening, party
вещь (f.)	thing
взро́слый	adult
вид	view, type
ви́деть/уви́деть	to see
вино́	wine
вку́сный	tasty, delicious
вме́сте	together
вме́сто (+ gen.)	instead of
внизу́	downstairs/below, down below
внима́тельный	careful, attentive

внук/внучка	grandson/daughter
вóвремя	on time
водá	water
водúть/вести (ведý, ведёшь)/повести	to lead, take (on foot)
возвращáться/вернýться (вернýсь, вернёшься)	to return
вóздух	air
возúть/везти (везý, везёшь)/повезти	to transport, take (by transport)
возмóжность (f.)	opportunity, possibility
войнá	war
вокзáл	(railway) station
волновáться/взволновáться	to be agitated, upset, worried
вóлосы (gen., pl. волóс)	hair
воскресéнье	Sunday
востóк	east
вот	here/there is/are
врач	doctor
врéмя (n., pl. временá)	time
всегдá	always
всегó	in all, only
всё	everything
вспоминáть/вспóмнить	to recollect, reminisce, remember
вставáть/встать (встáну, встáнешь)	to get up
встрéча	meeting
встречáть/встрéтить	to meet
встречáться/встрéтиться	to meet one another
втóрник	Tuesday
вход	entrance
входúть/войти	to enter
вчерá	yesterday
вы	you (pl. or polite form sing.)
вы́глядеть (+ instr.)	to look (e.g. smart)
высóкий	tall, high
выходúть/вы́йти	to go out
выходнóй день	day off
гáлстук	tie
где	where
глáвный	main
глаз (pl. глазá)	eye

глу́пый	stupid
говори́ть/сказа́ть	to speak, talk, say
год	year
голова́	head
голубо́й	light blue
гора́	mountain
го́рло	throat
го́род (pl. города́)	town
горя́чий	hot (to the touch)
гости́ная	sitting room
гости́ница	hotel
гость (m.)/го́стья	guest/female guest
гото́вить/пригото́вить	to prepare
гра́дус	degree (of temperature)
грипп	flu
гроза́	(thunder)storm
гру́ппа	group
гуля́ть/погуля́ть	to stroll
да	yes
дава́й[те]	let's
дава́ть/дать (дам, дашь, даст, дади́м, дади́те, даду́т)	to give
да́же	even
далеко́	far, a long way
дари́ть/подари́ть	to give as a present
дверь (f.)	door
дворе́ц	palace
де́вушка	girl
действи́тельный	real, actual
дека́брь (m.)	December
деклара́ция	currency declaration
де́лать/сде́лать	to do, make
де́ло	matter, affair
делово́й	business (adj.), businesslike
день (m.; fleeting e)	day
день рожде́ния	birthday
де́ньги (pl., gen. де́нег)	money
дере́вня	village, countryside
де́ти	children

дешёвый	cheap
дли́нный	long
дли́тельный	long, lengthy
для (+ gen.)	for
до (+ gen.)	before, as far as, until
до свида́ния	goodbye
до́брый	good, kind
дово́льно	enough, quite
дово́льный	content, satisfied
догово́р	agreement, contract
договори́лись	agreed
доезжа́ть/дое́хать	to reach, travel as far as
дождь (m.)	rain
до́лго	for a long time
до́лжен, должна́, etc.	must, have to, duty-bound
дом (pl. дома́)	house, home
дома́шний	domestic
доро́га	road, way, journey
дорого́й	dear, expensive
достава́ть/доста́ть (доста́ну, доста́нешь)	to get, obtain
достопримеча́тельность (f.)	sight (e.g. tourist sights)
дочь (f., pl. до́чери)	daughter
друг (pl. друзья́)	friend
ду́мать/поду́мать	to think
дуть/поду́ть	to blow
духи́ (m., pl.)	perfume
душ	shower
ду́шный	suffocatingly hot
дя́дя	uncle
еди́ный (биле́т)	all in one (ticket)
жего́дный	annual
жедне́вный	daily
ездить/е́хать (е́ду, е́дешь)/пое́хать	to go (by transport), to travel
лка	fir/Christmas tree
сли	if
сть	there is/are
сть (ем, ешь, ест, еди́м, еди́те, едя́т)/ съесть	to eat
щё	still, again, more

жа́ловаться/пожа́ловаться (на + асс.)	to complain (about)
жа́ркий	hot
ждать (жду, ждёшь, ждут)/подожда́ть	to wait for
жела́ть/пожела́ть (+ gen.)	to wish
жёлтый	yellow
жена́	wife
же́нщина	woman
жи́вопись (f.)	painting
живо́т	stomach
жизнь (f.)	life
жить	to live
журна́л	magazine
за (+ instr.)	behind, beyond
заболева́ть/заболе́ть	to be/fall ill
забыва́ть/забы́ть	to forget, to leave
зави́сеть от (+ gen.)	to depend on
заво́д	factory
за́втра	tomorrow
за́втракать/поза́втракать	to have breakfast
загля́дывать/загляну́ть	to glance, to drop in
зака́зывать/заказа́ть	to order, book, reserve
закрыва́ть(ся)/закры́ть(ся) (закро́ю(сь), закро́ешь(ся))	to close
замеча́тельный	splendid
занима́ть(ся)/заня́ть (ся) (займу́(сь), займёшь(ся))	to occupy (be occupied)
заня́тие	occupation, activity
за́нятый	busy, occupied, engaged
за́пад	west
заполня́ть/запо́лнить	to fill in
запреща́ть/запрети́ть	to forbid
зато́	on the other hand
заходи́ть/зайти́	to pop in
звать/позва́ть, назва́ть	to call
звони́ть/позвони́ть	to ring, telephone
зда́ние	building
здесь	here
здоро́вье	health
здоро́вый	healthy (short form – well)

332

здра́вствуйте	hello
зелёный	green
зима́	winter
знако́миться/познако́миться	to meet
знать	to know
зна́чит	that means, so
зо́нтик	umbrella
зуб	tooth
зубно́й врач	dentist
игра́ть/сыгра́ть	to play
игру́шка	toy
из (+ gen.)	from (out of)
изве́стный	famous
извиня́ть/извини́ть	to excuse
изуча́ть/изучи́ть	to study, learn
и́ли	or
и́менно	namely, precisely
и́мя (n., pl. имена́)	(first) name
иногда́	sometimes
иностра́нный	foreign
интере́сный	interesting
интересова́ться/заинтересова́ться (за + instr.)	to be interested (in)
иска́ть (ищу́, и́щешь)	to look for
испа́нский	Spanish
ита́к	and so, so well
италья́нский	Italian
ию́ль (m.)	July
ию́нь (m.)	June
к (+ dat.)	towards, to the house of
к сожале́нию	unfortunately
к сча́стью	fortunately
кабине́т	office, study
каза́ться/показа́ться (мне ка́жется)	to seem (it seems to me)
как	how, as
как бу́дто	as if
как жаль	what a shame/pity
как то́лько	as soon as
како́й	which, what sort of

кани́кулы (f., pl.)	(school) holidays
ка́рий (soft adjective)	hazel, brown (eyes)
карти́на	picture
ка́сса	cash desk, ticket office
ката́ться на лы́жах	to ski, go skiing
кафе́ (indeclinable)	café
ка́ша	porridge
ка́шель (m.; fleeting e)	cough
ка́шлять	to (have a) cough
кварти́ра	flat
кинотеа́тр	cinema
колле́га	colleague
командиро́вка	business trip
ко́маната	room
коне́ц	end, direction, destination
коне́чно	of course
ко́нкурс	competition
конфе́та	sweet
конча́ть(ся)/ко́нчить(ся)	to finish, end
кори́чневый	brown
коро́бка	box
коро́ткий	short
костю́м	suit
кошелёк	purse
кра́жа	theft
краси́вый	beautiful
кра́сный	red
Кремль (m.)	Kremlin
крича́ть/закрича́ть (кричу́, кричи́шь)	to shout
кро́ме (+ gen.)	apart from, except
кру́пный	major, large
кто	who
куда́	(to) where
кури́ть/закури́ть	to smoke
ку́хня	kitchen
ла́дно	OK
лёгкий	light, easy
лежа́ть (2nd conjugation)	to lie, be lying down
ле́кция	lecture

летать/лететь/полететь	*to fly*
лето	*summer*
личный	*personal*
лошадь (f.)	*horse*
лучший	*better, best*
лыжи (f., pl.)	*skis*
любить	*to love, like*
любой	*any*
люди	*people*
май	*May*
маленький	*small*
мало (+ gen.)	*little*
марка	*(postage) stamp*
март	*March*
маршрут	*route, itinerary*
масло	*butter; oil*
мать (f., pl. матери)	*mother*
машина	*car*
мебель (f.)	*furniture*
медсестра	*nurse*
между (+ instr.)	*between, among*
международный	*international*
мелочь (f.)	*change*
место	*place*
месяц	*month*
метель (f.)	*snowstorm*
милый	*dear, sweet*
мимо (+ gen.)	*past*
мир	*world, peace*
много (+ gen.)	*a lot, many*
мода	*fashion*
может быть	*perhaps*
можно	*it is possible, one may*
молодой	*young*
молоко	*milk*
море	*sea*
мороженое	*ice cream*
мороз	*frost*
морской	*sea (adj.), marine*

москви́ч[ка]	*Muscovite*
мост	*bridge*
мочь (могу́, мо́жешь, мо́гут; past tense: мог, могла́)/смочь	*to be able*
музе́й	*museum*
мы	*we*
мя́гкий	*soft, gentle*
мя́со	*meat*
на (+ acc.)	*to, onto, (intended) for*
на (+ prep.)	*on, at*
набира́ть/набра́ть	*to dial*
над (+ instr.)	*over, on top of*
надева́ть/наде́ть (наде́ну, наде́нешь)	*to put on*
наде́яться (наде́юсь, наде́ешься наде́ются)	*to hope*
на́до	*it is necessary*
наза́д	*ago*
назва́ние	*name*
называ́ть/назва́ть (назову́, назовёшь)	*to name, call*
наконе́ц	*finally*
напи́ток	*drink*
наприме́р	*for example*
наро́д	*people, nation*
насчёт (+ gen.)	*as regards to, concerning*
находи́ть/найти́	*to find*
находи́ться	*to be situated*
нача́ло	*beginning*
начина́ть(ся)/нача́ть(ся) (начну́, начнёшь)	*to begin*
не	*not*
неде́ля	*week*
не́который	*some, certain*
нельзя́	*it is forbidden, not possible*
нет	*no*
нетерпе́ние	*impatience*
нигде́	*nowhere (position)*
никогда́	*never*
никто́	*no one*
никуда́	*nowhere (motion)*
ничего́	*nothing, never mind*

но́вый	new
но́вости (f., pl.)	news
нога́	leg, foot
носи́ть	to wear
носи́ть/нести́ (несу́, несёшь; past tense: нёс, несла́)/понести́	to carry
носо́к (fleeting o; pl. носки́)	sock
ночь (f.)	night
ноя́брь (m.)	November
нра́виться/понра́виться	to please, be pleasing
о/об (+ prep.)	about
обе́дать/пообе́дать	to have lunch
о́бувь (f.)	footwear
объясня́ть/объясни́ть	to explain
обы́чный	usual
обяза́тельно	without fail, certainly
о́вощи (m., pl.)	vegetables
оде́жда (sing. only)	clothes
одея́ло	blanket
одна́ко	however
о́зеро	lake
окно́ (pl. о́кна)	window
о́коло (+ gen.)	near, approximately
октя́брь (m.)	October
он	he, it
она́	she, it
оно́	it
они́	they
опи́сывать/описа́ть	to describe
опуска́ть/опусти́ть	to drop, lower
опя́ть	again
ора́нжевый (adj.)	orange
о́сень (f.)	autumn
осо́бенно	especially
оставля́ть/оста́вить	to leave
остана́вливать(ся)/останови́ть(ся)	to stop
остано́вка	(bus) stop
от (+ gen.)	(away) from
от и́мени (+ gen.)	on behalf of, in the name of

отвеча́ть/отве́тить	to answer
о́тдых	rest, holiday
отдыха́ть/отдохну́ть	to rest, have a holiday
оте́ц (fleeting e)	father
отка́зываться/отказа́ться от (+ gen.)	to refuse
открыва́ть(ся)/откры́ть (откро́ю, откро́ешь)(ся)	to open
откры́тка (gen., pl. откры́ток)	postcard
отли́чный	excellent
о́тпуск	leave
отсю́да	from here
отту́да	from there
отходи́ть/отойти́	to leave, move away from
о́тчество	patronymic
о́чень	very
о́чередь (f.)	queue
очки́ (m., pl.)	spectacles, glasses
ошиба́ться/ошиби́ться	to be mistaken
оши́бка	mistake
пала́тка	tent
па́мятник	monument
па́мять (f.)	memory, remembrance
па́смурный	overcast
перево́дчик/перево́дчица	translator, interpreter
переса́дка	change (e.g. of train)
пе́рвый	first
пе́ред (+ instr.)	in front of
переда́ча	programme
передава́ть/переда́ть	to pass, pass on
переу́лок (fleeting o)	lane, alleyway
переходи́ть/перейти́	to cross
пи́во	beer
пиро́г	pie
писа́ть (пишу́, пи́шешь)/написа́ть	to write
письмо́ (pl. пи́сьма)	letter
пить (пью, пьёшь)/вы́пить	to drink
пла́вать/плыть (плыву́, плывёшь)/поплы́ть	to swim, sail
пласти́нка	record
пла́тье (gen. pl. пла́тьев)	dress

племя́нник/племя́нница	nephew/niece
плохо́й	bad
по (+ dat.)	along, according to
пого́да	weather
под (+ instr.)	under
пода́рок	present
подпи́сывать/подписа́ть	to sign
по́дпись (f.)	signature
подтвержда́ть/подтверди́ть	to confirm
по́езд (pl. поезда́)	train
пое́здка	journey
пожа́луйста	please
по́здний	late
пока́зывать/показа́ть	to show
покупа́ть/купи́ть	to buy
пол	floor
по́лдень (m.)	midday
полице́йский	policeman
по́лночь (f.)	midnight
полови́на	half
полоте́нце	towel
получа́ть/получи́ть	to receive
помидо́р	tomato
по́мнить/вспо́мнить	to remember
помога́ть/помо́чь (+ dat.)	to help
по-мо́ему	in my opinion
по́мощь (f.)	help
понеде́льник	Monday
понима́ть/поня́ть (пойму́, поймёшь)	to understand
поня́тно	clear, understood
пора́ (+ infin.)	it is time to
поря́док (fleeting o)	order
поса́дка	boarding (of train, plane, etc.)
посети́тель (m.)	visitor
посеща́ть/посети́ть	to visit
по́сле (+ gen.)	after
после́дний	last, latest
послеза́втра	the day after tomorrow
посте́ль (f.)	bed

постоя́нный	constant
посыла́ть/посла́ть (пошлю́, пошлёшь)	to send
посы́лка	parcel
пото́м	then, next, after
потому́ что	because
почему́	why
почему́-то	for some reason or other
по́чта	post office, post
поэ́тому	therefore
пра́вда	truth
пра́вило	rule
пра́вильный	correct
пра́здник	holiday, celebration, festive occasion
предлага́ть/предложи́ть	to suggest, propose
предпочита́ть/предпоче́сть (past tense: предпочёл, предпочла́)	to prefer
преподава́тель (m.)	teacher
преподава́ть/препода́ть	to teach
при (+ prep.)	at the time of, in the reign of, in the presence of
привози́ть/привезти́	to bring (by transport)
приглаша́ть/пригласи́ть	to invite
приём	reception
приме́р	example
приме́ривать/приме́рить	to try on
принима́ть/приня́ть (приму́, при́мешь)	to receive, take, accept
приноси́ть/принести́	to bring
приро́да	nature
прихо́д	arrival
приходи́ть/прийти́	to arrive, come
прия́тный	pleasant
пробле́ма	problem
проводи́ть/провести́	to spend (of time)
прогно́з	forecast
продава́ть/прода́ть	to sell
продаве́ц (fleeting e)	shop assistant (male)
продавщи́ца	shop assistant (female)
производи́ть/произвести́	to produce
происходи́ть/произойти́	to happen

проси́ть/попроси́ть (+ acc.)	to ask, request
просто́й	simple
про́сьба	request
про́тив (+ gen.)	against
прохла́дный	cool, chilly
проходи́ть/пройти́	to go through, past
про́шлый	last, past
проща́ть/прости́ть	to forgive, excuse
путеше́ствие	travel, journey
путеше́ствовать	to travel
путь (m.)	journey, way
пя́тница	Friday
рабо́та	work
рабо́тать	to work
рад	glad
ра́ди (+ gen.)	for the sake of
разгово́р	conversation
разме́р	size
ра́зный	different, various
ра́неный	hurt, wounded, injured
ра́нний	early
ра́ньше	earlier, formerly
расска́зывать/рассказа́ть	to tell, relate
ребёнок (pl. де́ти)	child
результа́т	result
река́	river
рекомендова́ть/порекомендова́ть	to recommend
ремо́нт	repair
реша́ть/реши́ть	to decide
роди́ться	to be born
ро́дственник	relative, relation
ро́зовый	pink
роль (f.)	role
рот	mouth
руба́шка	shirt
рубль (m.)	rouble
рука́	hand, arm
ру́сский	Russian
ру́чка	pen

ры́ба	fish
ряд	row, series, rank
ря́дом с (+ instr.)	next to
с (+gen.)	from, since
с (+ instr.)	with
сад	garden
сади́ться/сесть	to sit down, to catch (e.g. bus)
самолёт	aeroplane
све́жий	fresh
свети́ть	to shine
све́тлый	light
свобо́дный	free, vacant
се́вер	north
сего́дня	today
седо́й	grey (hair)
семья́	family
сентя́брь (m.)	September
се́рдце	heart
се́рый	grey
сестра́ (pl. сёстры)	sister
сиде́ть	to sit, be seated, to stay (at home)
си́льный	strong
си́ний	dark blue
скри́пка	violin
ску́чный	boring
сли́шком	too, too much
сло́жный	complicated
случа́ться/случи́ться	to happen
слу́шать/послу́шать	to listen to
слы́шать (слы́шу, слы́шишь)/услы́шать	to hear
смешно́й	funny, amusing
смотре́ть/посмотре́ть	to watch, look at
снача́ла	at first
сно́ва	again
соба́ка	dog
собира́ть/собра́ть	to collect, gather
собира́ться/собра́ться	to prepare oneself, intend, assemble
сове́т	advice, council
сове́товать/посове́товать (+ dat.)	to advise

совеща́ние	meeting, conference
совреме́нный	modern, contemporary
совсе́м	quite, entirely, at all
согла́сный	in agreement
сок	(fruit) juice
сообща́ть/сообщи́ть	to communicate, announce
состоя́ние	condition
спа́льня	bedroom
спаси́бо	thank you
спина́	back
спосо́бный	talented
спра́шивать/спроси́ть (+ acc.)	to ask, enquire
спустя́	later, after
среда́ (pl. сре́ды)	Wednesday
среди́ (+ gen.)	among
сре́дний	average
сро́чный	urgent
станови́ться/стать (ста́ну, ста́нешь; + instr.)	to become
ста́нция	station (bus or underground)
ста́рый	old
стара́ться/постара́ться	to try
столи́ца	capital
сто́ить	to cost
стоя́нка	parking
стоя́ть	to stand
стра́шный	terrible (dreadful)
стул (pl. сту́лья)	chair
суббо́та	Saturday
сухо́й	dry
сходи́ть/сойти́	to get off
чёт	bill
счита́ть(ся)	to consider (to be considered)
сын (pl. сыновья́)	son
сыр	cheese
так	so
та́кже	also
тако́й	such a, so
такси́ (n.)	taxi

там	*there*
телеви́зор	*television*
тёмный	*dark*
тепло́хо́д	*ship*
тёплый	*warm*
теря́ть (теря́ю, теря́ешь)/потеря́ть	*to lose*
тётя	*aunt*
ти́хий	*quiet*
то есть (т.е.)	*that is (i.e.)*
това́ры (m.)	*goods, wares*
тогда́	*then, in that case*
то́же	*also*
то́лько	*only*
то́чка	*point, full stop*
трамва́й	*tram*
тру́дный	*difficult*
туда́	*to there*
тума́н	*fog, mist*
тури́ст	*tourist*
ты	*you (informal singular)*
у (+ gen.)	*by, at the house of*
уважа́емый	*respected*
уваже́ние	*respect*
уве́ренный	*certain, sure*
увлека́ться/увле́чься (+ instr.)	*to be enthusiastic about*
у́гол (fleeting o)	*corner*
ударя́ть/уда́рить	*to hit, strike*
удиви́тельный	*surprising, amazing*
удо́бный	*comfortable, convenient*
удово́льствие	*pleasure*
уже́	*already*
у́жин	*supper*
у́зкий	*narrow*
узнава́ть/узна́ть	*to find out, to recognize*
у́лица	*street*
улучша́ть/улу́чшить	*to improve*
умира́ть/умере́ть (past tense: у́мер, умерла́)	*to die*
у́мный	*clever (intelligent)*

универма́г	department store
универса́м	supermarket
уника́льный	unique
усло́вие	condition
успе́х	success
устава́ть/уста́ть (уста́ну, уста́нешь)	to get tired
я уста́л[а]	I'm tired
у́тро	morning
уходи́ть/уйти́	to leave; be spent (of time)
учи́тель (m.)	teacher
учи́тельница	teacher
фами́лия	surname
февра́ль (m.)	February
фотоаппара́т	camera
хлеб	bread
ходи́ть/идти́ (иду́, идёшь; past tense: шёл, шла)/пойти́	to go (on foot), to walk
ходьба́	walk, walking
холо́дный	cold
хоро́ший	good
хоте́ть (хочу́, хо́чешь, хо́чет, хоти́м, хоти́те, хотя́т)/захоте́ть	to want
хотя́	although
цвет (pl. цвета́)	colour
цвето́к (pl. цветы́)	flower
цель (f.)	goal, aim
це́рковь (f., fleeting о)	church
цирк	circus
час	hour
ча́сто	often
часы́ (pl.)	watch, clock
чей, чья, чьё, чьи	whose
челове́к (pl. лю́ди)	person
че́рез (+ acc.)	across
чёрный	black
чесно́к	garlic
четве́рг	Thursday
че́тверть (f.)	quarter
число́	date, number

чита́ть/прочита́ть	to read
что	what
чу́вствовать/почу́вствовать себя́	to feel
чуде́сный	wonderful
широ́кий	wide, broad
шкаф	cupboard
шко́ла	school
шу́ба	fur coat
шу́мный	noisy
шу́тка	joke
щи	cabbage soup
эта́ж	floor, storey
ю́бка	skirt
юг	south
я	I
язы́к	language, tongue
янва́рь (m.)	January
я́ркий	bright

English–Russian vocabulary

able (to be, can)	мочь (я могу́, ты мо́жешь)/смочь
accident	ава́рия
activity	заня́тие
adult	взро́слый
advise (to)	сове́товать (я сове́тую, ты сове́туешь)/
	посове́товать (+ dat.)
aeroplane	самолёт
after	по́сле
again	опя́ть
ago	наза́д
agreed!	договори́лись
air	во́здух
all	весь (вся, всё, все)
already	уже́
also	та́кже, то́же
always	всегда́
and	и, а
and so	ита́к
annual	ежего́дный
answer (to)	отвеча́ть/отве́тить
any	любо́й
April	апре́ль (m.)
arm	рука́
arrival	прихо́д (on foot); прие́зд (by transport)
arrive (to)	приходи́ть/прийти́(on foot), приезжа́ть/
	прие́хать (by transport)
as	как
as far as	до (+ gen.)
as if	как бу́дто
as soon as	как то́лько
ask (to)	проси́ть/попроси́ть (+ асс.)
August	а́вгуст
aunt	тётя
autumn	о́сень (f.)
back	спина́
bad	плохо́й

bank (money)	банк
bank (shore)	бе́рег
be (to)	быть
beard	борода́
beautiful	краси́вый
because	потому́ что
because of (+ noun)	из-за (+ gen.)
bed	крова́ть (f.)
bedding	посте́ль (f.)
bedroom	спа́льня
beer	пи́во
before	до (+ gen.)
begin (to)	начина́ть/нача́ть
beginning	нача́ло
behind	за (+ instr.)
best	лу́чший
better	лу́чше
bicycle	велосипе́д
big	большо́й
bill	счёт
birthday	день (m.) рожде́ния
black	чёрный
blanket	одея́ло
blow (to)	дуть/поду́ть
blue (dark)	си́ний
blue (light)	голубо́й
boarding (of train, plane)	поса́дка
book	кни́га
book (to)	зака́зывать/заказа́ть (я закажу́, ты зака́жешь)
boring	ску́чный
bottle	буты́лка
box	коро́бка
bread	хлеб
breakfast	за́втрак
bridge	мост
bright	я́ркий
brother	брат
brown	кори́чневый

brown (eyes; hazel)	ка́рий
building	зда́ние
bus	авто́бус
bus stop	остано́вка авто́буса
business	би́знес
businessman	бизнесме́н
but	а, но
buy (to)	покупа́ть/купи́ть
cabbage	капу́ста
cabbage soup	щи
café	кафе́
camera	фотоаппара́т
car	автомоби́ль (m.); маши́на
careful	внима́тельный
carry (to)	носи́ть/нести́/понести́
cash desk	ка́сса
century	век
chair	стул
change (e.g. of a train)	переса́дка
change (money)	ме́лочь (f.)
cheap	дешёвый
cheerful	весёлый
cheese	сыр
chemist's shop	апте́ка
child	ребёнок (pl. де́ти)
cinema	кино́
colour	цвет (pl. цвета́)
condition	состоя́ние
Christmas	Рождество́
Christmas tree	ёлка
church	це́рковь (f.)
clever	у́мный
clock	часы́
close (to)	закрыва́ть(ся)/закры́ть(ся)
closed	закры́т (закры́та, закры́то, закры́ты)
closest	ближа́йший
clothes	оде́жда
coffee	ко́фе
cold	холо́дный

comfortable	удо́бный
competition	ко́нкурс
complain (to)	жа́ловаться/пожа́ловаться (на + асс.)
computer	компью́тер
concert	конце́рт
convenient	удо́бный
cool (chilly)	прохла́дный
cost (to)	сто́ить
countryside	дере́вня
cross (to)	переходи́ть/перейти́ (on foot); переезжа́ть/перее́хать (on transport)
cupboard	шкаф
currency (foreign)	валю́та
currency declaration form	деклара́ция
dad	па́па
daughter	дочь (f.)
day	день (m.)
day off	выходно́й день (m.)
dear (expensive)	дорого́й
dear (sweet)	ми́лый
December	дека́брь (m.)
delicious	вку́сный
department store	универма́г
depend on (to)	зави́сеть от (+ gen.)
describe (to)	опи́сывать/описа́ть
die (to)	умира́ть/умере́ть
dining room	столо́вая
do (to)	де́лать/сде́лать
doctor	врач
don't mention it	не́ за что
door	дверь (f.)
dress	пла́тье
drink	напи́ток
drink (to)	пить/напи́ть
dry	сухо́й
ear	у́хо (pl. у́ши)
earlier	ра́ньше
early	ра́нний
east	восто́к

easy	просто́й
eat (to)	есть/съесть
even	да́же
evening	ве́чер
every	ка́ждый
everything	всё
example	приме́р
excellent	отли́чный
except	кро́ме (+ gen.)
excuse me, please	извини́те, пожа́луйста
exit	вы́ход
eye	глаз (pl. глаза́)
factory	заво́д, фа́брика
far (a long way off)	далеко́
father	оте́ц
February	февра́ль (m.)
feel (to)	чу́вствовать/почу́вствовать себя́
fill in (to; e.g. a form)	заполня́ть/запо́лнить
finally	наконе́ц
finish (to)	конча́ть(ся)/ко́нчить(ся)
first	пе́рвый
fish	ры́ба
flat	кварти́ра
floor	пол
floor (storey)	эта́ж
flower	цвет (pl. цветы́)
fly (to)	лета́ть/лете́ть/полете́ть
fog	тума́н
foot	нога́
footwear	о́бувь (f.)
forbid (to)	запреща́ть/запрети́ть
forget (to)	забыва́ть/забы́ть
form	бланк
fortunately	к сча́стью
free	свобо́дный
fresh	све́жий
Friday	пя́тница
friend	друг (m.)/подру́га (f.)
from (away from)	от (+ gen.)

from (out of)	из (+ gen.)
from here	отсю́да
from there	отту́да
frost	моро́з
fur coat	шу́ба
fur hat	мехова́я ша́пка
future	бу́дущее
garden	сад
garlic	чесно́к
get up (to)	встава́ть (я встаю́, ты встаёшь)/встать (я вста́ну, ты вста́нешь)
girl	де́вушка
give (to)	дава́ть (я даю́, ты даёшь)/дать (я дам, ты дашь)
go (to)	ходи́ть/идти́/пойти́ (on foot) е́здить/е́хать/пое́хать (by transport)
go out (to)	выходи́ть/вы́йти
good	хоро́ший
good (kind)	до́брый
goodbye	до свида́ния
granddaughter	вну́чка
grandfather	де́душка
grandmother	ба́бушка
grandson	внук
grateful	благода́рный
green	зелёный
guest	гость (m.)/го́стья (f.)
hair	во́лосы
half	полови́на
hand	рука́
happen (to)	происходи́ть/произойти́
head	голова́
health	здоро́вье
healthy	здоро́вый
hear (to)	слы́шать (я слы́шу, ты слы́шишь)/услы́шать
heavy	тяжёлый
hello	здра́вствуйте
help (to)	помога́ть/помо́чь (я помогу́, ты помо́жешь) (+ dat.)

her	её; свой (своя́, своё, свои́)
here	здесь
here is / here are	вот
his	его́; свой (своя́, своё, свои́)
home	дом (до́ма, at home; домо́й, homewards)
hospital	больни́ца
hot	жа́ркий (weather); горя́чий (to the touch)
hotel	гости́ница; оте́ль (m.)
hour	час
house	дом
how	как
how many / how much	ско́лько
husband	муж
ice cream	моро́женое
if	е́сли
ill	больно́й
impatience	нетерпе́ние
impossible	невозмо́жный
in	в (+ prep.); на (+ prep.)
interesting	интере́сный
interpreter	перево́дчик/перево́дчица
into	в (+ acc.); на (+ prep.)
invitation	приглаше́ние
invite (to)	приглаша́ть/пригласи́ть
January	янва́рь (m.)
jeans	джи́нсы
joke	шу́тка
juice	сок
July	ию́ль (m.)
jumper	сви́тер
June	ию́нь (m.)
kitchen	ку́хня
know (to)	знать
lake	о́зеро
last, latest	после́дний
late	по́здний
left (on the, to the)	нале́во
leg	нога́

letter	письмо́
like (to)	люби́ть (я люблю́, ты лю́бишь)
listen (to)	слу́шать/послу́шать
live (to)	жить
lose (to)	теря́ть/потеря́ть
luggage	бага́ж
lunch	обе́д
magazine	журна́л
make (to)	де́лать/сде́лать
many/much	мно́го (+ gen.)
March	март
May	май
meat	мя́со
midday	по́лдень (m.)
midnight	по́лночь (f.)
milk	молоко́
minute	мину́та
mist	тума́н
mistake	оши́бка
Monday	понеде́льник
money	де́ньги (m., pl.; gen., pl. де́нег)
month	ме́сяц
monument	па́мятник
more	бо́льше (+ gen.)
morning	у́тро
mother	мать (f.)
mouth	рот
museum	музе́й
must (to have to)	до́лжен, должна́, должно́, должны́
my	мой (моя́, моё, мои́)
near	бли́зкий
necessary (it is …)	на́до (+ infinitive)
nephew	племя́нник
never	никогда́
never mind	ничего́
new	но́вый
newspaper	газе́та
next	сле́дующий
niece	племя́нница

night	ночь (f.)
no	нет
no one	никто́
noisy	шу́мный
north	се́вер
nothing	ничто́, ничего́
November	ноя́брь (m.)
nowhere	нигде́ (position); никуда́ (motion towards)
nurse	медсестра́
obtain (to)	доставать/достать (я достану, ты достанешь)
occupied	за́нятый (за́нят, занята́, за́нято, за́няты)
occupy (to; to be occupied)	занима́ть(ся)/заня́ть(ся)
October	октя́брь (m.)
of course	коне́чно
often	ча́сто
OK	ла́дно
old	ста́рый
open	откры́тый (откры́т, откры́та, откры́то, откры́ты)
open (to)	открыва́ть/откры́ть
opinion	мне́ние
opinion (in my)	по-мо́ему (по моему́ мне́нию)
order (to)	зака́зывать/заказа́ть
our	наш (на́ша, на́ше, на́ши)
over there	вон там
palace	дворе́ц
pancakes	блины́
parking	стоя́нка
party	ве́чер
pay (to)	плати́ть/заплати́ть
perfume	духи́ (m., pl.)
person	челове́к (pl. лю́ди)
petrol	бензи́н
piece	кусо́к
place	ме́сто
play (to)	игра́ть/сыгра́ть
please	пожа́луйста

policeman	полице́йский
poor	бе́дный
possible	возмо́жно
post office	по́чта
postcard	откры́тка
prefer (to)	предпочита́ть/предпоче́сть
prepare (to)	гото́вить/пригото́вить
present (gift)	пода́рок
problem	пробле́ма
purse	кошелёк
rain	дождь (m.)
read (to)	чита́ть/прочита́ть
receive (to)	получа́ть/получи́ть
reception	приём
red	кра́сный
rest (to)	отдыха́ть/отдохну́ть
restaurant	рестора́н
return (to)	возвраща́ться/верну́ться
rich	бога́тый
right (on the, to the)	напра́во
ring (to)	звони́ть/позвони́ть (+ dat.)
river	река́
room (hotel)	но́мер (pl. номера́)
Saturday	суббо́та
school	шко́ла
sea	мо́ре
see (to)	ви́деть/уви́деть
sell (to)	продава́ть (я продаю́, ты продаёшь)/ прода́ть (я прода́м, ты прода́шь)
September	сентя́брь (m.)
shirt	руба́шка
shout (to)	крича́ть (я кричу́, ты кричи́шь)
show (to)	пока́зывать/показа́ть (я покажу́, ты пока́жешь)
sister	сестра́
sit (to, to be seated)	сиде́ть (я сижу́, ты сиди́шь)
sit down (to)	сади́ться/сесть (я ся́ду, ты ся́дешь)
skirt	ю́бка
smoke (to)	кури́ть/закури́ть

snow	снег
snowstorm	метéль (f.)
sometimes	иногдá
sock	носóк (pl. носкú)
south	юг
speak (to)	говорúть (e.g. по-рýсски)
spring	веснá
stand (to)	стоя́ть
station	вокзáл (railway); стáнция (metro)
still	ещё
straight on	пря́мо
street	ýлица
suddenly	вдруг
sugar	сáхар
suit	костю́м
summer	лéто
sun	сóлнце
Sunday	воскресéнье
supper	ýжин
surname	фамúлия
swim (to)	плáвать/плыть (я плывý, ты плывёшь)/ поплы́ть
take (to)	брать (я берý, ты берёшь) / взять (я возьмý, ты возьмёшь)
tea	чай
television	телевúзор
tell (to)	сказáть (скажúте, пожáлуйста, tell me, please)
terrible	ужáсный
thank you	спасúбо
then	потóм (next); тогдá (at that time)
there	там
there is/are	вот
think (to)	дýмать/подýмать
this	э́тот (э́та, э́то, э́ти)
this is / these are	э́то
throat	гóрло
Thursday	четвéрг
ticket	билéт

tie	га́лстук
time	вре́мя
today	сего́дня
tomorrow	за́втра
tooth	зуб
towel	полоте́нце
town	го́род
trousers	брю́ки
try (to)	стара́ться/постара́ться
Tuesday	вто́рник
understand (to)	понима́ть/поня́ть (я пойму́, ты поймёшь)
unfortunately	к сожале́нию
usually	обы́чно
very	о́чень
waiter/waitress	официа́нт/официа́нтка
want (to)	хоте́ть (я хочу́, ты хо́чешь)/захоте́ть
warm	тёплый
water	вода́
weather	пого́да
week	неде́ля
west	за́пад
when	когда́
where	где (position); куда́ (motion towards)
which	како́й
who	кто
whose	чей (чья, чьё, чьи)
why	почему́
wide	широ́кий
wife	жена́
wind	ве́тер
window	окно́
wine	вино́
winter	зима́
with	с (+ instr.)
wonderful	чуде́сный
work (to)	рабо́тать
worry (to)	беспоко́иться/побеспоко́иться
write (to)	писа́ть (я пишу́, ты пи́шешь)/написа́ть

yes	да
yesterday	вчера́
young	молодо́й
your	ваш (ва́ша, ва́ше, ва́ши); твой (твоя́, твоё, твои)

Credits

Front cover: © Thinkstock images

Recorded at Alchemy Studios, London

Cast: Sarah Sherborne, Natasha Radski, Andrei Nazarenko

"Global scale" of the Common European Framework of Reference for Languages: learning, teaching, assessment (CEFR)

Advanced	CEFR LEVEL C2	Can understand with ease virtually everything heard or read. Can summarise information from different spoken and written sources, reconstructing arguments and accounts in a coherent presentation. Can express him/herself spontaneously, very fluently and precisely, differentiating finer shades of meaning even in more complex situations.
Advanced	CEFR LEVEL C1	Can understand a wide range of demanding, longer texts, and recognise implicit meaning. Can express him/herself fluently and spontaneously without much obvious searching for expressions. Can use language flexibly and effectively for social, academic and professional purposes. Can produce clear, well-structured, detailed text on complex subjects, showing controlled use of organisational patterns, connectors and cohesive devices.
Intermediate	CEFR LEVEL B2 (A Level)	Can understand the main ideas of complex text on both concrete and abstract topics, including technical discussions in his/her field of specialisation. Can interact with a degree of fluency and spontaneity that makes regular interaction with native speakers quite possible without strain for either party. Can produce clear, detailed text on a wide range of subjects and explain a viewpoint on a topical issue giving the advantages and disadvantages of various options.
Intermediate	CEFR LEVEL B1 (Higher GCSE)	Can understand the main points of clear standard input on familiar matters regularly encountered in work, school, leisure, etc. Can deal with most situations likely to arise whilst travelling in an area where the language is spoken. Can produce simple connected text on topics which are familiar or of personal interest. Can describe experiences and events, dreams, hopes and ambitions and briefly give reasons and explanations for opinions and plans.
Beginner	CEFR LEVEL A2: (Foundation GCSE)	Can understand sentences and frequently used expressions related to areas of most immediate relevance (e.g. very basic personal and family information, shopping, local geography, employment). Can communicate in simple and routine tasks requiring a simple and direct exchange of information on familiar and routine matters. Can describe in simple aspects of his/her background, immediate environment and matters in areas of immediate need.
Beginner	CEFR LEVEL A1	Can understand and use familiar everyday expressions and very basic phrases aimed at the satisfaction of needs of a concrete type. Can introduce him/herself and others and can ask and answer questions about personal details such as where he/she lives, people he/she knows and things he/she has. Can interact in a simple way provided the other talks slowly and clearly and is prepared to help.